50 YEARS
of
CORONATION STREET

50 YEARS

of

CORONATION STREET

THE (very) UNOFFICIAL STORY

SEAN EGAN

BOOKS

First published in Great Britain in 2010 by
JR Books, 10 Greenland Street, London NW1 0ND
www.jrbooks.com

A catalogue record for this book is available from the British Library.

Picture credits (T = Top; M = Middle; B = Bottom)
p. 1, p. 7, p. 11 (M, B), p. 12 (M, B), p. 13: Trinity Mirror/Mirrorpix/Alamy
p. 2 (T), p. 3, p. 5, p. 6 (B), p. 8 (T): Bob Thomas/Getty Images
p. 2 (B): Pictorial Press Ltd/Alamy
p. 6 (T), p. 14, p. 15 (T, B), p. 16: Getty Images
p. 8 (B): Jim Hutchinson/*Mail On Sunday*/Rex Features
p. 9 (T,B): TopFoto
p. 10: Pictorial Press Ltd/Alamy
p. 11:(T): TopFoto/UPP

ISBN 978-1-906779-80-1

1 3 5 7 9 10 8 6 4 2

Printed in Great Britain by the MPG Books Group

Contents

Introduction

In 1996, it was announced that BBC1's long-running music chart programme *Top Of The Pops* was being relocated in the schedules to the slot opposite the Friday broadcast of ITV's *Coronation Street*. By now, people knew what that meant. *Tops Of The Pops* was being consigned to the same fate as had another generations-spanning but increasingly out of favour programme – *Doctor Who* – a decade before when it too had been forced to go head-to-head with the exploits of the denizens of the fictional Greater Manchester district of Weatherfield.

That this scheduling actually killed off the aforesaid BBC programmes is probably more myth than reality: BBC1 controller Michael Grade seems to have been determined to cancel *Doctor Who*, a programme he found laughable, regardless of the five million viewers it continued to attract, while the all-encompassing reach of the internet and its instant sales news would have eventually done for the archaic weekly chart run-downs of *Top Of The Pops* whatever the time slot in which it was broadcast. However, it is the symbolism that is important. For a channel to transmit a show opposite *Coronation Street* was a sign of either contempt (*Doctor Who*) or despair (*Top Of The Pops*). Schedulers had long been *au fait* with the fact that putting something in the time slots occupied by the continuing drama serial that had started broadcasting on ITV in December 1960 was futile: since its inception, its episodes were almost always in the list of top 10 rated shows of their particular week, let alone days, and – when the show was on form – one or more of its episodes would be at the very top of those charts. The very fact that in their heyday *Doctor Who* and *Top Of The Pops* had themselves been giants of the schedules only emphasised the fact that *Coronation Street's* popularity was remarkable not just for how intense it was but how enduring.

That popularity is now, after half a century, so ingrained in British culture that we no longer think anything of it, not least because of the way the show's format has been purposely replicated so often, most successfully by the BBC's *EastEnders*. However, on reflection, the esteem in the nation's affections that *Coronation Street* claimed upon its launch seems to conform to no televisual logic. It did not have the mythology and chiselled features of *Wagon Train*, the glitz and glamour of *Sunday Night At The London Palladium*, the cockle-warming merriment of *Morecambe And Wise*, the flash and larger-than-life nature of *Dallas* or the freak-show qualities of *Pop Idol*, to name a few other examples of television phenomena, both before and after. It was a modest, quiet and parochial drama set in an English Northern street whose protagonists were often – in the way of all ordinary people – markedly flawed, both psychologically and physically. On one level, the success of *Coronation Street* is strange indeed.

On the other hand, it's not strange at all. It is that very spurning of showbusiness convention that has made *Coronation Street* the most successful and longest-running drama in the history of UK television. Glamour and escapism has its place, but few are the people who do not require or enjoy a reflection of their own circumstances in the art they consume. Though The Street was not the first British continuing serial drama (now more commonly referred to as 'soap opera'), it was the first to feature a working class locale and characters. However, the mere fact of the reflection of proletarian life was not why it maintained its popularity even while the definition of working class changed beyond recognition with the passing decades – as the failure of subsequent serials in its gritty vein from *Market In Honey Lane* to *Brookside* attests. When creator Tony Warren scripted the first 12 episodes of *Coronation Street*, he created a template of unashamed obsession with the minutiae of life, vividly drawn characters, scathing wit and compelling but unforced storylines so strong that it remains recognisably in place today, even though parts of the titular street itself have physically been demolished and rebuilt several times and the society depicted in its early years has gone forever. Even when other working class serials have vied with The Street for viewers, none have been in its league aesthetically. Would a figure like poet laureate John Betjeman say of *EastEnders* (as he did of The Street in 1979) that it contained, 'the best writing and acting I could wish to see'?

So adept has been the programme makers' (initially independent television company Granada, now ITV Studios) retention of The Street's original essence while simultaneously and perpetually reflecting societal changes that the 'How long can it last?' talk that dogged the programme in its first decade or so has now receded into the mists of time. Initially semi-weekly, five new episodes per week are now broadcast. Entire generations have grown up on a diet – directly or by osmosis – of *Coronation Street*.

This book does not attempt to detail every storyline *Coronation Street* has ever featured nor recite the name of every character to have inhabited its buildings: not only is this impractical in a book of this length but an endless parade of 'Then this happened…' would hardly make riveting reading. Instead, it analyses and explains via both discussion of the major events in its history (on-screen and off-screen) and new and exclusive interviews with its top writers, producers, directors and actors how and why the programme has reached the simultaneously unbelievable and inevitable milestone of a Golden Jubilee.

Part One
Birth of the Street

With the exception of a brief period in the mid-Sixties when he fell out with the programme's makers, Tony Warren's name has been seen in the credits of every single one of the 7,000-plus original screenings of *Coronation Street*. Said appearance is now in conjunction with the words 'Created by...' Previously it was, 'From an idea by...' Before that it was the very similar 'From an original idea by...' All are rather bland phrases that do not do justice to his immense importance to this television phenomenon.

It's been more than three decades since Warren last put dialogue into the mouths of The Street's characters, but thousands of actors, scriptwriters, directors, producers and other crew found employment – even careers – because of the industry he kick-started, an industry that has generated millions of pounds. He devised the concept of *Coronation Street*, dreamt up its original characters, scripted the programme's first 12 episodes and guided its fortunes as consultant for its first few years. Following those initial dozen scripts, he scripted 59 further episodes from 1961 to 1976. Though his subsequent influence on the programme went no further than proffering general ideas and observations at lunch dates with programme producers who, one feels, met up with him for sentimental reasons, *Coronation Street* even in its modern incarnation remains undeniably his baby. As Derek Granger – the second-ever producer of *Coronation Street* – says, 'If twelve scripts and a complete set of characters and an environment aren't an extraordinary creative achievement, I don't know what is.'

Warren was born Anthony McVay Simpson in Eccles in 1936. Contrary to understandable popular assumption, he was not the product of the grim terraced housing depicted in *Coronation Street*'s early days but was brought up in a semi-detached home in pleasant Pendleton, near Salford. Granger, a close friend of Warren's, says, 'Tony wasn't working class. Tony Warren's father was quite middle class and he had married working class, so Tony had this extraordinary thing of having all these working class aunts and things and it was his fascination with the working class end of the family which enabled him to see these characters. Elsie [Tanner] is absolutely based on an aunt of his and old Ena [Sharples] is based on his granny from his mother's side. Tony is quite posh to meet.' The original interiors of the houses in *Coronation Street* were all based on the layout in Warren's maternal grandmother's modest home.

Warren's fruit importer father – initially rendered distant by work in military intelligence – was not a huge part of his son's life, nor judging by Warren's autobiography was any other male much of an influence during his childhood. Not that Warren has ever disliked male company. Though homosexuality was not decriminalised until he himself was around 30, unlike many gays of his generation he appears not to have been tormented by the fact that he was not (his own words) 'the marrying kind'. In Warren's 1969 autobiography *I Was Ena Sharples Father* (a book which, like, famously, the Rovers Return, lacked a logical apostrophe), he was more than a little disingenuous about his sexuality ('There isn't too much of a whiff of lavender about me'). In his day-to-day life he was less circumspect. Actor Alan Rothwell – one of the original cast of The Street – recalls, 'He was definitely gay and obviously gay and didn't seem to want to hide it'. Ken Irwin, a *Daily Mirror* journalist who got to know Warren well over the years, says, 'He was very camp. He did stick out like a sore thumb in a way but he was quite funny and he could be very amusing. A bit over the top always. He was not victimised or anything because of that.'

Entertainment was always in Warren's genes and he became a successful child actor. He tried to make it as an adult entertainer, moving down to London to that purpose, but after acquiring good notices for a performance in a television play, the flood of expected work never materialised, partly because he was by now a beanpole with a baby face. While his acting career was floundering, his parallel cabaret act came to an end voluntarily. Though he began writing for fun, the impetus to pay the rent saw him turning it into a paying job – he provided other performers with cabaret material. Homesickness took Warren back to

Manchester, where, lost as to what to do, he approached Margaret Morris, a casting director at the recently formed Granada Television.

Granada was one of the regional television companies – or franchises – set up when the Independent Television network (ITV) became the first small-screen rival to the British Broadcasting Corporation in 1955. Granada – owned by the wealthy but left-wing Bernstein family that had created the Granada cinema chain – had begun transmitting from May 1956 to the North of England, Monday to Friday. (Associated British Corporation had the region's remit on weekends; in 1968, Granada's transmission area was restricted to the North-West of the country to allow the creation of a new franchise but it also gained the weekend remit.) As with the other franchises, Granada sold some of its output to the other franchises, and vice versa, although unlike most BBC output the franchises' programmes were not necessarily broadcast across the entire country. Though the introduction of television that, unlike the BBC's output, screened paid advertisements between and during its programmes seemed a rather vulgar and Americanised move to many Britons at the time, it went hand in hand with a leftist approach that was particularly incongruous considering the fact that ITV's inception took place only four years into 13 years of unbroken Conservative government.

Sir Denis Forman was a founder member of and big cheese at Granada, although had no formal title until he was appointed Managing Director in 1965. He says of the franchise system, 'The virtue of it was that if a programme company didn't produce programmes of quality, they could lose their licence. This was the only reason that ITV sustained such a high quality as it did from its inception to about 1990…. I don't believe in golden ages but I think from 1960 to 1990 ITV made far, far better programmes than it's made since. It's because of the demise of a system of franchising that only gave a franchise if you made worthwhile programmes. When that went, quality went.' He dismisses the suggestion that this was paternalistic and that viewers should decide what makes the airwaves. Forman: 'That's rubbish. If you allow commercial people to have their heads, they will make popular programmes the whole time. They will not intersperse it with any programmes of quality. They think – and they're wrong – that that in the end will be more profitable.'

Additionally, in what appears in retrospect like an ostentatious attempt to get in tune with a *zeitgeist* in which 'the regions' were being acknowledged by a media that had previously suffered from a middle class metropolitan hegemony, the new commercial television companies of the

United Kingdom – which were staggered in their introduction but by 1960 numbered 10 – had a statutory obligation to make 25 per cent of their programming oriented around local issues. Though *Coronation Street* wasn't part of this 25 per cent local matter for Granada, the self-consciousness about serving the community that the franchise system engendered may have been an impetus for commissioning it. Forman: 'The fact that certain programme companies had their base in Yorkshire, Lancashire and in the Midlands meant that they became oriented toward those areas or their audiences. If we had been in London, I don't think we would have made *Coronation Street*. I don't think anyone in London would have made *Coronation Street*.' Something else about Granada lent itself to commissioning a programme like *Coronation Street*. Granger recalls of the ambience, 'You had a lot of freedom. You could talk to your bosses. Sidney and Cecil [Bernstein] used to have lunch in the canteen with everybody, Denis Forman. There was no separation, there was no hierarchy. That was part of the Granada socialist principle. Nobody even had titles. It was like a little family group.' While The Street was never particularly leftist, this corporate social conscience must surely have played at least a subliminal part in Granada's willingness to bring it into the world.

Warren had approached Morris with furthering his acting career in mind, but upon learning of his writing sideline she sent him in the direction of Harry Elton, then producing a semi-weekly detective series called *Shadow Squad*. In a move that would have been cringe-makingly presumptuous even if he hadn't been just 22, Warren wrote half of a specimen *Shadow Squad* episode and left it for Elton at the reception desk with the message, 'If you want to know how this episode ends, contact Tony Warren at the telephone number below.' However, after a slight hiccup when the script didn't reach its intended target, Warren's presumption was proven justified: Elton contacted Warren within two hours of coming into possession of the semi-script. Warren was commissioned to write a *Shadow Squad* episode based around prostitution and the result was broadcast. Warren received a handsome £150 for his efforts, over £2,500 in today's coinage.

However, that impressive start did not immediately inaugurate a glorious scriptwriting career. Though he had a couple more *Shadow Squad*s broadcast, Warren's exulting in a *wunderkind* status that saw journalists present him with a tin crown inscribed with the legend 'Britain's Youngest Script Writer' led Elton to punish him by taking him off scriptwriting duties and making him a staff employee in the Granada promotion department, where he wrote on-screen voice trailers. Though a demotion, it involved no little power, as he had full access to all studios. Not only that, but Warren seems to have enjoyed his time in the job, not least for the discipline acquired by having to distil a programme's points of attraction into 30 visionless seconds. However, when he got a chance to work for daily Granada Northern news programme *People And Places*, he took it, despite the fact that he was required to be a jack-of-all-trades in a role that didn't involve much writing. One piece of writing he did come up with for the programme was a script for an edition about Christmas pantomimes. The fact that it was a subject that greatly interested him was reflected in the quality of his words. The script so impressed Denis Forman that he offered Warren a year's exclusive writing contract on the strength of it. Said contract was considered something of an experiment at the time. It gave Granada full ownership on anything Warren produced for 12 months. Warren was perfectly happy to agree to these conditions for weekly wages of £30 and a year's financial security. Neither he nor Granada had any inkling he would shortly create, as Derek Granger puts it, 'The banker for the whole of ITV.'

Warren was asked to be one of the scriptwriters on *Biggles*. Captain W.E. Johns' tales of airborne derring-do were completely beyond his frame of reference and the work made Warren miserable, even ill. Warren told Harry Elton this, rather dramatically from atop a filing cabinet. According to Warren, the producer told him to then bugger off out of sight for 24 hours and come back to him 'with an idea that will take Britain by storm.' Some, of course, after such a performance would have been inclined to tell the young writer to bugger off, full stop. Granger feels Elton's patience with Warren played a key part in the story of *Coronation Street*: 'He must get a lot of praise. He was the one who really held onto Tony and encouraged him, and I think that if it hadn't been for his tutelage it would never have happened. Tony was quite highly strung and was very young. He could be difficult and temperamental. Harry was wonderfully understanding and he persevered.'

Warren did precisely what Elton asked him to in the taking-Britain-by-storm stakes, presenting himself at his desk a day later with the script for the first episode of what would become *Coronation Street*. It wasn't quite such a pat, let's-do-the-show-right-here scenario as that makes it sound, though. The idea had been germinating in Warren's brain for a while. Even to some extent all his life: Warren even claims that *Coronation Street* would never have happened without a 'show' he put on as an eight-year-old called

The Air Raid Shelter Follies. Warren has also put forward a case that the germ of the idea for *Coronation Street* was an old Lancashire song called 'Bolton's Yard'. A poem by Samuel Laycock set to music by Eddie Crotty, it describes the characters who lived in the titular yard in Castle Hall, Stalybridge in the middle of the 19th century. (The yard disappeared in the slum clearances of the 20th century.) There is indeed something not too dissimilar to the house-by-house intrigues documented by The Street (especially in its early days) in the way the song explains who lives at each dwelling and what their jobs and/or personality traits are. The song – written in the local dialect, in which Bolton's is pronounced 'Bowton's' – depicts a varied cast of characters against an impoverished and strife-filled background, although does so with some humour – again a description that applies to early *Coronation Street*. However, Warren has admitted that the inspiration of the song would only have been subliminal. The notion of it as a stimulus only occurred to him when he heard Violet Carson – who played prominent *Street* character Ena Sharples – sing the composition during a technical breakdown at the recording of the 100th episode of The Street; he suddenly remembered he had heard her play (she was an accomplished pianist) and sing the ditty many moons before The Street was conceived during another technical breakdown when the two were working together in radio and Warren was a child actor.

Around 18 months before that cop-movie-style 24-hour ultimatum from Harry Elton, Warren had submitted a pilot script for a proposed series called *Our Street* to BBC Leeds, only to have it turned down by producer Barney Colehan. (Another legend says he never received a reply.) While *Our Street* was more of a comedy show, it itself was an adaptation by Warren of a drama script about a Northern backstreet that he wrote in 1956, aged 19, called *Where No Birds Sing*. Additionally, this doesn't even seem to have been the first time Warren had tried to sell at least the idea to Granada: director Herbert Wise later related how, having rejected a play of Warren's, he had found the young writer trying to convince him of the worth of the idea of a series depicting people's ordinary lives in a particular street, a concept that Wise told Warren had no dramatic potential.

Though Warren has been happy to acknowledge the possibility of the influence of the public domain 'Bolton's Yard', he does not seem to be on record with regard to the notion that *June Evening* – a play by Bill Naughton very much in copyright – may have helped him shape *Coronation Street*. Naughton (1910–1992) was a superb writer whose stories, novels and plays chronicled the lives of the working class. His startlingly wide spectrum of work included famous children's short story collection *The Goalkeeper's Revenge, Alfie* (yes, *that Alfie*), a play – *Spring and Port Wine* – that made an implausible transition to Broadway and another, *All in Good Time,* that became the movie *The Family Way. June Evening* was a Naughton play that portrayed the inhabitants of Holdsworth Street, Bolton, Greater Manchester on one particular evening in 1921. The street in question was in no sense noteworthy in the grand scheme of things but buzzed with all the things that daily life is made of, albeit against a pre-Welfare State backdrop that made the residents of 1960 Weatherfield look like relative millionaires. At one end of this street on the wrong side of the tracks is a corner shop, while one of the families depicted has the surname Tatlock. (Note: the only commercially published edition of the play was a much revised 1972 version with a reduced cast and the Tatlock family name changed to Kippax.) Considering that *Coronation Street* appeared six months after the transmission of a BBC Manchester production of *June Evening* and that that production featured faces that would crop up in The Street (Jennifer Moss and Violet Carson), it's little wonder that many (including apparently Naughton himself) became convinced that Warren was influenced by Naughton's play.

'He wasn't,' insists Daran Little, future *Street* archivist, scriptwriter and close friend of Warren. 'He said this to me the other day. We didn't know the name of the play but we were talking about the Bill Naughton play. It's not the first time I've heard that. I think it's just coincidence.' Leaving aside the argument that depictions of humdrum and proletarian life in any medium were hardly Naughton's invention and that the overlap of actors was possibly due to the fact of a relatively small pool of thespians having the right accents, it should be remembered that it seems likely that *Coronation Street* was in development by the time that the aforesaid BBC Manchester production was screened in June 1960, for two pilots had been filmed by the time it was formally commissioned in August of that year. If Warren was influenced by *June Evening*, it would probably have been by the July 1958 BBC radio version that was *June Evening*'s entrée to the public (and which also featured future *Street* actors, in this case Carson and Jack Howarth). While this may have been prior to Warren's *Our Street*, it was preceded by the 1956-vintage *Where No Birds Sing*.

The formal process of writing *Coronation Street* (as opposed to *Our Street* or *Where No Birds Sing*) started during a three-week period shortly before the day of the 24-hour ultimatum. During a stay in the Highlands, Warren began scribbling down notes in a diary for a new 'programme about a backstreet'. The location of this backstreet in Warren's head was 'four miles in any one direction from the centre of Manchester.' The district would be named Weatherfield because had the programme been set in a real suburb its stories would have been circumscribed by that area's by-laws. Despite these facts, few seem to doubt (including, judging by many of his comments, Warren himself) that Coronation Street is notionally located in his hometown of Salford. This itself raises an interesting geographical point. Though Salford is in the Greater Manchester area, and though it is located just a half-mile walk away from Piccadilly (the dead centre of Manchester), Salford is not *within* the city of Manchester. How ironic that *Coronation Street* and football club Manchester United are generally perceived as the two most famous things about Manchester: like The Street, Manchester United is not located in the city to which it is attached in the popular imagination, its Old Trafford ground actually being situated in the Greater Manchester borough of Trafford.

Before embarking on his rail return from the Highlands, Warren purchased a notebook and six pencils on the station platform. A yardstick for artistic inspiration – becoming so engrossed with a project that the world recedes into the distance – attended Warren's mapping and fleshing out of his backstreet drama idea on the journey home. Looking up from his furious scribbling, he was surprised to find Granada's neon sign shining back at him.

When Elton gave him that ultimatum, therefore, to deliver him a great programme idea within the space of a day, he didn't know that Warren was already more than halfway there. Which is not to slight in any way the 42-page script bashed out on his bedroom floor that Warren gave him the next day. That Elton was bowled over by Warren's idea was not because, unlike some at Granada, he had a sense of mission about the North of England – he was Canadian, one of several North Americans recruited by Granada because television was such a new medium in Britain that it was felt the company needed to cast its recruitment net outside the country's borders to acquire relevant talent. Rather it was because he knew great drama when he saw it. He later said of Warren, 'He has the most remarkable talent for dialogue and character creation of any writer I have ever worked with.' Such was the script's quality that though its title of *Florizel Street* was subjected to what is these days called 'finessing', and save for the addition of two characters, it was broadcast largely unchanged. Such also was its quality that the producer, after reading it, spurned his normal convention of getting his secretary to summon the individual he wanted to see and personally made haste to Warren's office to tell him to write a memo to accompany the script for consumption by the decision makers upstairs. Surprisingly for someone who had in his continuity days mastered the art of distilling a programme to its essence, Warren's memo was somewhat less impressive than the script. It read, 'A fascinating freemasonry, a volume of unwritten rules. There are the driving forces behind life in a working class street in the North of England. The purpose of *Florizel Street* is to examine a community of this nature and, in so doing, entertain.' Following that peculiar introduction, The Street's architecture and its residents were detailed.

This precise layout of the street of Warren's imagination was not all in place by the time of his first script. It would take a later process of Warren and designer Denis Parkin driving around Manchester before he decided upon its architecture. Though there was a Coronation Street in Salford, the road on which the pair physically based the fictional Coronation Street was not that but Archie Street in Ordsall, a road with rows of terraced houses and an off licence (Daniel Clifton & Co. Ltd) at the end of one. The off licence was changed for the programme because it was thought that a general shop would enable a wider variety of activity and the type of gossiping that could advance the plots. Meanwhile, a pub was added at the other end of the fictional Coronation Street. The Rovers Return was divided between the Public Bar and the Snug, the latter an unofficial woman-only zone where the old biddies tended to nurse their drinks for an inordinate length of time that reflected the meagre means of pensioners. (There was also the Select – a function room – but it was rarely seen.)

The bay windows and single front steps of the Archie Street houses and the presence of St. Clement's Church in the background also became part of Coronation Street (albeit the latter was renamed St. Mary's). Though there would be a studio set of the exterior of Coronation Street, it was slightly ridiculous (especially to modern eyes), with its painted, picture book-like backdrops. Accordingly, the programme would sometimes shoot on location in Archie Street in the early Sixties. Archie

Street was also seen in a panning shot in the first title sequence, which ran until 1964 (film stock of the time was so bad that its lack of a pub down the far end wasn't apparent). Additionally, its back alley was shown in the second title sequence, which ran until 1968. By coincidence, the latter was both the year that the Archie Street residents were moved out to prepare it for its demolition and the year Granada built their own outdoor *Street* set, making location visits to Archie Street – increasingly difficult as the programme's fame had grown – unnecessary. Archie Street was demolished in 1971, and is not to be confused with an extant Archie Street in, ironically, Salford.

While Archie Street had terraces on both sides, one side of the fictional Coronation Street was occupied by the back wall of Elliston's factory, which manufactured raincoats, and the back entrance of Victoria Street's Glad Tidings Mission Hall (the Vestry). *Coronation Street*, in fact, has always effectively been a story of two streets, for while the architecture of the terraced side has remained unchanged since 1960, the opposite side has been redeveloped several times as different producers have opted for a new landscape in order to enable an influx of new characters and/or modernise the show.

The road surface between the two opposing pavements was, like many Northern streets of the period, cobbled rather than tarmacked. There was a notional local school called Bessie Street, which many *Street* characters have attended. Warren made it abstract by situating it around the corner of Coronation Street itself, an overhang of his hatred of his own truancy-pocked schooldays. However, Ken Barlow would later be seen teaching in it. Rosamund Street ran across the mouth of Coronation Street at the Rovers Return end and Viaduct Street was the road parallel to Rosamund Street at the Corner Shop end, its name a reference to the railway bridge through whose arches one could (originally) walk or drive to reach Jubilee Terrace, a street physically very similar to Coronation Street.

The seven houses of Coronation Street's terraced side were, it was decided, built at the turn of the 20th century. Their structural design was uniform: no front path, but rather a door that opened directly onto the street, and no back garden but rather a yard (colloquially called the 'coal hole' in reference to its status as storeroom for the means of keeping warm in pre-central heating days), three downstairs rooms – a front parlour, a combined living room/kitchen and a scullery – and three rooms upstairs. Those who had not converted the back bedroom did not have the pleasure of a bathroom, while all the houses had outside lavatories. This tin-bath-and-outhouse arrangement was in no way unrepresentative of many parts of working class Britain at the time, nor was the fact that all of the houses were rented: a Britain that was, or aspired to be, a 'property owning democracy' was a long way into the future. The weekly rent went into the coffers of one Edward Wormold. The latter charged 19 shillings per week, a sum that was never established on screen but which was stated in a pull-out guide to The Street that appeared in ITV's schedule listings magazine *TV Times* when the programme began.

Warren peopled his fictional street with an extraordinarily colourful and varied cast, their names, according to Denis Parkin, taken from gravestones in the grounds of Salford's Pendlebury Church.

'The Rovers', as it was colloquially referred to by all locals, was run by Jack and Annie Walker. Annie's steely blonde tresses – dyed, obviously, as she was like her husband late middle-aged – and haughty manner were things many would be put in mind of several years later when a politician called Margaret Thatcher began acquiring fame. Others were reminded more of battleaxe TV chef Fanny Craddock, especially considering the resemblance of Annie's good-natured and slightly henpecked husband to Craddock's other half, Johnny. The Walkers' grown-up children were daughter Joan, a schoolteacher, and son Billy. The latter was initially away doing his National Service but in later years would be one of the few alpha males on The Street.

No.1 Coronation Street, situated right beside the pub, was occupied by retired elderly widower Albert Tatlock. Tatlock was only created at the insistence of a Granada executive who felt that Warren's first script lacked someone of 'age, charm and dignity.' In truth, the first of that trio of qualities was the only one this harrumphing grouch with a symbolically appropriate Hitler moustache possessed. Somehow, though, he was endearing and would be a decades-spanning fixture of The Street.

Coronation Street adhered to the British tradition of odd and even house numbering on opposite sides, so the next house in the terrace was No.3. This was the home of the Barlows. Frank Barlow was a man in his mid-forties who worked as a sorter at the General Post Office. His wife Ida was kitchen hand in a Manchester hotel. Younger son David was an apprentice mechanic. Like Tatlock, he was added to the cast after that first script, his introduction designed to give the show a male teenage presence. David's brother – at 21, older by two years – was Kenneth. He was the character who in the programme's early days most captured the *zeitgeist*, not just via his brooding youthful intensity (i.e., an angry young man, even if his anger was as much directed at his folks, whose simple ways he looked down on, as the Elders and Betters who had made such a mess of the world) but in his status of university student: Ken was representative of the millions who had benefited from the post-war education reforms which provided free further education for those academically gifted enough to continue their studies.

Spinster Esther Hayes was the resident of No.5. An office filing clerk in her early forties, she had a motherly affection for Ken Barlow. Harry Hewitt, a bus inspector in his late thirties, occupied No.7. He had been widowed a year earlier. In a day and age where it was assumed that raising children was exclusively women's work, his 10-year-old daughter Lucille was initially in a local authority orphanage. Next door's No.9 was unoccupied, the consequence of the producers not being able to decide on whom to inhabit it with, although they were conscious of the opportunity the vacant property would give them to alter the alchemy of the show if the current mixture was found wanting.

No.11 was occupied by Elsie Tanner and her son Dennis, 25. Elsie was an auburn-haired woman in her mid-forties who worked in the dress department of a Manchester store. The term 'chav' did not exist in 1960, but the Tanners were the first example of a *Coronation Street* tradition that has been maintained down the years by the Ogdens, the Duckworths, the Battersbys and the Windasses. Dead common, ne'er-do-wells, deadbeats, tramps, yobs, pikies – call them what you will, but they are the type who are looked down on even by people who haven't got much to feel snobbish about. In those more genteel times, the Tanners' crimes against society were rather less wicked than those of their modern day equivalents. Elsie, vaguely shockingly for the age, was separated from her seaman husband Arnold, and – somewhat more shockingly – was not averse to 'gentleman callers'. Dennis was a bequiffed and seething individual with an already chequered past in his young life: he had a couple of convictions for crimes against property and had spent time in prison for one of them. They would occasionally be visited by Elsie's beautiful and likeable daughter Linda – one year Dennis' senior – who was married to burly Polish-born metal worker Ivan Cheveski. The latter couple lived in Warrington at the show's outset but would move into the vacant No.9 (i.e., right next door to Elsie) in 1961.

The last house, No.13, had only one occupant when The Street started, as the mother of Christine Hardman, May, was in hospital suffering from a nervous breakdown, and in fact would soon depart both The Street and this world. Christine was a cheerful, intelligent and pretty girl who worked as a machinist in the raincoat factory. Her father had died five years before.

The shop beside No.13 would have many owners, and hence names, down the years but is consistently referred to in this text as the Corner Shop for the sake of convenience. There were living quarters to the rear of the shop reserved for the owners and a flat above it, which could be rented out. The first episode of the programme would capture the shop on the cusp of a change of ownership, with good-natured ex-barmaid Florrie Lindley having just purchased it.

On the opposite, more barren side of The Street, Ena Sharples could often be seen emerging from the door of the Vestry of the Glad Tidings Mission Hall, at which she was caretaker. Aged 70, Sharples was The Street's conscience, but not in the modern touchy-feely way. Rather, she was the self-appointed upholder of the censorious and judgemental mores of the day and executed her job with an appropriately grim face. Not that this meant she didn't have her own vices: much to the embarrassment of the Chapel committee of the Mission Hall, she frequented the Rovers as much as she absented herself from church services. They put up with her because nobody else seemed to want her job, even though it came with free accommodation.

There were a few non-residents who were nonetheless major characters. Martha Longhurst and Minnie Caldwell were drinking companions of Ena Sharples in the Snug and formed an often hilarious Greek chorus with her. Leonard Swindley was chairman of the committee of the Mission Hall, as well as owner of a haberdashery shop on Rosamund Street. He was a rather clipped but essentially decent old cove and provided much comic relief.

In 1960, it was of course impossible for the fictional street to feature a gay character. Warren got round this by inserting elements of the personalities of gay men into those of The Street's women. 'I'd known all these queens in the village,' he later said. 'Some of their dialogue was too good not to use. I remember giving Elsie lines that they would say. When you think of some of the things she came out with, how many straight women have you heard say that?'

arren's first episode was taken to Denis Forman, the man who had been instrumental in giving Warren a contract. Forman heard a considerable stir in the open area outside his office just before Elton and drama director Stuart Latham burst in. They demanded that he read a script they excitedly thrust at him. Forman says he had to 'calm down' Elton and Latham, but could see the merits in what he read. Forman's verdict on *Florizel Street* was, 'Good characters, good dialogue', which slightly disappointed the pair, who had sat waiting outside his office for the 20 minutes or so he took to get through it. They considered it to be 'a knockout'. Does Forman now concede that the pair were vindicated? Forman: 'Yes. certainly. Of course they were right. But there's no point in being over-excited, however successful you're going to be.' Forman's shortness with Elton and Latham is what one would expect of a brisk, upper class and slightly intimidating man, yet his ultimate receptiveness to the backstreet story is in another sense logical in that, surprisingly, he shared the socialist Bernstein values and was married to a Labour Party campaigner.

Forman had a surprise when he was informed who had written this gritty script. 'I knew Tony only as a willowy figure with a long cigarette holder and a cane, who affected the style and manner of speech of Noel Coward,' he wrote in his book *Persona Granada*. 'He was unmistakably a grown-up child actor and this was not at all the sort of stuff I would have expected of him.' Forman told the pair to distribute two scripts to the Television Committee (decision-making forerunner to Granada's Programme Committee) and to try to think of a title better than *Florizel Street*.

The Committee was not enthusiastic, with words like 'dreary' being thrown around. Forman says that there was a fear 'that people wouldn't understand the argot.' About the only yea-sayer was Granada's deputy chairman Cecil Bernstein, who liked what he read and thought it would at least play well locally if it transpired not to be network-friendly. Forman denies that there was ever a worry that the natural demographic for the programme were low-waged people who the advertisers wouldn't be interested in. He also refuses to condemn the apparent contradiction of the programme committee of a Northern television company being so nervous about Lancastrianisms. 'They were dead right,' he says. 'It was a terrific gamble. Everyone was surprised that the nation was prepared to accept such a tough accent as there was in *Coronation Street*.' Forman must take some credit for that gamble. He later claimed, 'I worked the meeting round to a reluctant agreement to let the show go ahead as a seven-parter.'

The seven-parter reference rather adds to a confusion surrounding just how long this programme was originally intended to run, with some citing the figure of 12 episodes (the number of shows Warren wrote before a writing team was brought in), some 16, and Daran Little stating, 'They commissioned a run of thirteen episodes.' *Street* actor Alan Rothwell adds, 'As far as I was concerned we had six scripts and we were doing six, so I'm sorry if that throws another spoke in the wheel.' Also victim of conflicting accounts is whether the programme was ever seriously envisaged as something in which the other franchise holders would be interested rather than a thing of solely parochial interest for Granada's transmission region. At some point in all of this, a message was sent down from the bigwigs that they were thinking of *Florizel Street* as something that would have two episodes per week – which slightly adds to the confusion, because when some have spoken of a projected 12- or 13-week run, it's not clear whether they were factoring in an extra episode each week.

Before the programme could make it to air, a pilot – also known as a dry run – was required, a sample programme not for public consumption. The reception to the dry run from the Programme Committee was if anything even less enthusiastic than their feelings about the initial script. Light entertainment producer Eddie Pola seemed to have been prejudiced against the programme from his viewing experiences in his native United States, dismissing it as 'soap opera' and the sort of 'crap' that should be on in the afternoons, not evenings. The term soap opera derives from the 1930s when American soap and detergent manufacturers advertised heavily in and around daytime radio drama serials because of their housewife demographic. Pola was way off: there is clearly little resemblance between the sophistication and poise of the domestic dramas played out in The Street and the simplistic plots and melodrama of then-traditional soap operas. Interestingly, Granada – especially David Plowright, who went from programme controller to MD to chairman – was subsequently always very touchy about the pejorative connotations of the phrase soap opera, preferring descriptions like 'drama serial' or 'continuing drama.'

General manager Victor Peers stated that he couldn't find a single redeeming quality about the pilot and offered the advice that people wanted to be lifted out of their dreary lives, not to have their noses rubbed in them. Deputy chairman Cecil Bernstein said nobody would ever take it seriously because of cartoon north-country dialect reminiscent of the likes of buck-toothed Wigan comedian George Formby. Perhaps rather patronisingly, he allowed that Elton couldn't be blamed for a 'horrible mistake' because he was not from round these parts. Denis Forman felt it fell between the two stools of comedy and documentary. In his judgment, Granada chairman Sidney Bernstein seemed to be gravitating more toward the mindset of the first half of his contradictory status of millionaire socialist when he noted that the houses on The Street weren't very nice and hardly the sort of image that his company should be purveying to those within its company's broadcast reach, which he had tagged Granadaland. Questions were posited by some about whether such a show would drive away advertisers. Forman is not surprised by the negativity, saying that the pilot was very 'messy'.

It was a unanimous thumbs-down, one ostensibly devastating. Forman, though, says there was no question that The Street would not make it to people's screens. 'It had a pulse like a canon,' he says. 'I think it was going to make the air.' However, others have stated that only one thing saved The Street: Elton had nothing else to screen, as *Biggles*, failing in the ratings, was due to end in early December; the committee therefore agreed that *Coronation Street* would receive a short, limited run but Elton was instructed to devise something quickly to replace it.

What caused Granada to break with precedent and permit a second pilot is uncertain. This pilot was subject to the sort of test screening now common in the field of cinema but not widespread in television even now. A broadcast on closed circuit television was arranged to which everybody in the Granada building from cleaners upwards were invited, with questionnaires being provided for their verdicts. (Some reports state that both pilots were shown on this day.) Warren has said, 'More than anything else, the comments on those questionnaires put *Coronation Street* on the screen.' Yet according to Elton (admittedly in testimony later than Warren's, with the attendant possibility of less reliable recollection), the show had already been commissioned, albeit for a limited run. (It's not clear whether or not this is lent credence by the fact that one of the dry runs was of episode three.) But that in itself begs the question of why the show needed a second pilot if it was already destined for the air. Would Granada have permitted a second dry run merely so that Elton could 'get some positive feedback for our efforts'? Forman is not sure, but suspects that the second pilot was commissioned to get the casting right. Whatever the reason for it, the second pilot was rapturously received by those who saw it, and perhaps this is why *Coronation Street* did not transpire to be merely the stop-gap originally envisaged. The programme was formally commissioned on 25 August 1960. The core of its production team was executive producer Harry Elton, producer Stuart Latham, writer Warren and script editor Harry Kershaw. Latham was actually known by his real name of Harry. Kershaw, meanwhile, had been brought in by Latham to be a sounding board: because Elton was a Canadian and Latham a Southerner, it was felt a Northern point of view was needed. Kershaw did not originally receive a credit until his wife came up with a title for his job that Granada could live with: serial editor. When he did, it was as H.V. Kershaw. Kershaw remembered a certain amount of hostility or scepticism within Granada, with people (who he implied were very high up) convinced that no programme could be successful without middle class appeal, which is presumably why pressure was unsuccessfully applied to have a young doctor living in the street.

Warren has stated that the 11 episodes following the first one were written not on his bedroom floor, like the first, but in his glass-walled Granada office. Bill Podmore (*Street* producer from 1976), however, claimed that those 12 episodes were written on a settee of a pub called the Lantern Pike (Warren often on his stomach) in Warren's home of Little Hayfield in Derbyshire. Of course, writers often go through many drafts of their creations – not to mention the note-jotting process that precedes and/or complements those drafts – so both stories could be true. Warren also said that he was told to 'plan a possible bulldozing of The Street for what might prove to be a final, 13th episode.'

Though the dry runs had had beneficial results, they also brought about casualties. One, according to former Granada Press Officer Norman Frisby, was overt Lancastrianisms; he felt the programme was 'a bit watered down' as a result of the notes on the questionnaires. Meanwhile, Nan Marriott-Watson, who played Ena Sharples in the dry run of episode three, turned that part down, while Nita Valerie, the actress who depicted Ena in the other pilot, was deemed unsuitable. Because Warren and co. found all other applicants wanting and rehearsals for the first episode were shortly to begin, Granada instructed Warren to delete the part. Warren and his colleagues were united in disbelief and indignation and appealed the decision, only to be met with indifference. It seems to have been Warren's desperation that made his brain suggest to him the name of a woman who had latterly become as much known for playing the piano on folksy, audience-participation radio show *Have A Go* as for acting. Though not quite the flint-faced battleaxe she would portray in The Street, Violet Carson had once terrified the kids with whom she appeared in a Children's Hour serial, one of whom was Warren in his child thesp days. That Warren didn't bear a grudge is evident in the fact that Carson passed the audition to which he ensured she was called. Carson's heavyset frame was the opposite to Warren's original vision of a thin woman but that it was a perfect piece of casting is illustrated by the fact that to anyone of a certain age one of the first images that springs to mind at the mention of the phrase *Coronation Street* is that of a woman whose tresses are bound in a transcendentally unflattering hairnet and whose timeworn face is set in chilly disproval. This was the image of Ena Sharples that would grace TV screens for two decades. The woman who lost out in the battle to be Ena, incidentally, did make it onto The Street eventually, if fleetingly: Nita Valerie played a factory cleaner named Polly Sagan in a 1966 episode, as well as appearing in *Street* spin-off *Pardon the Expression* the same year.

The process of casting *Coronation Street* had been exhaustive. Those proletarian Southerners who were wearily used to seeing posh actors shoving glottal stops into their normally impeccable diction to portray cockney barrow boys and gangsters might think they bore a unique grievance, but residents of the North of England were themselves despairingly familiar with the sight of actors with Received Pronunciation going all ecky-thump as they took on the fictional personas of people who hailed from north of the Watford gap and south of the actors' own social caste. Warren, Elton, casting director Margaret Morris and Morris' assistant José Scott decided that there would be none of this in The Street. They also decided that The Street would feature no well-known faces so as to assist the quest to convey realism. 'There was only one famous person in the cast originally and that was Maudie Edwards,' says Daran Little. 'She played Elsie Lappin.' The crew began drawing up a list of Northern thespians. The statistic of 600 people ultimately auditioned by them for the programme's 23 roles stands as an indictment of all the casting directors who had previously reached for the telephone numbers of people who spoke 'laake thet' in their real lives when looking for somebody to play a character from Lancashire. For all that, though, some Mancunians weren't impressed when the show aired: those in the know could spot the improbability of one street housing people with accents as far-flung as Bury, Oldham and Rochdale.

The most famous line ever uttered by Elsie Tanner was in The Street's inaugural episode wherein she said to her mirror reflection, "Ee, Elsie. You're just about ready for the knacker yard.' Warren first heard the line from the mouth of his aunt Lily, and years later began to develop Elsie's character from that single quote. Not that Lily was the only inspiration for the character who was 'a slice off a cut loaf', Northern parlance for a woman who is not a virgin and to whom by implication sexual intercourse is no big deal. Warren used three separate women as source material for the character who would be the programme's totem in its first two decades. 'Tit and glitter' were what Warren considered necessary for the role. When actress Patricia Phoenix turned up to read, he felt she was 10 years too young. She did, though, visibly possess both parts of his twin requirements. Not only was she busty, she arrived at the audition in a fur coat, in an era when such an accoutrement was apt to bring sighs of admiration rather than gasps of horror. That Phoenix had scrimped for such a garment almost in defiance of a lifetime in acting that had made her the battered survivor of countless rejections and periods of semi-starvation rather suggests that in real life Phoenix was exactly the type of person she was auditioning to play: a woman who wrested happiness and glitz from the maws of a dreary and unfulfilled existence. Little wonder she got the role.

Some of the casting decisions were simplicity itself. Warren had always had Doris Speed in mind for Annie Walker – a character based, according to Phoenix and Podmore, on the landlady of the Lantern Pike hostelry that Warren is supposed to have written the early episodes in. (Podmore named her as Josephine Paterson.) Though such networking might strike some as distasteful, nobody would now either say that Speed was inadequate to the part or be able to envisage anyone else in it. In real life, incidentally, Speed was completely different to her character, bereft of airs and a firm Socialist. For Warren, Christine Hargreaves was also a cinch as Christine Hardman: she was a local girl born within a mile of Warren's Salford home and possessed of a smile that could light up a room.

Derbyshire-born William Roache was cast as Ken Barlow. He had appeared in Granada's Marking Time, an instalment of the prestigious Play Of The Week slot. Recalls Roache, 'When I was doing Marking Time, apparently Tony Warren took the casting director down to the studio and pointed to me and said, "That's the guy I want to play Ken Barlow." I was called in for an audition…. Didn't particularly want to do it because

I thought other things would be happening. But we all thought it was only going to run for thirteen weeks [sic].... I didn't want it so you're very relaxed, aren't you? That went alright, then they asked me to do a pilot, which I got paid for and I did that. Then they offered me the part.' Little did he know, 50 years later Roache would still be in the show that was planned as a two-month instalment in his career and indeed would constitute its one surviving link to that original cast.

'Just something that's in you,' is Roache's explanation for his decision to go into acting. 'My family were all doctors, so I'm the black sheep of the family, but I did acting at school. I was in the army for six years. I didn't think it was a proper job or I'd be good enough, but it was burning away so when I came out of the army, aged 26, I thought I've got to give it a go. So that's what I'm doing: I'm still giving it a go. I did two, three years in the theatre, mainly repertory, which was a great training ground and was why we produced so many great actors. You can't have [a] better training ground than the rep. I did lots of film bits, television bits, then I had a lead in *Marking Time*.' As can be gleaned from the above, Roache is not exactly from a *Coronation Street*-style backstreet. 'I'm a middle class background, cut and dried,' he says. Did that make him apprehensive about taking on the role? 'Not at all. I'm an actor.' The actor part was evident in the early days via an accent noticeably broader than it is today. Roache: 'In those days we all worked on the accent, much more so. I always thought Ken Barlow was the sort of guy who would want to better himself anyway, so it was partly that and partly laziness, it sort of slipped a bit. But a lot of regional accents are breaking down anyway with the communications being what they are.'

The role of Ken's little brother was given to 23-year-old Alan Rothwell. Like Roache, Rothwell had been picked out beforehand. 'I did a play called *Love On The Dole* for the BBC and that went out just at the time they were casting for *Coronation Street*,' Rothwell recalls. 'I didn't audition for it. They just offered me the part of David Barlow.' He feels that the working class milieu of the adaptation of Walter Greenwood's classic novel is what won him the role. That milieu matched Rothwell's upbringing by cotton mill workers in a village just outside Oldham. 'I was thrilled by them,' Rothwell says of Warren's *Street* scripts. 'The echoes of my own life were just there on the page.' Like several *Street* actors and many Granada staff, Rothwell knew Warren from his previous life: 'I'd known him for years actually, because we'd done radio programmes together for the BBC when he was a performer.'

Though Rothwell's background couldn't have been more different to that of Roache, he says the two men 'were actually really good mates' off-screen in marked contrast to the underlying antagonisms between the characters they played. There was an extra layer of irony in this. Of Ken, Rothwell says, 'He was the one that had got all the advantages. He'd gone to university and [my character] hadn't gone to university. Now curiously, that reflected what my father used to say. He was one of two brothers and his elder brother went to the better school and carried on at school longer and went to work in the cotton mill office, whereas my father, they couldn't afford to have him spending any more time at school. They took him out of school and put him in the cotton mill. So my father always resented that and there was always great antagonism between my father and his brother, just as there was this underlying antagonism between Ken and David.'

Only a couple of actors beat the Northern bias. One was Ken Farrington, a Londoner by birth who got his part by taking the advice of José Scott not to mention his roots and imitating Albert Finney, with whom he had attended drama school. Though he failed to land the role of Dennis Tanner that he auditioned for, he was soon to become known as Billy Walker. The other was Ernst Walder. Inspired by the example of Charles Laughton, who went to drama school in London, Walder moved to England from his native Austria and learned the language while engaged in domestic work before getting into the Royal Academy's preparatory school. After Harry Corbett recommended him to an agent, he appeared in a number of films, including *The One Who Got Away*, before getting his first television role in The Street. Though Austrian, he would play Italians, Czechs and Germans in his career, so it's no surprise that the climate of the times dictated that he be considered suitable for the role of Linda Cheveski's Polish husband Ivan. (Anne Cunningham played Linda.) Walder, who would become a good friend of Warren's, explains of Ivan, 'Apparently there were lots of Polish people in Manchester from the War still and I think that's what made him think of [writing in] a Pole.' Walder says he was not irritated by his generic Continental status. 'I had an Austrian accent,' he explains. 'A bit like Welsh. Softer. Not as hard as German English. I got most of my parts because I had an accent.' It should also be pointed out that the people least likely to find his casting plausible in fact seemed to do so. Walder: 'I had many times in Manchester when I walked about, Polish people came up to me talking to me in Polish and I couldn't speak a word of

Polish.' Walder also makes an observation that puts the above comments about casting locally into context. Asked if he found his fellow cast members difficult to understand, he says no: 'They spoke perfectly beautiful English but they just used the accent for the show. Most of them.' Clearly, Northern actors knocked the edges off their natural accents in their everyday lives. Walder also, incidentally, recalls less than luxurious conditions at Granada when rehearsals got underway: 'The first big building wasn't there when we started off…. Barracks were there. Those who weren't actually rehearsing had to sit outside on the stairs 'cos there wasn't enough room.'

The programme was still being referred to as *Florizel Street* in late November 1960. Florizel is the most common of the names of the prince in the Sleeping Beauty fairy tale. Warren had a picture of him working his way through the enchanted forest on his office wall. *Florizel Street* certainly doesn't trip off the tongue. Though Warren, according to Daran Little, pronounced it 'Flor-e-zel', there was confusion as to how to say it. Little: 'Bill Roache couldn't pronounce it in the dry run so it was decided to change the name.' Additionally, a Granada tea lady called Agnes rang alarm bells when she observed that it sounded like a disinfectant.

Warren decided to step back as Elton, Latham and Kershaw went about re-christening the programme. Many will assume that the title decided upon alluded to the coronation of Queen Elizabeth II. It is an understandable assumption: her ascension to the throne had taken place only seven years previously and had been the biggest event in the history of British television so far, to such an extent that many of the people who had decided to branch out from a hearth dominated by the 'wireless' and buy one of these new-fangled tellies (as they were only just beginning to call them) had specifically done so in order to watch it take place. However, the notion is a mistaken one. Kershaw has said the title was decided in Latham's office, a bottle of whisky between he, Latham and Elton. (Some anecdotes have the title of the show being discussed in a pub in Bootle Street at a *Biggles* farewell party.) The trio decided that the street name should derive from its late 19th-century vintage. There were two contenders: Jubilee Street, in reference to Queen Victoria's Diamond Jubilee, and Coronation Street, an allusion to the ascension to the throne of Edward VII that occurred shortly thereafter. A heated debate ensued, then a vote. Kershaw and Elton went for Jubilee Street. Latham announced the following day in a memo that the new name of the programme and its titular street was…*Coronation Street*. By Latham's account, he had already made up his mind before the aforesaid drunken meeting: he recalled deciding upon it after 'much lonely concentration' in Granada's New Theatre Tavern and settled on *Coronation Street* because trisyllabic names like *Florizel Street* and *Jubilee Street* felt wrong, following which he returned to the studio and told only the Graphics Department of the new title.

The *Coronation Street* theme music has not changed in the half-century of the programme's existence. This is testament to the fact that it is perfection. It was provided by Eric Spear, a film and television composer whose credits so far included the Frankie Howerd vehicle *Touching The Sun* and *Meet Mr. Callaghan*, the latter theme covered by guitar legend Les Paul. Accounts of how Spear's music came to be used – as with so many things surrounding The Street's early days – differ. Some stories say that the script of the programme's first episode was posted to Spear's home in Capri and that within a week Spear had sent Granada the sheet music and a tape with a piano arrangement of what he had come up with. Others say that his home in fact was in the Channel Islands, from where he travelled reluctantly to watch one of the pilots. Latham was of the opinion that Spear's theme had already been written and was an unsold property. If that is the case, it's little short of miraculous because it was so appropriate. It was a piece of music that was sedate, somewhat mournful and almost wistful. Slightly jazzy musically, it was dominated by a cornet, and it was this latter element which probably helped seal its feel of complete appropriateness, for one of the things for which the North of England was then (and to some extent still is) known is brass bands.

So embedded is The Street's theme tune in our consciousnesses that it's difficult to examine it completely clinically, but it does genuinely seem the case that Spear could not have done better in tone, memorability and aesthetic worth. A television show's greatness is not dependent on a great title theme and it is not spoiled by it having a bad one – the fact that *Frasier* was cursed with a stupid, *apropos*-nothing ditty about tossed salads and scrambled eggs makes us remember one of history's finest comedy programmes no less fondly – but a pleasing sense of completeness is achieved when a show's dramatic brilliance is bookended by equally fine music.

Paradoxically, this apparently quintessentially English brass band music may actually have originated as a musical tribute to the somewhat different environs of the Deep South of America. The most prominent motif bears more than a passing resemblance to 'Dear Old Southland', a jazz song originating in 1921 whose music was composed by Turner Layton. However, lifting themes from other works is a tradition in musical composition going back centuries – underlined by the fact that the melody of 'Dear Old Southland' itself clearly owes a debt to that of the spiritual 'Deep River'.

It now seems barely conceivable, but The Street's producers did not immediately fall in love with Spear's theme and there was some debate about whether to employ music from a commercially available album by the CWS Brass Band, until it was decreed that Spear's work would be used because it had been paid for.

The instrumentation on the recording of the theme tune comprised trumpet, clarinet, four trombones (probably muted with cups), and a rhythm section of drums (played with brushes), stand-up bass and acoustic guitar. The source for the details of this line-up is David Browning, who, though he didn't play on the session, recalls that when he took part in the theme's 1970 re-recording he was cognisant of the fact that the line-up was the same as it had been in 1960. However, he thinks there may be an exception. Browning's trumpet cornet is the most prominent part of the instrumentation of the modern theme and he thinks that its equivalent on the original was most likely an ordinary trumpet, which has a smaller sound.

Trumpet or trumpet cornet, that part on the original was played by jazz sessioner Ronnie Hunt. The latter only appeared because he was sent to deputise for more celebrated player Stan Roderick, who had no reason to believe that the programme would be anything other than something that disappeared into the ether almost as soon as broadcast. Writing in *Jazz Professional* in 1994, Ron Simmonds claimed, 'I believe that an attempt was made in later years to re-record that solo, using Stan Roderick, but it sounded too good, and they reverted to the old one.' This is ironic according to Dave Browning. 'Nobody's heard of Ronnie Hunt in the music business,' he says. 'He wasn't what you would call a top class player. When you're talking about Stan Roderick, you're talking about the absolute top shelf of the business, as good as it gets.' Browning also reveals that, rather contrary to the spirit of the franchise system, the original theme recording was not done locally. 'I do know for a fact that it was recorded down in London,' he says. 'The first years of ITV, most of the shows themselves – particularly light entertainment shows as opposed to documentaries – were made in London and then sent up here for final touching up.'

Snippets of the theme tune were used for the show's 'break bumpers': the climatic bobbing descent was isolated to provide a sort of aural mini-cliffhanger at the close of part one, and the start of the theme briefly flared following the commercial break. There was no incidental music (music employed within the programme to underscore the drama) in The Street, a now prevailing tradition in continuing drama serials that is possibly rooted in economic reasons: theme music requires only one-off payments to the musicians, whereas incidental music necessitates residual payments in perpetuity.

Though the 20 seconds of music at the start of the programme these days is roughly the same amount as was heard when it was first broadcast, the inordinately long advertising break necessitated by The Street's sky-high ratings makes it impossible to let the theme run to the full minute it did over the closing credits of that inaugural episode. Now, less than half a minute is heard at the end. Even that closing credit music often has a vocal trailer over much of it. All of this means that sadly, the half-wispy, half-jaunty clarinet passages between the blare of the trumpet are now never heard.

The first episode of *Coronation Street* was due for transmission on Friday 9 December 1960 at 7pm. Not all the franchises had agreed to show the programme. While Anglia Television (the licence holder for the East of England), Associated-Rediffusion (London), Scottish Television (Central Scotland), Southern Television (Southern and South-East England), TWW (Wales and West of England) and Ulster Television (Northern Ireland) all felt that the show (or the sound of it) had something to offer viewers in their region, Tyne Tees Television (North-East of England) and ATV (the Midlands) had opted out. Transmitters, of course, recognised no geographical borders other than the limits of their signal and if they had a mind to and were handily located, people in those areas could pick up the programme.

The day of the transmission found Warren a bag of nerves, although the fact that a bad dress rehearsal is according to showbusiness tradition a harbinger of a good performance proper ensured that he at least wasn't too worried about a shaky run-through. There was much to be nervous about. From today's perspective, it seems inconceivable that television companies would want to screen a programme live when the technology existed even then to record them, but that's what Granada had decided to do. It seems even more inconceivable that Granada would want to film the second episode 'as-live' 15 minutes later (i.e., recorded, but shot right the way through with no second takes), as that would seem to negate the benefits to be had from recording, namely making fluffed lines, missed cues, malfunctioning scenery and misbehaving technology cease to be part of the equation. But this is a demonstration of the fact that The Street has been around almost as long as television has existed in any meaningful way.

Live TV drama was not uncommon in the era, despite its practical drawbacks, one of which had been demonstrated in 1958 when actor Gareth Jones died during the transmission of an episode of *Armchair Theatre*. 'It was an economic decision,' explains Michael Cox, who directed his first *Street* in 1965. 'You could record it, fine. Once you started to edit it though, you were costing money both in terms of an electronic editing suite and also in terms of the tape you used, because in those days tape was edited physically. You would cut with a razor blade and once it had been cut the tape couldn't be used again. So there was a history for the company of saying, "Well it worked very well, it was live, not much went wrong did it, let's do it that way." And of course it's a time-saver.'

Certainly the production team had to be on their toes. In a scene in episode three of The Street, Ena's cocoa milk boiled over. On a live show, there is no such thing as post-production, so the sizzle that alerted her to this calamity was something that had to be effected at the time by an individual alert for his cue. The production staff did their jobs amazingly well considering the technology available: very impressive camera tricks and sound effects accompanied the collapse of May Hardman in episode seven, another live broadcast, with us being made privy to the thudding in the character's head and her blurring vision.

There were logistical scriptwriting issues with live broadcasts unimaginable to writers today. John Finch, a *Street* scriptwriter from 1961 onwards, recalls, 'We had to write into the scripts what we called verbal transitions, where you'd write a couple of lines extra on the end of the scene to give the actor time to get across to another set. You had to be aware of all these technical problems.' During the respite of the commercial break, the actors would be told by the floor manager or director what the current running time was and to slow down or fill out accordingly.

Ironically, 1960 TV audiences would have been forgiving of the mistakes the crew frantically attempted to prevent. With the tradition of multiple takes yet to be properly established, the audience perceived a television drama as akin to a stage play that happened to be transmitted. Additionally, it wouldn't have occurred to many of the actors to think about this aspect: the days of dedicated television actors in Britain had barely started and most thesps viewed television as a nice bonus on top of their normal theatre work.

The Street's procedure of one live, one as-live, persisted right up until February the following year. Mercifully, Granada did not adhere to another common practice of the day in treating the tapes of their live or even as-live transmissions as though they were the televisual equivalent of a newspaper. *Coronation Street*'s past is intact. Unlike early episodes of the BBC's *Doctor Who*, almost all Sixties and Seventies episodes of ITV's *Crossroads* or indeed the entirety of The Street's spin-off *Turn Out The Lights*, no *Street* episodes were ever wiped on the orders of cost-conscious executives. Only the dry runs have not survived.

That mournful but attractive theme music was cued. It drifted across opening titles consisting of a panning shot from the roofs to the front doors of The Street. As it faded away, programme director Derek Bennett cued the actors in the first scene.

The first sight that greets the eyes of the programme's viewers is an exterior scene (albeit shot in the studio) depicting two small girls bouncing a ball and chanting a song in the dark street outside the Corner Shop. Elsie Lappin comes out to serve a boy a bubblegum from a dispenser, then gazes up at the sign over the shop door bearing her name. She goes in and tells the woman inside that the first thing she will need to do is change the sign to her own name. Elsie Lappin was a character who would never be seen again after the second episode as she was selling her shop to one Florrie Lindley, the woman inside, whom the viewers most certainly were to become better acquainted with.

Florrie rearranges some cans in an eye-catching pyramid shape, somewhat to Elsie's amusement. Florrie is clearly struck with child-like excitement at owning her own little business. She thanks Mrs Lappin for agreeing to stay on and help her get her bearings. Mrs Lappin gives her advice on allowing tick and on the Tanners at No.11, whom she hints are a bad lot. Coincidentally, Linda Cheveski then comes in for some ham. Mrs Lappin is obsequious to her but when introducing her to the new owner Elsie pointedly says, 'Linda Tanner that was.'

Cut to an establishing shot of the front door of No.11. Inside, Elsie Tanner and Dennis are coming down the stairs having a row about two bob missing from Elsie's handbag, which happens to be the price of a packet of fags that Dennis had been badgering her for without success not an hour before.

> Elsie: 'So you stoop to going in a lady's handbag.'
>
> Dennis: 'Just listen it! A lady? Is that what you crack on you are these days?'

It is established that Dennis is unemployed and that this is as much to do with his bone idle nature as the fact that he is only seven weeks out of prison. Elsie unfavourably compares Dennis to young Kenneth Barlow at No.3 ('He's got it up here, in the upper storey'), causing Dennis to storm out. Cut to the Barlows' front room, where Frank, Ida and Kenneth Barlow are eating their tea. We soon find out that Kenneth would probably bristle at the use of the word 'tea' in favour of 'dinner'. Wearing a tie, he declines brown sauce on his meal and can't quite keep the disdain off his face when his shirt-sleeved father pours some on his.

> Frank: 'Don't they do this at college then?... Oh I've been noticing you looking at me.... We're not good enough for you.'
>
> Kenneth: 'Look, I never said a word and he starts.'
>
> Ida: 'Look dad, can't we have one meal in peace for a change?'

Frank: 'Now you know he doesn't like you calling me "dad". It's common.'

Ida: 'Oh give over, the pair of you....'

Kenneth says he will be meeting a girl from his 'year' later. When he reveals their rendezvous will be at the Imperial Hotel, his father forbids it, infuriated by the irony of the money Ken has for treating his girlfriend at that venue having come from the meagre wages his mother gets from her kitchen work there. David Barlow enters. Though, or because, he is more rough and ready than Kenneth, their father is clearly fonder of him than Ken. End of part one follows – in the days when these words were actually spelt out before the centre-break started, in this case against a photographic backdrop of brickwork with the abbreviated nameplate 'Coronation St' affixed above it. 'Part Two' before the resumption of activities is spelt against the same shot. There follows an establishing shot of the outside of the Rovers Return Inn. Annie Walker greets Kenneth warmly as he comes in for some cigarettes, although her smile drops at the sight of Dennis Tanner, who approaches the bar at the same time. There is some banter between the two wildly contrasting contemporaries (Dennis: "ow's our local genius then? Not seen your name in paper recently. Haven't you been winning any more scholarships?') but Kenneth gives Dennis one of his packs of 10 cigarettes, much to Mrs Walker's bewilderment. 'It's Elsie I'm sorry for,' says Annie.

Cut to Elsie's front room, where Mrs Tanner is examining her visage with some dismay. "Ee, Elsie,' she mutters. 'You're just about ready for the knacker yard.' She is dragged away from the reflection in her compact by the sound of her dustbin being knocked over and goes out to remonstrate with the guilty child – Christine Farrer – who is unseen but whose departing footsteps are accompanied by her calling Elsie a 'silly old bag'. (Actually the voice of Jennifer Moss, who would appear as Lucille Hewitt from episode four and was brought in to say the line to give her some studio experience.) Linda enters and it emerges that it was she who took the missing two shillings to buy the ham. It also emerges that the reason Linda has come to stay for the week is because she has left her husband Ivan Cheveski over their frequent rows.

Linda: 'He's *that* moody.'

Elsie: 'Ah well, foreigners are.'

A discussion follows on legs and whether Linda's are bandy. Subsequent talk of the new woman at the shop leads to a cut to said premises where Lappin and Lindley are discussing the former's retirement bungalow. (Florrie: 'Me, I never could take to a bungalow.... Not going upstairs to bed. Seems all wrong somehow.') Ena Sharples enters and after the briefest of introductions ('I'm a neighbour... I'm the caretaker at the Glad Tidings Hall') interrogates Mrs Lindley about her religious beliefs, in between barking out her shopping requirements – all of which it transpires she expects to be put on her slate.

Back in the Barlows' front room, Frank and David are trying to fix the puncture of a bicycle wheel in front of the fire. David goes off to borrow a pump. Ida enters and starts knitting. Frank indicates he is experiencing pangs of guilt about forbidding Kenneth the right to go to the Imperial Hotel but doesn't know how to back down. Frank: 'We've certainly raised a rum 'un.' There is then an establishing shot of No.1, where the conversation between Frank and Ida has confirmed Kenneth is located, chatting with Mr Tatlock. Inside, Albert Tatlock is tending to his coin collection. Ken is quiet and broody. Albert guesses it is about 'this business at the Imperial Hotel', which Ida has told him about. Kenneth says he has got to go because, 'There's a number to ring if I couldn't but Susan's bound to have left by now.' Albert suggests bringing her back to his house, but Kenneth doesn't want her round here.

Albert: 'What's wrong with Coronation Street?'

Kenneth: 'I just don't fancy the idea of her actually seeing it.'

Albert: 'I never thought the day'd come when I'd have to say this, but I reckon that that college has turned you into a proper stuck-up little snob, Kenneth Barlow.'

Ida suddenly comes in the back door with the news that Susan has unexpectedly turned up at the Barlows' house, a turn of events much to Albert's hilarity. Cut to the Barlows' front room, where Susan is volunteering to help Kenneth's dad and brother with the puncture. Kenneth and mum enter. Ken and Susan say hello to each other, their tones edgy – the cliffhanger on which the programme ends. After the credits, a caption informs the viewers when the next edition will be broadcast.

Looking at the first episode through modern eyes, an overwhelming patina of age affects the proceedings. This is not due simply to the fact that the street pictures in the credits look grimy enough to originate in the 19th century or the stygian gloominess of black and white TV. The show creaks with age in just about every scene: the iron till in the shop; the open fire in the Barlows' home; Albert Tatlock's unlocked back door; Ida calling Frank 'Dad' in an age before Freudian self-consciousness made such spousal terms of endearment obsolete; dialogue peppered with references to pounds-shillings-pence currency; everyone spurning their front parlours and instead sitting around in the back room; adverts for what we now call ketchup reading 'catchup'; the cigarette and pipe smoke in which the characters are wreathed; the reference to 'The Labour [Exchange]' rather than Jobcentre Plus; a grown man like Kenneth Barlow meekly accepting his father's authority; Linda being informed that she needs to get a job now that she has left Ivan – implying that she is a housewife even though she has no children; the fact that Annie Walker is able to come out with the phrase – vis à vis Dennis Tanner – 'Some mothers do 'ave 'em' without the irony that the 1970s Michael Crawford television comedy series of that name has now made requisite....

There would be other things over the coming weeks and months that would make early *Coronation Street*'s age almost painfully obvious within less than a couple of decades, such as the talk that establishes that the General Post Office has a monopoly of all telephone and mail services; the fact that Ena's drink of choice at the Rovers' is an unearthly/sickly sounding brew called a milk stout; the fact that the Walkers' son is doing his National Service (abolished on the last day of 1960); the revelation that the Rovers has a sign on its wall reading 'Ladies are kindly requested not to remain at the bar after being served'....

However, that is all a reflection of the fact that when *Coronation Street* hit the screens, it was achingly, amazingly Now. It was Now not just in the sense that it accurately captured the society of the time, but in that it showed the hitherto hidden parts of that society. Forman says that Granada had always been looking for a 'working person's' show. It can't be denied that they got that. Astonishing as it may seem today, in those days the people who made up the majority of the public – those who did unskilled jobs – almost never saw themselves represented in television drama. The transmission of *June Evening* earlier that year proves that the working class milieu was not completely unknown in TV. So does the 1958 production of John Finch's coalfields play *Dark Pastures* by Associated-Rediffusion. Ditto for Alun Owen's 1959 *No Trams To Lime Street* and other bleak plays in the *Armchair Theatre* ITV series produced by Granada's sort-of sister station ABC from 1956 onwards. However, The Street provided a window on a world whose sight were still very uncommon in the medium – and, crucially, did so on a regular and continual basis. *Coronation Street* was the permanent extension to TV of the Angry Young Man/Kitchen Sink movement that had sprung up in the late Fifties and early Sixties when John Osborne's play *Look Back In Anger*, Alan Sillitoe's fiction *Saturday Night and Sunday Morning* and *The Loneliness of the Long Distance Runner*, John Braine's novel *Room At The Top* and the subsequent film adaptation and Stan Barstow's novel *A Kind Of Loving* had seen a long overdue acknowledgment of a class below that which tended to hog the media. 'It was cutting edge,' says Roache of The Street. 'On television, it was really the first [programme] showing the raw side of life. Tony Warren was a man of his time.' Michael Cox says, 'I remember thinking, "Gosh, that's a revolutionary piece, that's like a bit of British cinema." I don't think you get that feeling from it now. You get a lot more sensational stories but they don't quite have the impact of Dennis Tanner coming back from prison.' John Finch says. 'It was a fabulous thing Tony did…. It was very different. Television drama up to then had been largely classics. [There were some] series like *Knight Errant* and *Family Solicitor* but they were all basically middle class.'

The BBC's Fifties Children's Hour show *The Appleyards* is cited by some as the first UK television drama based around the lives of ordinary people. However, the Corporation's *The Grove Family* (1954–1957) is the first example of the genre intended for an adult medium. The way the scripts tended to end as a morality tale was typical of society, and particularly the BBC, at the time. ITV's first foray into the area came the day after its launch in 1955 with a daily 15-minute morning show called *Sixpenny Corner*. Largely rural, it followed the lives of a couple who owned a garage and lasted just under a year. ITV's semi-weekly *Emergency Ward Ten* (1957–1967) could also plausibly be bracketed with such programmes, although as its title implies was more a workplace drama. Unlike with all of those, *Coronation Street*'s proletarian ambience was undiluted. It would be much imitated in drama serials from here on. As future *Street* scriptwriter Adele Rose points out, 'Tony created a completely new genre really.'

Novelty, however, is not the first episode's only attribute. Although it is amazingly hard-hitting for its era, the programme does not in any way solely rely for its power on that fact. It leans just as much on sheer verisimilitude and fine writing. The cross-section of domestic life is miraculously even-handed, favouring no particular character, and with such a varied array of personalities – all of whose values and worldview are treated as equally valid – every viewer has at least someone with whom to identify. The trivia about which the characters converse is acutely convincing and yet not boring, no more so than in the first scene with Florrie and Mrs Lappin. At more than two-and-a-half minutes, it's a long opening section, but it doesn't drag because the dialogue is so vibrant. The strongly delineated female characters for which The Street has always been famous – often reduced by media commentators to a lazy caricature of brassy ladettes – is present from the get-go. The exchange between Elsie and her daughter about whether Linda has bandy legs has a complete distaff verisimilitude. Meanwhile, the argument between Dennis and his mother crackles with superbly conveyed tension, fine dialogue and – like the rest of the episode – skilful exposition.

Almost as if fate was providing a sign of the fact that this programme was blessed, technical and set problems in the first episode are just about zero. Save for the banister on the stairs in the Tanner's house wobbling, there is almost nothing to betray the fact that this is a live broadcast. The cutting between scenes is as slick as one would expect of recorded TV drama today. There is even what seems to be an impressive piece of ad-libbing when Pat Phoenix tucks Anne Cunningham's visible bra strap back inside her sleeve, with neither woman commenting on the manoeuvre. It's difficult to see how The Street's first episode could have gone any better.

There were contrasting responses to the new show from two left-of-centre (and therefore theoretically sympathetic) papers. Mary Crozier, critic on the posh *Guardian*, loved The Street and predicted a long life. The opinions of Ken Irwin, the television critic of the Northern edition of the tabloid *Daily Mirror*, were diametrically opposed to that. His review following the second episode remains the most famous – or more likely only famous – review of the programme, simply because he got it so spectacularly wrong. He expressed incredulity at the advance publicity that had stated Warren had spent a couple of months going around meeting the ordinary people of the North before he wrote the first episodes, asserting, 'Frankly, I can't believe it. If he did, he certainly spent his time with the wrong folk. For there is little reality in his new serial, which, apparently, we will have to suffer twice a week.'

'I watched the first episode and then the second episode,' recalls Irwin today. 'It was a Friday the first episode went out and I don't think we had a crit column on the Saturday. So I reviewed the second episode. It got a lot of response. It was pretty dire the first few episodes. I just thought at the time what a dreary bit of nonsense it was. I wrote a crit and I didn't think it would last, and I still stand by that crit.' His assertions in print that the people depicted were not convincingly normal Northern folk and judgment of Spear's music as 'dreary' are of course subjective opinions and impossible to empirically prove or disprove. What it is possible to definitively pronounce upon is his prediction that 'The programme is doomed from the outset.' It became obvious several decades ago that this forecast was about as wrong as could be. Irwin: 'It did last… and it became a joke. Pat Phoenix, who became a great friend of mine, used to send me a postcard every year on the anniversary saying, "Another year's gone, Ken. Who was it who said it wouldn't last?"' The review is usually exhumed and parts reprinted when a *Street* anniversary is covered in the media. 'You get things wrong sometimes,' says Irwin. 'I wasn't embarrassed by it.… I suppose I was in a minority.'

Irwin's condemnation of the programme's alleged inadequacies wasn't restricted to that review. For instance, in September 1961, he was writing another feature that the *Mirror* headlined, 'Haven't We Just About Had Enough Of *Coronation Street*, Anyway?' For Warren, Irwin's aversion to The Street actually benefited the programme in a perverse way. He later wrote, 'His printed dislike was so frequent, fervent and definite, that people began to watch the programme out of curiosity.'

Such is the forward planning involved in television that it must have been at a point well before The Street mushroomed in popularity that Granada decided to indefinitely extend the programme's run. Stuart Latham seemed to indicate that the initial idea was for Warren to write the programme *ad infinitum* when he once wrote, '…it became clear that Tony had temporarily shot his delighted bolt, and the original scripts – hardly four weeks' air time – were just about all we had, or were likely to have, for a while.' Derek Granger confirms this, adding, 'It's an exhausting thing writing scripts. He did get very, very exhausted. You could almost say he got a bit over-excited too. There was a slight question there of nervous exhaustion. He just couldn't carry on.'

Though Warren would write more episodes, it would only be as a member of a writing team. It's therefore tempting to view that inaugural dozen episodes as a self-contained part of the programme's history. The creator's undiluted vision, they were all written before a single episode had been filmed and were free of the compromises dictated by the exigencies of broadcasting, advertising, practicality and cost requirements, as well as all untainted by the whiff of the self-consciousness that must inevitably come once the public and critics have been let in on the secret. Certainly, many are the people who find a grittiness about those early episodes that would never be replicated. Alan Rothwell says he noticed a change in quality when he found himself reading the lines of the new writers: 'I think we all felt that Tony knew the characters intimately. I did feel that there was a certain reduction in the standard of them. There were some really good new writers found but I think they had to work themselves into it a bit and they certainly at the beginning weren't up to the standard of Tony Warren's scripts, which were just literary gems.'

It is the supreme irony that the authenticity that made The Street a success with the public was the first casualty of the longevity that that success engendered. Once a drama has been running for a while, its realism becomes eroded by what we might call the likelihood factor. Restricted to those opening 12 episodes, the dramatic events portrayed could be posited – just about – as what might happen in such a street in such a space of time. In order to keep the show interesting, the scriptwriters have to keep up the rate of dramatic occurrence in characters' lives – a rate far more frequent than would ever take place in the existences of the average person in reality. With a programme so ostentatiously concerned with portraying ordinary folk, this is a contradiction in terms. Adele Rose: 'That was a fine line we always had to tread between keeping it real and plausible and bearing in mind that we were in the entertainment business. If we just sort of plodded on with the routine details of everyday life, the show would have folded years ago.' While there's no doubting that Rose and her fellow writers did work hard to walk this fine line, there's also no doubting that with every broadcast episode, the original authenticity of *Coronation Street* was unavoidably, incrementally diluted. In addition to those things, a natural softening up occurs, something identified by Kershaw in the Eighties: 'The mere fact that the programme had lasted for twenty years has imposed its own restrictions. What is acceptable in the short term is unbearable in the long.' It's tempting, therefore, to speculate how The Street would be remembered had it not survived beyond Warren's first dozen scripts. The evidence of our eyes suggests that, though it would be known of by far fewer people, it would have a reputation as a very powerful landmark in television, one far more firmly embedded in that kitchen sink drama tradition it brought to TV from film and literature than is now perceived to be the case.

Though *Coronation Street* quickly became popular with British television viewers, set against its swelling numbers of fans were the not insubstantial piles of hate mail Warren began receiving telling him he was a disgrace to the North, some of which threatened violence or even death. The Street was one of the first times people in the South had seen the North represented at length on the box and many Northerners were accordingly over-sensitive that their region was not necessarily being shown in a good light. Says then-journalist and future *Street* scriptwriter John Stevenson, 'You used to get letters to the *Manchester Evening News*: "What people in London must think of us. They must think we've all got whippets and wear flat caps and live in slum houses. This is terrible for the image of the North".'

Others had a less chauvinistic point to make. It has to be acknowledged that despite the 'cutting edge' qualities that Roache and others correctly mention, right from its very first episodes a criticism that has dogged The Street is that it is in a time lag. As David Browning observes, 'Even when it first came out, I can remember thinking, "Well it's going back to my aunties. It's more redolent of their era, rather than the era I was in at the time."' John Finch: 'I think it was a passing way of life. It was a lifestyle that was changing at that time. Of course, things changed very rapidly at that time in the Sixties, but The Street tended to lag behind the changes. It was so popular that they were scared of it going out on a limb and doing something else.' Even with the passing years and conscious attempts by the programme makers to update the show, the whiff of being left behind by the times has hovered for a variety of reasons: that increasingly antediluvian theme tune; the fact that terraced rows like that in The Street became increasingly less common in the UK with the rise of tower blocks; that even on surviving terraced rows neighbourly familiarity was more and more rare in an increasingly fragmented and insular culture; the disinclination of The Street's producers to address social issues in the way that newer serials were gleefully happy to…. All of these things gave ammunition to the programme's detractors and culminated in 1992 in a report by William Rees-Mogg, then chairman of the Broadcasting Standards Council, in which The Street was lambasted for not accurately representing the ethnic make-up of Britain and for harking back to an increasingly distant time when everybody knew who their neighbours were. While it is rather amusing that Rees-Mogg – alumnus of Charterhouse and Oxford – should pontificate about life on the streets, he has by no means been alone in making this point.

Yet *Coronation Street* has survived where the once trendy *Brookside* – a hard-hitting continuing drama serial that was deemed on its 1982 entrée to be making The Street look old-fashioned – has disappeared into TV history, while those programmes like *EastEnders* and *Emmerdale* that have attempted to ride the social fashions have never consistently matched the success of The Street. It may broadly spurn crime-related storylines, the self-conscious introduction of ethnic minorities and the depiction of fragmented neighbourhoods, but The Street is convincing on a micro level in a way that the other serials rarely if ever match: the exchanges of dialogue are realistic and the character motivations organic, not the result of a desire to make a didactic point or to engender exciting action. As Patrick Stoddart of *The Times* wrote in response to Rees-Mogg's broadside, 'The millions who watch *Coronation Street* – and who will continue to do so despite Lord Rees-Mogg – know real life when they see it.'

Part Two
The Sixties

The last live broadcast of *Coronation Street* (at least for 39 years) occurred on Friday 3 February 1961. The impetus for the switch was a technician's strike which prevented the broadcast of the Friday 10th edition: for some reason, when activities resumed after this short hiatus, they were exclusively pre-recorded.

Alan Rothwell was glad of the change. For him, the live episodes were 'very' nerve-wracking. 'You could tell which one was live because the live always had an enormous amount of nervous energy behind it,' he says. 'Then you recorded the next one after that and that was always slightly down. You always think, "Phoo, you've got that one over and this is only a recording so they can stop it and do it again if anything goes wrong" so there was a difference in the level of intensity.' He also says of the live transmissions, 'The nerves were quite tremendous and I would imagine for older people it was quite exhausting because it was every week relentlessly.' There were other reasons why going over to recording made sense. Says Rothwell, 'I remember one time two of the characters were carrying a table through a door and this door just wouldn't open, so they had to carry it round the set through the place where the cameras are, where there was supposed to be a wall of course.'

When Rothwell talks of the comfort blanket with the recorded episodes of being able to stop and shoot a scene again, he knows it was little more than a notional one. With as-live episodes, barring an absolute disaster, each half of an episode would be recorded all the way through without interruption. Said disaster would mean filming the episode-half from scratch again – which meant actors' nerves were always on edge in the final scene of an episode-half in case they made the fatal clock-resetting mistake. Conversely, as time went on some actors cottoned on to the fact that they could compel the director to reshoot something they weren't happy with by swearing.

There were other restrictive parameters that made it surprising that Granada managed to produce a show of such high quality. Because only six sets could be mounted at any one time in Granada's Studio Two, where The Street was shot, and even allowing for the fact that the commercial break gave opportunity to take some sets down and erect others, designer Denis Parkin found himself having to attend story conferences so that he could raise objections if a story idea required a combination of sets that he knew would be physically impossible.

*C*oronation Street's introduction had not been the subject of any kind of fanfare on the part of Granada: Cecil Bernstein refused to allow a press launch or press releases in case the show failed. This made all the more astonishing the turn of fortunes for the programme in March 1961. On the 6th of that month, the approximately thirteen million viewers the evening's episode (written by Warren, poetically enough) attracted put *Coronation Street* in the ratings top 10 for the first time. (There was no top 20 until later on in 1961.) Not coincidentally, it was the first episode broadcast by the ATV franchise: that The Street remained lodged in the top 10 was assisted mightily by the capitulation of ATV and the other network holdout Tyne Tees. The former was owned by the famous cigar-chomping impresario Lew Grade whose wife happened to be from Manchester. Legend has it that Mrs Grade saw an episode on a home visit and had a word in hubby's ear, although considering the London viewing figures she may have been pushing at an open door when it came to the ever-populist Grade. Westward Television, which formed in April, held out for a month but then also broadcast The Street. (It should also be noted that not all televisions on the market could yet receive ITV, as some were manufactured when there was only one broadcaster.) Also in March, the programme's Wednesday and Friday schedule was changed to Monday and Wednesday and transmission times were changed from 7pm to 7.30, a capitulation to the requirements of the previous refuseniks.

As The Street's ratings climbed, so did the recognition factor of its actors. This may have been something of a surprise to the production team, who had emphasised to the casting directors that The Street itself was the star. It must also have been disconcerting to the thesps, whose theatre backgrounds had not prepared them for the experience of their roles translating into open mouths in department stores and being buttonholed by people of whom they'd never had the pleasure. Warren has estimated the period before these hitherto unknown commodities found normal life a thing of the past to be 'within a month' of the first episode. Warren himself became a bit of a celebrity, not only contacted by entertainment correspondents but canvassed for his opinion on the state of the nation by political journalists. Perhaps not surprisingly, this man who affected the lofty, effete air of Noel Coward had no socio-political insights to offer them.

In an era of just two television channels, fame was a far more intense affair than today. Says Adele Rose, 'One of my closest friends in those days was Pat Phoenix and you only had to go anywhere with Pat and the screaming hordes just showed you in how much esteem she and the cast and the programme was held. It made its mark very quickly on the public consciousness.' Says Alan Rothwell, 'It's hard to realise now how big it was. It was absolutely huge.' In August, Pat Phoenix and Philip Lowrie, who played Dennis Tanner, visited Leeds to open a fashion store in the usual *quid pro quo* arrangement whereby they would receive a handsome fee for their trouble while the store got the benefit of a massive first day crowd. Four thousand people – obviously, far more than the store could physically accommodate – turned up and chaos ensued involving traffic jams, fainting women and the summoning of mounted police.

Such was the show's popularity that it could not mathematically be possible that its demographic was restricted to the type of people who would identify with it on a regional basis: the Scotsman, the Welshman, the Ulsterman and the Londoner clearly loved it as much as the North-Westerners. Additionally, though it was theoretically possible that the programme was only watched by the working class – in those days two thirds or more of the population described themselves as such – it was somewhat implausible, taking into account that one prole's meat is another's poison. The bourgeoisie clearly enjoyed it too, even if it was something of a guilty or inadmissible pleasure in a society whose class divisions were of a rigidity and pitilessness unimaginable in today's relative meritocracy. It became a running joke with *Street* staff how people with formal enunciation professed never to have seen the show while exhibiting intimate knowledge of its storylines.

Was it a surprise that such an apparently parochial show could be popular nationwide? Rose: 'I don't think so.... And don't forget it was the first of its kind, a complete novelty, so it had a clear field. Which isn't to say if it hadn't been any good it would still have succeeded, but it was completely new and different and people took it to their hearts very quickly.' 'I don't think it surprised us,' says John Finch, even though he also says, 'I don't think we were ever writing for that big audience out there. If we imagined our viewer panel, it would be largely Northerners.'

In an age before the internet and camera phones, the public were reliant upon the mass media for information about their favourite stars, yet that mass media at that juncture in history had a finite amount of space and interest to devote to such matters as a TV programme. Which meant that in the year that *Coronation Street* really began to take off, it was easy for outlandish rumours to take hold. If a character was written out or an actor was on his holiday entitlement, it was enough to start talk of them having been involved in a horrific accident or even killed. Sometimes, such speculation made the papers. Cecil Bernstein had to visit a distraught Doreen Keogh to reassure her that a report that her character, Rovers barmaid Concepta Riley, was to be killed off was in fact untrue. Meanwhile, many members of the public were seething with envy for a while when a rumour began circulating that *Coronation Street* episodes were screened in Scotland several weeks before their transmission south of the border.

At the head of this rapidly expanding empire was a 25-year-old man who has readily admitted that it all went to his head.

Tony Warren was not completely unreasonable for longing for acclaim: he had precious little else in the way of reward for what he had created. The stars of the show were being paid handsomely for their endeavours by both Granada and private clients. ITV franchises were raking in the advertising revenue. Warren had no such revenue streams: *Coronation Street* was a property he had devised under his flat £30 per week contract and was 100 per cent owned by Granada. 'It became the most valuable show in the ITV firmament and by rights Tony should be enormously rewarded,' says Derek Granger. 'The tragedy is that circumstances have somehow deprived him of that. If an American had done this he would have been hugely, hugely, hugely rich and successful. There's the theory that, "Oh, this in the end became a Granada show and everybody did it." I don't quite subscribe to that.... It was his creation and I think Granada were a bit dismayed about this. That this slightly frail, gay young man from the promotions department could have actually done this. I think there was a degree of embarrassment there.' Granger states that the embarrassment was not because Warren was homosexual ('Granada was always pro-gay'). He says, 'They were rather puritanical days. For a long time none of us producers or directors got credits: "We don't want to upset audiences with [this] kind of information." It was part of that kind of thinking mode which resulted in the fact that Tony's contribution was never acknowledged. It's the greatest creative contribution to ITV that has ever been made. [Granada] was a great company. It gave us enormous freedom, we had a very good time, it was great fun to work for, it was a very benevolent company in lots of ways, it was a very egalitarian company. You kind of forgot that it wasn't terribly well rewarded. David Plowright was very concerned that Tony had had a raw deal and I felt this for a long time.'

While Warren's friends are quick to take offence on his behalf on this matter, Warren himself has always insisted that he felt no bitterness over not owning a percentage of his money-spinning creation. In his autobiography, he wrote, 'People have gone so far as to say that I think I was robbed. I don't.' He pointed out that the investment that Granada had made in him with that first contract could have transpired to yield them nothing of substance. He has stuck to this line ever since. However, in 1961, with that one-year contract with Granada approaching its end, he also knew his worth. He took on the Music Corporation of America (MCA) – then the biggest talent agency in the world – as his representatives. Granada offered him an exclusive seven-year contract involving what he has claimed were 'alluring sums of money.' Warren baulked at the exclusivity and by the time he/MCA had thrashed out a compromise, the contract was for one year. The appended 'options' were meaningless in that, like all options they are what they sound like – optional – and therefore legally unenforceable, but the contract did give him the right to take three months off if he wanted to work on another project.

MCA also wrung another concession from Granada: the 'From an original idea by Tony Warren' line in *Coronation Street*'s end credits. Granger is not impressed. 'Tony Warren's agent was a nice man but not immensely tough,' he says. 'Granada said that Tony could either have a royalty or a credit but he couldn't have both.' Warren opted for the credit. Granger: 'It's rather Tony-ish to say, "I want the glory of the credit and if they don't want to give me a [royalty] they're mean bastards but let that be." That's when he first got a credit on screen. It happened sometime during my watch [as *Street* producer]. I think it was an absurd attitude to take as an agent. An agent's supposed to fight for you. He should have been saying to Tony, "Don't be ridiculous – you've got to have both…." They were bending over backwards to take the credit away from him. They didn't want him to have the credit for creating that show. They didn't actually want to say this had been done by this frail, neurotic youth.'

After the last of his inaugural 12 *Street* scripts went out on 18 January 1961, Warren provided 13 further episodes that year, 15 in 1962, nine in 1963 and seven in 1964. However, the programme was now the subject of more than a hundred individual broadcasts per year. Though Warren has said he accepted the need for a writing team in the absence of his ability to write all the episodes, he has also said he felt 'like a parent who had handed a child over to an adoption society and was still dithering.' Forman says Warren couldn't bear the fact of suddenly merely being a part of a writing team, and not the foremost part either. 'His original idea was absolutely great but he was no longer important to the show after the idea had taken root….' he states. 'He was piqued that he was not given star status, which in a way he deserved. He thought he should be given a higher status than other writers because he'd invented it.'

Warren's new contract with Granada granted him an advisory role on The Street that seems to have been rather vaguely defined. Finch: 'I think what Tony did really, he was *there*. He was there for people to say, "Is this character developing as you see it?" Perhaps coming up with other characters. He was a presence.'

Another cause for Warren's dislike of the writers, which he was not able to publicly admit until many years later, was their quasi-homophobia. The 'quasi' qualification is made because it can't be denied that in showbusiness ridicule of gays has often gone hand in hand with nonchalance about and tolerance of their lifestyles – certainly far more tolerance than the type of working class people depicted in *Coronation Street* would be inclined to display. Nonetheless, it wasn't easy for Warren to take this ridicule. 'They were some of the largest verbal queer bashers I'd ever come across,' he recalled in 2007. 'It was all back-to-the-wall stuff. On one occasion at a conference I sat there and listened and listened until I got to my feet and said, "I have sat here and listened to three poof jokes, an actor described as a poof, a storyline described as too poofy, and I would just like to remind you that without a poof you wouldn't be in work".'

He despised, also, a succession of new producers – one of the first of which was Harry Kershaw – whose ideas he felt inconsistent with the *Coronation Street* premise. As early as May 1963, he was talking in a *Woman's Hour* radio interview of the programme's decline from its original realism into something more stylised. 'What goes on now bears very little relation to the original idea,' he said. 'It's a glamorised working class life now. It wasn't intended to be. They are almost working class pipe dreams. It's gone completely away from the original conception.' Considering he was still contributing scripts to the programme at this point, this was pretty eyebrow-raising stuff and potentially embarrassing for Granada. Judging by the fact that he remained on the roster of writers, the company doesn't seem to have immediately taken against him. 'I think we took it in our stride,' says Forman. Though he states that he likes Warren, he says, 'Tony was a child actor and child actors always have throughout life a temperament that's different from other people's.' Even if he had not come from that peculiar template of child thespian, Warren would still have been someone catapulted to fame and acclaim, if not wealth, when still not a fully rounded human being. As John Finch observes, 'To become successful at that age is quite a shattering thing, I think. It's hard to cope with. I was 35 before I got anywhere.' Warren may have been unusually intelligent and observant but that didn't necessarily make him any better able than anyone else of his tender years to deal with setbacks, disappointments and general adversity after seeming to have had it made professionally with that first big success.

Despite Granada attempting to display equanimity in the face of Warren's criticisms, something was certainly brewing. 'Tony Warren was a bit of a drama queen,' says Ken Irwin. 'The whole thing went to his head when it took off. They brought in a scriptwriting team and he was left to write only so many scripts and he didn't like this. He actually quit and walked out. He just lost his way. He couldn't produce the scripts anymore and he then began to believe his own publicity…. I don't think they could put up with his tantrums.' The 1964 Christmas edition of The Street – broadcast on 23 December – was Warren's last script for the show for several years. In an act of unintended symbolism, it featured the cast performing a panto – the subject matter of the script that had first got him noticed by Denis Forman.

Warren's star would never shine so brightly again as it had in those first few months of the programme's life when the world beat a path to the door of a man who had created a television sensation and cultural landmark. His name had a cachet for a while, enough to get a theatrical play on (*Strumpet's Daughter*) and to be commissioned by Beatles manager Brian Epstein to write *Ferry Cross the Mersey,* the movie debut of another of his charges, Gerry and the Pacemakers. Both projects were a disaster, with the play stalling a metaphorical thousand miles from the West End and Warren driven almost to the point of a breakdown over the Pacemakers' film script and abandoning it, parting with Epstein by mutual consent. Meanwhile, he was being pursued by the Inland Revenue over unpaid taxes and in an act of naiveté that was as much an indicator of his youth as his preternaturally astute *Coronation Street* scripts belied it, he decided to go abroad to escape their clutches.

Ken Irwin recalls, 'A year or two later he was doing a drag act around the clubs in Europe making jokes about *Coronation Street* because he thought he couldn't live with it. He was almost suicidal he told me once, trying to get away from it. Wherever he went: "Oh, you're the man who invented *Coronation Street*." He got fed up with this.' 'There was a nervousness about him always,' says Rothwell. 'I think it might have been one of the things that stopped him ever being a performer and would have affected him in some way in the rest of his life.' Including writing? 'I think it could have done, yeah. Actually sitting down and doing the work.' It's difficult, though, to find anybody who actually dislikes Warren. Derek Granger was also not unaware of his faults but says, 'I don't want to make Tony sound a complete flake. He was a terribly clever, bright person. He was such a wonderful witty, funny companion. He was a very alive and brilliant young man with a very bright mind.'

Warren turned down an invitation to attend a party celebrating The Street's 500th edition in 1965. Granada removed his name from the credits, and Warren responded by saying, 'I'm only too happy not to have my name associated with the programme as it is today. I did not go to its 500th birthday, but I wouldn't mind attending its funeral.'

After that symbolically low ebb, there was a turnaround of sorts. Irwin: 'I remember going to Tony and interviewing him when he was on the dole in London, living in a flat, within a few years of The Street starting. I went to see Tony to do a piece on "What's happened to Tony Warren?" He was on his uppers. He poured out his heart to me. I wrote a big piece in *The Mirror*, a full-page piece saying, "Here's the man who invented *Coronation Street*, doesn't make a penny out of it now, Granada have disowned him, etc." His agent then phoned me a couple of weeks later saying Lord Bernstein, who was the chairman of Granada, had read my piece and they felt sorry for Warren and they decided to put his name back on the credits.' Warren accepted an invitation to the sixth birthday celebrations, partly mollified by a friendly meeting with the aforesaid Granada chairman Sidney Bernstein. He had always resented Bernstein's failure to hook up with him before, considering he had created the company's greatest asset. At the party, he realised, surrounded again by television people, that he was having a good time – helped by a surreal interlude on the train journey up wherein a fellow traveller in his compartment (unaware of who he was) sniffily observed of him that he needed to watch *Coronation Street* to find to what real life was about. Warren asked Harry Kershaw, now the programme's executive producer, if he could come back. He was slightly shaken when Kershaw told him the programme had changed slightly and that he would have to commission a script from him on a trial basis. However, he passed the test and provided scripts for 15 episodes of The Street from 1967 to 1976. His reinstated creator's credit has remained.

There was, though, no great resurrection of Warren's career. He wrote a trilogy of plays for Granada about a black marketer called *The War Of Darkie Pilbeam*, broadcast to acclaim and good ratings in 1968, but it was a false dawn and Warren again slipped off the public radar. By 1977, the creator of the most famous British television programme of all time was reduced to writing the novelisation of TV sitcom *Rising Damp*. Though in 1980 he worked with future poet laureate Carol Ann Duffy on a Granada vehicle for actress Margi Clarke called *Love Margox,* it never got past the pilot stage. Another idea seems to have never got past the stage of a mad rush of whimsy, according to the recollection of Ken Irwin. At a point that he dates somewhere between 1970 and 1980, Irwin says he received a call from Warren in his *Mirror* office in London. Warren told him, 'I've got a marvellous idea for a television series. I want to be the first for you to know it.' Irwin met him at the BBC's Portland Place building. Irwin: 'He said, "I want to do *The Seven Deadly Sins*. It'll be a seven-week series, and every week a different sin, I'll write a drama around it." He then said, "Okay, can you lend me a few quid? I'm going to start tonight on the research for this. I'm going down to Soho. I've got to buy a bottle of champagne and you never know what else. I'm going to commit my first sin. I can't do anything without proper research. I've got to experience everything I write about." I got the money back but I never, ever saw *The Seven Deadly Sins*. But that was Tony. He was a bit mad.'

Warren all but disappeared off the radar again for decades. Daran Little says, 'If you read [Warren's] second novel, *Foot Of The Rainbow*, I think you'll understand more about what happened to him. He had other things going on in his life at the time.' As said novel is a picaresque tale that follows the multi-coloured trail from Swinging Sixties London to psychedelic San Francisco, you can guess what those others things were, or were tinged by. Stimulants ensnared a troubled Warren in their clutches for a long time, until a second act to his life began in 1991 when he embarked on a career as a novelist. His entrée was *The Lights Of Manchester* a doorstep-sized affair that was reasonably well-written if never exactly enthralling. Its protagonist seemed to be a thinly disguised Pat Phoenix whose male best friend seemed to be a thinly disguised Warren. The publishers packaged it in such a way as to suggest they were aiming for the Catherine Cookson market. Though his books are now out of print, they did well enough for him to get four under his belt, excluding *Rising Damp*. Warren picked up an MBE in 1994 and took the Landmark Achievement Award at the 2006 National Television Awards.

In his autobiography – published nearly a decade after the transmission of The Street's first episode – Warren wrote, 'Like it or not, all these years later, that programme was and still is my own. I no longer write it, in my own mind I've tried to give it away but I have only to walk through the studio doors to find someone who was in on the beginning….' Those days, of course, are gone. *Coronation Street's* original backroom crew have all long moved on, retired or died, while the original cast members have dwindled to one. His entry into the portals of Granada Television (now actually part of ITV Studios) would produce few flickers of recognition. Though his name appears in the closing credits and though he is interviewed in every documentary ever broadcast on the history of The Street, many must be the people working on *Coronation Street* today who don't actually know who Tony Warren is.

David Liddiment, Carolyn Reynolds and Tony Wood are three modern-day *Street* producers who had sufficient knowledge of and respect for Warren to lunch with him regularly. Liddiment: 'He had a strong sense of its rootedness, of its values, and was a great champion of the show. He always expressed his views and it was always valuable to hear them. He tended not to say, "Why don't you do this and do that?" He would talk in more abstract terms about when the show was on form and not on form and when characters and stories were hitting a mark and when they weren't.' Says Reynolds, 'It became a bit of a joke that we had to sit somewhere quite quiet because we'd have heated conversations. It was great to get his take on things. He's still got a good eye for what works.' Nonetheless, both Liddiment and Reynolds say that Warren never expressed interest in contributing scripts. Reynolds: 'I never asked him and he never volunteered. We talked about doing something else 'cos I still think he's got a great voice and I don't think he should be confined to books.'

It could plausibly be said that Warren peaked professionally before his mid-twenties and that he is a one-hit wonder. Warren himself seems amazingly unembittered by the course of his life. Perhaps this is because he takes the view that being 'merely' the father of the biggest phenomenon in the history of British (and arguably world) television would suffice for most in the fulfilment stakes.

The person chiefly responsible for ensuring that *Coronation Street* more or less seamlessly picked up the thread from the original Warren episodes and consolidated its immediate splash was H.V. Kershaw. Says *Street* scriptwriter and later *Street* producer John Finch, 'The Street wouldn't have survived if Tony had been in charge. Tony was too young and too much up in the air to carry The Street forward.… It needed somebody like Harry Kershaw. Without Tony of course there wouldn't have been a series but Harry got it all together and he totally devoted himself to *Coronation Street* for the rest of his life. Without Harry, I don't think *Coronation Street* would have survived to its present position. He sort of shaped it, guided it and we all owe him an enormous debt, anybody who worked on The Street.'

Kershaw – born in 1918 – was a pipe-smoking, moustachioed, scholarly and conventional man who was a complete contrast to the hyperactive and semi-callow Warren. Yet Granada could not have picked a more appropriate individual to take *Coronation Street* forward. For one thing, he had a commitment to the North that was as much as ideological as sentimental. So much so that he was one of the brains behind a company of scriptwriters called Group North, set up in 1963, all of whose members had written for The Street. Nobody could be as important in *Coronation Street*'s story as its creator, but Kershaw comes a very close second. He bestrides *Coronation Street* from its beginning to his retirement in 1988. Over the course of more than a quarter of a century, he seems to have had a hand in its every conceivable facet except appearing on screen. He started out as the programme's script editor in 1960, became one of its writers the following year – in so doing, becoming the first person other than Warren to have a *Street* script broadcast – and the programme's producer in 1962, a role he would fulfil for four periods, alternating it with the executive producer's role up until 1972. Graduating to producer was itself a titular matter, for as 'serial editor' he had fulfilled several of the functions one would expect of a producer, not merely editing scripts but being ultimately responsible for all the stories and hiring and firing writers. From 1961 through to 1988, there were only two years – 1964 and 1967 – in which he did not pen at least one *Coronation Street* episode. He scripted exactly 300 *Streets* (including three co-writes), in the process riding multitudinous cast, style and social changes that took place across this timeframe. He was executive producer of *Street* spin-off series *Pardon The Expression* and wrote and produced the never-broadcast pilot for another proposed *Street* spin-off called *Rest Assured*.

Kershaw was also responsible for the very first *Coronation Street* novelisations – *Early Days, Trouble at the Rovers* and *Elsie Tanner Fights Back* – which appeared from 1976 to 1977. These books – all tracing story arcs from early Sixties episodes – served an important function at the time. It's astonishing to think that, three episodes excepted, no *Coronation Streets* were ever repeated in full until May 1981. This meant that in the days before commercially available *Street* videos (and recordable video tapes that were anything less than hellishly expensive), the general public simply had to rely on their memories of previously viewed shows, while those who had not seen them the first time round had to rely on those viewers' second-hand relaying of events.

Amazingly, Kershaw achieved all he did with The Street while maintaining a prolific writing career outside of it. He subsequently wrote – among other things – *City 68, Family At War, The Villains, Crown Court, Love Thy Neighbour, Oh No, It's Selwyn Froggitt, Life Of Riley, Village Hall, Leave It To Charlie* and *The Spoils Of War*. In some cases he was producer or deviser of said programmes. Finch explains, 'He got weary from time to time and changed his job and always came back to it.'

Kershaw's long reign in many senses added to that perennial *Coronation Street* problem of lagging slightly behind the times. Being a conservative can be discounted as a reason for him not wanting socio-political commentary to be brought into the show – the line from his autobiography

'Governments tend to curb any outside power when they feel themselves under threat' suggests he was hardly a mindless reactionary. Rather, it was his innate populism that made him veer away from controversy or didacticism. Over the years, this meant mass immigration was not reflected in a *Street* that remained resolutely white and then prevalent UK-wide industrial unrest generally failed to reach the apparently harmonious Weatherfield. Finch: 'I'm slightly left of centre and I wanted The Street to be more realistic and Harry's main aim was to entertain so we occasionally fell out…. Very early on – round about '62, '63 – I put forward the idea that we have a coloured family in The Street and Harry was totally against it. Came up with all sorts of arguments why not, none of which convinced me. He said things like, "If you're going to be real about it, you're going to have the coloured people called yobbos and they're going to be racial remarks directed at them in the Rovers Return and so on and you'll sort of destroy the thing you set out to do." Which is a fairly substantial argument but I still think it would have been worth doing. My idea was that you simply brought in coloured actors and forget about the fact that they were coloured and just played them as characters….'

Yet for Finch the fact that The Street's ratings and longevity achievements are greater than those of any edgy or PC competitor is the positive flipside of Kershaw's cautiousness: 'He was responsible for it being popular and maintaining that popularity. He was always very tough on the entertainment aspect of it and he always used to maintain that the audience identified with the characters…. Whether it would have achieved the kind of popularity that has carried it through these fifty years doing it the way I wanted to do it is very much open to debate. I don't think it would. Harry was right in seeing it as he did: as a long-running, money-earning television series.'

Tony Warren may have had valid emotional reasons to hate the roster of scriptwriters employed by Granada to work on The Street, but artistically it can't be denied that they were a formidable team. Several of the team's members would go on to achieve acclaim for their writing outside of The Street – far more so, it has to be said, than Warren himself. The spine of the first *Street* writing team – established over the first few years, with many writers tried and discarded – was Warren, Kershaw, John Finch, Harry Driver and Vince Powell (who wrote as a pair), Jack Rosenthal, Adele Rose, and later arrivals Peter Eckersley and Geoffrey Lancashire.

Driver was a paraplegic struck down by polio at age 27 who began writing by hitting typewriter keys with a knitting needle held in his teeth. Lancashire would become part of a *Street* dynasty when his daughter Sarah took on the role of the much loved Raquel Wolstenhulme three decades after he wrote the first of his 171 scripts for the show. Like Lancashire (and indeed Warren), Jack Rosenthal came up through Granada's promotion department. Rosenthal enjoyed writing for The Street but it was too small to contain him, and after penning 129 scripts for it in its early years (he also produced The Street in 1967), he spread his wings to write TV shows like *The Dustbinmen, The Lovers, Spend, Spend, Spend, The Knowledge* and *London's Burning*, among many others, as well as co-writing the screenplay of *Yentl* with that movie's star, Barbra Streisand. Peter Eckersley took what some might consider a step down to write for The Street. Recalls Derek Granger, who was then the producer, 'He came to me in the *Coronation Street* office. He said, "My name's Eckersley, I'm from *The Guardian*." I thought, "Oh, it's an interview." He said, "I came in to ask you if you thought I could have a shot at writing this?"'

Though Esther Rose was a (to use the phrase of Stan Barstow, who observed her in action when employed as a consultant to the programme in the late Sixties) 'Queen Bee' figure in The Street's storyline department for a quarter-century, for a long time the unrelated Adele Rose was The Street's only female writer. Salford-raised, she was a former Granada employee. Rose says, 'I worked as a secretary to the head of Press, Publicity and Public Relations and that's where I met Jack Rosenthal and Geoff Lancashire and we all became friends.… We always liked writing, all three of us, and fiddled about with it at an amateur level.… Jack rang me up and said, "I've just been paid money – the magnificent sum of a hundred pounds – to write a script for the new programme, and if I can do it you can".' Rose was told to call Kershaw. Rose: 'I rang him and I said, "I've no professional experience but I was born and brought up in Salford, plus I noticed all your writers are men", and that's all I could say in my favour. It got me an interview and Harry gave me a trial script to write and then commissioned me to write one. In the first year I didn't do many – nobody did, they tried about thirty-odd writers – and then in the second year they decided to have a small team of regulars and I was fortunate enough to be asked to be one of them.'

Rose's last *Street* script was broadcast in 1998. Her long career with the programme got off to a good start: in the episode broadcast on 8 November 1961 there was a showdown in the street involving a conflict of moralities between Elsie Tanner and Ena Sharples preceded by a preamble where the two women were psyching themselves up for the battle, Ena finishing her milk stout in the Snug and Elsie her cigarette in No.11. 'The *High Noon* scene, as we called it,' says Rose. This segment from what was only Rose's third broadcast script has become one of the most screened in the programme's history, included in many a compilation programme as representative of The Street's early days or its strong women or both.

Rose also says, 'We all brought our own personal experience. [Fellow writer] Jim Allen had been a bricklayer and John Finch had been in the navy. I was a housewife with two children. So we all had our feet rooted firmly in the ground. We weren't products of theatre school or media degrees at university. We had very varied backgrounds. All the writers were from the North. We all had a strong feeling of connectedness with the show and with what was real and what worked for it.' Southerners were not banned from working on The Street but rarely made the cut. Finch: 'Harry was in those days specifically trying for Northerners but there were so few of us that they had to widen the search.... We had London writers coming up desperate to work on The Street and they just couldn't do it. They just couldn't handle the Northern idiom. Tony's characters were so accurate, Northern expressions like "Ecky thump" and so on were things they'd never heard. And the general feel of being a Northerner as opposed to a Southerner plays a big part in writing.' Not that being an Northerner and an acclaimed dramatist (*The Long And The Short And The Tall, Billy Liar*) automatically made for a successful *Street* writer, as Michael Cox points out: 'One or two distinguished writers did try their hand at it and came unstuck. I remember Willis Hall trying to write for The Street and not finding it something he could tackle. It's a special skill.' The Street's writers were encouraged to mix with the actors socially so as to effect a cross-fertilisation whereby the writers could get into the groove of the thespians' mannerisms and tics.

The Street's strength in depth in writing was not just down to good writers. The story conference process played a huge part. After the first dozen Warren episodes, Kershaw and John Finch were responsible for devising the storylines for a brief period. 'We had two storyline writers from round about episode eighteen, nineteen, something like that, Harry

Driver and Vince Powell, who were basically comedy writers,' recalls Finch. The quartet of Driver, Powell, Kershaw and Finch would gather in Kershaw's office and all would chip in with ideas for the next six or so episodes. Finch: 'Then Harry and Vin went away and turned the discussion into storylines which were then handed out to the writers as a sort of guide.' Though Driver and Powell provided a scene breakdown to the scriptwriters, Finch points out, 'What you did with it was optional as long as you stuck to the same number of sets. There was a lot of flexibility in those days because nobody quite knew where we were going.'

The work of this quartet was a stepping stone to something that has become probably the single most important factor in The Street maintaining its high quality over the years. Finch: 'What Harry [Kershaw] started – which continues to this day and made things much easier for us and brought up a large variety of different ideas because there were so many people involved in it – was the story conference. Which was writers, story editors, script editor and Harry. That was a big breakthrough. That helped to carry The Street forward because it was becoming an impossible burden for a couple of people like Harry and myself and then Vincent and Harry Driver. They were very exhausting days just keeping it going apart from maintaining the quality. Now it's done with other series too. It's become a staple thing in television drama.' Finch estimates that the first ever formal *Street* story conference occurred somewhere between the writing of the 40th and 50th episodes and was attended by around 10 people. He recalls them as having a monthly schedule. They would later become three-weekly and in more recent years, with an increased number of episodes, have become more regular than that. The normal story conferences have since the Seventies been augmented by others. Separate commissioning conferences interleave the story conferences. There are also long-term conferences for planning large issues – such as who is the landlord of the Rovers – ahead by six months.

The 'story editors' to which Finch refers above are formally titled story associates and generally colloquially known as storyliners. Their job is to build on the work of the scriptwriters by knitting the episodes together. Finch says, 'It's always puzzled me that, because it's not a job I could have done myself. People came in over the years to do that and very rarely developed as scriptwriters. It's very strange.' Nonetheless, storyliners are very important to the process of crafting The Street, even if the story associates' title, or the 'Stories by…' credit they once received, is a misnomer that suggests they, and not the scriptwriters, devise the programme's plots. Finch: 'The writers' input at the story conference was considerable. The to-ing and fro-ing, the arguments, largely took place between the writers. Gradually, the story writer's job became less important because the writers' contribution at script conferences carried most of the weight.' John Stevenson – a *Street* scriptwriter of a different vintage to Finch, his first story conference being in 1975 – says, 'The stories are not invented by people sitting in a room who dole them out to the writers. This is what they do on *EastEnders*, I gather. They tell a writer, "Here's a storyline – go away and do the dialogue." It's never been like that on *Coronation Street*.' Though Stevenson acknowledges that storyliners do come up with some story ideas, he says, 'You're talking about five per cent of ideas.'

'That's rubbish,' says Tom Elliott of Stevenson's 5 per cent figure for storyliners' contributions. As not only a friend of Stevenson's but someone who has worked as both storyliner and scriptwriter on The Street, Elliott has no appreciable vested interest in the debate. 'You weren't just stenographer,' he says of the storyliners' craft. 'You had to chip in with story ideas of your own. We came up with so many. You couldn't quantify that. It was a team game absolutely across the board.' Nonetheless, he does accept that the old 'Stories by…' credit was slightly misleading.

Elliott became a storyliner in 1983, by which time that one-way traffic Finch speaks of was becoming a thing of history because of a policy of recruiting seasoned scriptwriters (from other programmes) in the story department. Elliott took over from Peter Tonkinson, who had been Esther Rose's long-term collaborator. Tonkinson was a comedy writer who provided material and sketches for the likes of Ken Dodd and Mike and Bernie Winters and would write 10 *Street* episodes. Elliott had already written plays for theatre and radio when he was asked to join the programme, and would go on to write scripts from 1990. When Esther Rose retired in 1984, Elliott's new long-term storylining partner would be Paul Abbott, who also wrote for The Street and is today a very respected drama writer.

Elliott and whichever storyline partner he had would turn up at the story conference with a sheet of paper – similar in dimensions to wallpaper – on which story arcs would be noted in boxes, Elliott favouring the technique of using different coloured inks to differentiate stories. Elliott: 'You've got to go back then and talk this through with your fellow storyline writers and decide where to start and where to finish and try and knit it together.' Before the episode could be worked out, the practicalities needed to be addressed. Elliott: 'You've got a cast list and you've got to use these people. Some people are on holiday, so you can't use them – you had to weigh all that up. You've got to choose the sets. You have to choose the locations.' Then came the episode breakdown. 'The first thing you do when you're writing a storyline, you take a piece of A4 paper and just above the halfway point you put a line across,' explains Elliott. 'That's the ad break. You put crosses down the left-hand side, in the old days six in the first, seven in the second. You write your tagline – that's the scene whereby when the viewers have finished watching, they say "My word, we've got to see the next episode." It's a cliffhanger. Then you go up to just above your line across and you write the ad break. That's to bring them back after the interval.' Filling in the rest of the episode came next. The crosses were for the 13 scenes that were the average in The Street prior to the late Eighties. Each episode had a main theme and two secondary themes up until that late Eighties change of pace, when the subsidiary themes grew to three as the scenes doubled in number. Elliott: 'You'd write just little headlines, what the scene's about and who's in it, the mood of the scene. Ideally, the shorter the better but the more detail the better. Not what they said – we didn't write the dialogue. In the old days, you've got a fortnight to write these storylines. The week after, you'd have the commissioning conference when the scriptwriters and the story writers get together with the producer.' Of the scriptwriters, Elliott says, 'Each writer has been commissioned to write one of those scripts and they talk independently in turn about their storyline. They take it apart, or try to. "I'm not doing that." Occasionally, you'd say, "If you take that brick out of the wall in episode two, the biggie in episode four doesn't work." The storyline writer who's written all that block, who knows what that block of scripts should look like, he says, "I'm sorry, that's got to be there." Occasionally a scriptwriter would stray over into somebody else's episode. You can't do that. Then they'd go off and write the scripts and submit the script. It would come back to us in the story office to read for continuity. Little things or big things that you would correct and give to the producer. The producer had editorial responsibility – we couldn't change anything. Continuity was vital, because viewers would tell us where we'd got it wrong, or the press would. The Street when it's being watched by eighteen, twenty-odd million people, it's in the public consciousness all the time.'

Elliott says of the role of the storyliner, 'It's totally undervalued. If you're not a writer, you can make a scriptwriter, but you'd never make a story writer. It is perhaps the most difficult job that I did. Story telling is an art. Even the people that produce these shows, I don't think they put enough value on that job or recognise how much ability it takes. Having done all the writing jobs on The Street, I would recommend that [they] periodically rotate scriptwriters to have them do a stint in that story office. They would write better scripts.'

One thing that has changed since their inception is how heated the story conferences get. Finch remembers Sixties conferences as being civilised, with even his entreaties to reflect things such as the ethnic make-up of the population leading to disagreement rather than rows. However, they have since famously become far more fiery affairs. Equal measures of ego and passion for the programme seem to be behind the development of an adversarial atmosphere. Carolyn Reynolds, who became *Street* producer in 1991, says, 'Sometimes I used to feel I was more like a referee than a producer.' Elliott: '*Coronation Street* conferences were so violent that they had to wipe the blood off room 600 before anyone could use it.' Stormings-out became in no way infrequent, so much so that one of Reynolds' predecessors, Bill Podmore, would entertain himself by trying to guess how long it would take for someone who had thus dramatically departed to return to the fray.

The output of that first team was television gold. Daran Little became in the role of *Street* archivist that he took on in the late 1980s one of the few people in the world who has seen every single episode of The Street. For him, the period of 1960–1964 is the programme's golden age. 'You had a very tight cast of about seventeen characters,' he says. 'Everybody had done rep, so they were used to quick turnover and different sorts of stories and picking things up very easily…. Good characters, good strong stories.' He points out that his feeling is not motivated by sentimentality: 'I wasn't born then.'

Rovers' barmaid Nona Willis became The Street's first Londoner in 1961, though she was only there a couple of months before leaving because she couldn't understand anybody's accent. The prim Emily Nugent – played by Eileen Derbyshire – joined the cast in January, although initially as a colleague of Leonard Swindley rather than as a

Street resident. Additionally, her Christian name wasn't even revealed until a year later. However, a half-century on, she is still in the programme. With her insistence on referring to 'luncheon' – not even lunch – rather than dinner, she was clearly cut from somewhat more refined cloth than most *Street* regulars. Shortly after Miss Nugent amalgamated her baby linen business into Swindley's haberdashery, the latter got into financial trouble and he was taken over by one Spiros Papagopolous, who turned the shop into Gamma Garments. Mr Papagopolous would often be spoken of – usually in fear – but would never be seen. This scenario of an absentee landlord with an amusingly multi-syllaballed Greek name would several decades later be echoed – apparently deliberately – by the makers of *EastEnders*, who portrayed launderette worker Dot Cotton answering to (but never visibly) one Mr Papadopoulos.

Another non-resident who became a regular face this year was Len Fairclough. Played by Peter Adamson, he was a straight-talking, brawling, ruggedly good-looking builder in his mid-thirties and was one of the few alpha males in a programme where men – then as now – tend to shine more as hapless, comic characters. John Stevenson puts this down to the fact that even today with the redeveloped non-terraced side of The Street, it is difficult to bring professional workers into the programme: 'Even on the semi-detached side of The Street, the most you got was accountants or a bookmaker or a successful butcher, only a slight cut above the terraced side. So in terms of alpha males, they tend to be the local bit of rough who's got a bit of something about him.' Len would remain in the programme for nearly a quarter of a century and the fact that Adamson left the show not long before Phoenix's final departure was for many viewers appropriate, as across this timespan Len and Elsie conducted a sort-of love affair that never quite morphed into coupledom, formal or otherwise. Rose: 'The value of their relationship was always in the spikiness underneath the genuine affection they had for each other. It was far more profitable in terms of story and character to keep them with the love-hate relationship going on. He was the one who could say things to her that nobody else could and vice versa. If we ever brought it to any kind of conclusion, that would have been the end of both the characters' value to the show.'

Alf Roberts (Bryan Mosley) – at that point a Post Office worker – also made his first appearance this year. Ken graduated with a second. He briefly had a job in personnel before becoming a teacher. Linda Cheveski gave birth to baby Paul, who was played by Vicky Elton, son of Harry. The first *Coronation Street* baby was followed not long afterwards by the first big *Coronation Street* farewell when the Cheveskis left No.9. Ernst Walder: 'Linda wanted to come out of the show and we were written out. We emigrated to Canada.' Was he upset at losing his job because of colleague Anne Cunningham's wish to move on? Walder: 'Obviously, because it was a lovely time.' However, he continued to be a familiar face on British TV screens, appearing in the likes of *The Saint, Danger Man* and *Man In A Suitcase*, as well as making short returns to The Street in 1962, '66 and '67 when the Cheveskis came to visit Elsie. He also appeared in a Yorkshire Television soap opera of 1969/70 called *Castle Haven*. Additionally, 'The odd film. I was in *Darling*. The scene I had with Julie Christie, they showed in Hollywood when she got the Oscar.' Says Walder of The Street, 'It was quite an important part for me. It was my first television and I got known. I still get the odd fan letter through my agent. It's amazing. It's so long ago. I've been in Austria since 1983.' Walder is still close to Tony Warren, his former screen wife Cunningham and his former screen brother-in-law Philip Lowrie, and was close to his screen mother-in-law Pat Phoenix until her death.

Noel Dyson also declined a new contract. Kershaw decided to kill her character Ida Barlow off. It was a logical move. Finding a different way for such a loving couple as the Barlows to be permanently separated would have involved a bending of the character to suit a plot requirement the type of which did not mark The Street at this period in its history, though many lament now does. It was the first major *Street* death. Warren, of course, had killed off May Hardman, but she was always intended as a short-term character and hadn't been in the show long enough for her demise to have much meaning to the viewers. In the episode broadcast on 11 September 1961, a police officer informed Frank that Ida had been run over by a bus. The death had actually been postponed by a week because Kershaw had realised that Dyson would otherwise be turning on the Blackpool illuminations with her fellow cast members only two days after her screen death, so ordered hasty rewriting. Granada made up for Ida's rather sketchy off-screen death with her September funeral, whose audience of 15.6 million was *Coronation Street*'s highest so far, even if the extent of the programme's mushrooming popularity at that point meant that such records were no sooner made than broken.

Considering she was the first to jump ship, and showed nonchalance about sacrificing such a prime role in so doing, it's rather ironic that Dyson was not struck with the typecasting curse that so many actors leaving The Street would find themselves afflicted by in the future. Perhaps it was because she was in the programme for a sufficiently long period to be noticed by casting directors but not long enough to make her seem too associated with one role, but Dyson would go on to notch up plenty more television roles, including the *Street* spin-off *Turn Out The Lights* and, most notably, the Seventies generation-gap sitcom *Father, Dear Father* in the role of Nanny. She died the death all actors dream of when she collapsed on stage in 1995.

Derek Granger had succeeded Stuart Latham as producer in the second quarter of the year (Latham would be producer again for an eight-episode stretch in 1964) and he recalls that Blackpool illuminations ceremony as a revelation to himself and Warren. 'We drove from Granada in a bus and I was on the top deck with Tony Warren,' he says. 'The bus was disguised as a couple of Coronation Street houses. It was covered in sort of brick wallpaper. As we drove from Manchester, we saw there were people not only lining the streets but actually in fields, waving to us. I remember Tony turning to me and saying, "Good God Derek – what have I done?" We were gobsmacked at this extraordinary scene. Then as we got to Blackpool, we couldn't get in because the crash barriers were all up. Masses and masses of police. The crowds were absolutely enormous. It was at that point I think that we realised it had become a sort of national heritage. It was very peculiar that night, and very wonderful.'

In fact, it was Granada's realisation of just how big the programme was becoming that led to Granger's appointment. 'They hadn't entertained that it would suddenly be such a success,' he explains. 'I was brought in by Cecil Bernstein. They suddenly thought that this rather tentative little series had enormous possibilities. Cecil was very, very shrewd and [had] a very sharp eye for ratings, unlike Sidney who was much more highbrow.' In light of this comment, it seems little coincidence that Granger was appointed by Cecil Bernstein soon after that first appearance of the programme in the weekly ratings. Granger: 'I had been Head Of Drama. It sounded like a demotion but in fact it wasn't. Cecil said, "Derek, do you think you could give this a bit of bounce? We think it could be bigger and stronger than it is. Can you get this really going as a piece?" I was being sought after as a troubleshooter in a sense. I said, "It's like changing course on Cunard's liner. It'll take three to four months before you actually get a change." And I looked at countless episodes – not every episode, but I looked at a lot of them – and the stories were very, very small. The last story I looked at was a story about little Lucille Hewitt, who'd lost her purse in the Mission. They were all trying to find the missing purse. I thought, "My God, this isn't strong enough. It's got to have a bit more sex and drugs and rock 'n' roll." One of the things one did was develop hugely the character of Elsie Tanner. Nobody had done this before, but we really had Elsie having love affairs. I remember one famous episode when she's almost caught *in flagrante delicto* in a telephone box with a sailor. We were doing things like that. We were sharpening it up and making it much more strong and real and sexy. I think I did the first scene in *Coronation Street* where a husband and wife were in bed together: Ivan and Linda. And there was a wonderful scene in the bathroom with a terrific row between Bill Roache and his father. So it became much earthier.'

As well as the earthiness, Granger attempted to do away with what he perceived as a staccato approach. 'We tried to introduce really strong stories which went over several episodes,' he says. 'Very much like what *Coronation Street* does now and *EastEnders* does now. But we were in very early days, 'cos there hadn't been a series like this before. Shaking it up but in very specific ways. One of the ways was introducing a long-running storyline which built to a terrific climax. A famous one I did was a huge row between Ena and Elsie. Elsie had been getting poison pen letters and all the suspicion was on Ena.' The culmination of this storyline was the aforementioned 'High Noon' episode. Granger: 'We created a kind of parody of *High Noon* and they advanced towards each other with everybody twitching their curtains. I remember looking at the ratings immediately after that and I said, "Why do audiences respond like this? How did they know this scene was coming? I'm sure they knock on each other's walls." That was the high point of my tenure really, and I was very proud of that.'

The programme's first big wedding came on 1 October 1961, when Harry Hewitt tied the knot with Concepta Riley. It was quite a controversial story thread for the time as the characters were respectively Protestant and Catholic. Though the programme didn't show the actual ceremony, it made a big deal of the occasion, with the episode dominated by the wedding day preparations and the reception. The final shot lingered on the 'Mr and Mrs H. Hewitt' signed by Harry in the register at the couple's honeymoon hotel. Even the show's theme tune reflected the nuptials by being given a flowery arrangement in the opening titles and break bumpers.

In one way, the most interesting storyline of 1961 was that involving the discovery by Ena Sharples at the town hall that Coronation Street was scheduled for demolition. The residents of The Street rose up in arms against the plan to move them away from their happy community to impersonal 'streets in the sky' – until they realised that Ena had misread Coronation Terrace as Coronation Street. It was a conveniently happy ending, but in real life at this juncture in history 'slum clearances' were all the rage and streets like Coronation Street were being torn down all over Britain and replaced by tower blocks, which were then posited as sensibly clean and futuristic replacements of primitive backstreet housing. In some ways, it would have been better if in fact Coronation Street had been scheduled for bulldozing and its residents won the council over to the merits of it remaining intact, for then the programme makers would have an instant, unanswerable response to the recurring criticism down the decades about how increasingly unusual such a street is.

On 23 August 1961, The Street hit number one in the ratings for the first time. For his part, Alan Rothwell says he was 'Stunned' that the programme made the summit. 'Amazed by it. We were all amazed.' Roache says of The Street that he was 'amazed at the effect that it had', but not surprised at its ratings success: 'Not at all. We knew what it was.'

Though it has had the inevitable peaks and valleys of a life of half a century, extraordinarily, only twice since then has there been a year where The Street has failed to make number one at least once in the weekly most-watched charts – and usually it mounts the summit many more times than that *per annum*. The Street's peak Sixties viewing figure of 21.362 million (12 October 1964) was never improved upon before the advent of repeats, omnibus editions and aggregated statistics in the mid-Eighties confused the entire picture about ratings. However, the fact that *Coronation Street* usually pulled in between nineteen to twenty million viewers per episode for a quarter of a century (and probably longer) is remarkable considering that the increasing number of alternative channels and the steady rise in living standards in that timeframe meant that British homes ceased to be the captive market (for either a particular channel or television *per se*) they had been at the start of the Sixties. Today, The Street's viewing figures have been decimated by the fractured audience that goes with a multiplicity of channels and (like all television programmes) by other forms of entertainment like the internet, computer games and DVDs, as well as the access to entertainment outside the home conferred by more money in the family purse. Yet *Coronation Street*'s current official ten million viewers per episode means it remains the biggest consistent puller of the schedules: the likes of *The X Factor/Pop Idol* beat it when they are on, but those shows are not screened all year round.

That, though, was all in the future. In 1961, colour television wasn't even on the horizon, let alone VHS, DVD, satellite TV, cable TV, set-top boxes and the World Wide Web. In 1961, more than a third of Britain's then population of 53 million people were happy to snuggle down in front of the box (as the television was called for several decades, before the increasing prevalence of another new-fangled artefact – the flat screen – made the phrase seem old-fashioned) to watch the sepia-toned happenings in a street that could almost be their own.

CORONATION STREET

No sooner had Granger taken *Coronation Street* to number one in the ratings than Granada was faced with a crisis that could conceivably have signalled the programme's destruction. A strike was called by actors' union Equity and began on 1 November. While the programme made it to the airwaves throughout the dispute twice a week as usual, it was as a skeleton crew proposition with its storylines severely circumscribed by the reduced personnel. The reason for the strike was that the actors' union wanted a new pay deal which they said should reflect the fact that the existing one was agreed when commercial television was in its infancy and no one could foresee just how flush the

ITV companies would become. Granada employee David Browning observes of the franchises' profitably at this point, 'Trust me, it was a licence to print money. The money was just sloshing about like water.' However, the ITV companies found Equity's demand exorbitant and a stalemate had ensued. In the 'closed shop' industry of acting, the order to go on strike was not something that could be resisted even by the thespians who had a mind to. The only reason *Coronation Street* was able to be screened at all – and what probably saved its life – was the fact that 14 of the average cast of 25 had signed their contracts before the dispute. Granger: 'They couldn't break their contracts. It would have been illegal and any judge in any court would have found it so.'

Luckily for the programme, those 14 cast members were the ones playing the main stars: Frank Barlow, Ken Barlow, Minnie Caldwell, Len Fairclough, Harry Hewitt, Concepta Hewitt, Florrie Lindley, Martha Longhurst, Dennis Tanner, Elsie Tanner, Albert Tatlock, Ena Sharples and Annie and Jack Walker. What felt like the essential core of the programme, therefore, was maintained. Yet despite the retention of that nucleus, a lack of a sense of layering and a certain stagnant ambience could not be avoided as the strike ground on for five months. There was also a certain ghost town atmosphere: because extras were affected by the dispute, the Rovers suddenly seemed deserted. Some characters were hastily written out – a pair of Town Hall officials called Norman Dobson and Phil Braithwaite who had recently become tenants of Florrie's in the flat above the shop fled the bellyaching of Ena – while others whose absence would be more difficult to explain away were notionally still resident but unseen. Some simply disappeared without explanation but then reappeared, also without explanation, when the strike ended.

Says Granger, 'I was accused of making it very fanciful and far-fetched because it took a lot of ingenuity to get amusing or interesting stories out of so few people with nobody allowed in. You couldn't have a subsidiary character at all. Lucille Hewitt – who wasn't on contract – we used her as a sort of poltergeist. Concepta would say, 'Get off to school Lucille, you're late already, you know' and the door would bang and you'd hear the sound of a satchel hitting a wall. So it was quite silly in that kind of way. We also invented a lot of slightly bizarre stories. Dennis Tanner became very fascinated with animals. He got a chimpanzee from a circus. He got hold of a seal and suddenly realised that it needed a tank with water in it, so he put it in Annie Walker's bath. Annie Walker wakes up in the middle of the night and Jack Walker says, "Is there anything wrong, Annie?" and she says, "I thought I heard a seal bark" – which is a famous line from a cartoon by James Thurber. That's how silly it got. But it was quite funny.' The animals seen on screen, of course, did not require an Equity card. Granger: 'People said to me, "Really, it's just getting ridiculous." But we kept it going. I think it was pretty makeshift during that period. It was wearing a bit thin and ingenuity was wearing out and the stories got very far-fetched. The great thing about *Coronation Street* is its quality of realism and of course the strike rather stretched that. I don't feel particularly guilty but I took the point.' As the strike – and the gimmicks it necessitated – wore on, was Granger thinking he was ruining the gravitas he felt he had brought the programme? 'I don't think particularly I was,' he says. 'I was just getting on with it and I was finding it rather enjoyable in a kind of odd way because one had to be fairly ingenious.'

Yet there were advantages to the strike. With many other ITV shows off the air, it wasn't difficult for *Coronation Street* to remain at the top of the ratings.

With its first three months dominated by the increasingly desperate exigencies dictated by the Equity strike, 1962 was the single most difficult calendar year for *Coronation Street* in its history. There would be other strikes in the future, some nearly so long, but because the programme was by then part of the fabric of British cultural life, its return once the strike was over was not in question. In 1962, The Street might have been at the top of the ratings but this was partly by default and it was still new enough on the block to be susceptible to cancellation.

According to John Finch, that cancellation became ever more likely as the industrial action wore on. Though Granada had been canny enough to get latecomer Peter Adamson to sign a long-term contract when industrial action was in the wind, they hadn't anticipated how long the strike would last. As the months ticked by, the contracts that expired could not be renewed. 'We kept losing actors,' Finch recalls. 'By the end of it, we got down to something like seven or eight actors. It got to the stage where in the Rovers Return there was nobody there to serve behind the bar and one of the props men had to slide a pint of beer in out of the wings.'

The ever-diminishing number of characters and permutations of situations for them to interact within – plus the problem of having to make characters interact who normally wouldn't associate with each other – began to both reach farcical levels and provide nightmares to the storyliners Vince Powell, Harry Driver and John Finch. By the closing weeks of the strike, the people left dealing with this mounting problem in the storyline department had been reduced to two. Says Finch, 'The formal story conferences were abandoned to some extent in favour of more informal arrangements…. Vince got absolutely weary of it and then Harry was on his own and so Harry and I worked together, mostly just the two of us. Harry Driver and I worked with the producer and the tight group of writers involved on an almost day to day basis, but as the number of actors diminished and the story problems became more acute Harry and I were increasingly responsible for coming up with stories which could be shaped around whatever actors were left, and which were then presented to the producer and the writers involved. All in all it was a bit of a nightmare, and towards the end we were working almost round the clock…. I can remember being in the building up to two, three o'clock in the morning with Harry and we're both tossing ideas around about how to get stories for six, seven actors and the silences grew longer and in the end Harry said to me, "Well now we know how long a long-running series runs." We just felt it had come to the end, that we couldn't do any more. But fortunately a few days after that, the strike ended.' Asked if that cessation of industrial action hadn't occurred it would have spelled doom for The Street, Finch says, 'Oh yes, I think so. In the end of course we wouldn't have had a cast to work with.'

With an agreement between Equity and ITV reached, the strike effectively came to a halt at the end of March. Finch says the strike period was 'a very sad time.' He explains, 'All these actors, most of them hadn't done much before *Coronation Street*, certainly nothing like the regular work that it was for them, and the strike was done over their heads. It was potentially a disaster for them so when it finished they all came back highly delighted.' Not all. The dispute would be a bitter blow for several of the affected actors, several of whom found they were never called back after they had been written out *pro tem*. And, though he did make a return, spare a thought for Alan Rothwell. The previous year had seen the departure of David Barlow to professional soccer in London following his turning out for Weatherfield County FC. Rothwell recalls, 'At the end of six months I asked to be written out because Associated-Rediffusion were doing a detective thing called *Top Secret*, which was set in South America, and they were looking for somebody to play the main detective sidekick. I was chosen for that. It was before the Equity strike.' Recalls William Roache, 'I remember we were envious at the time, 'cos we never knew how [The Street] was going to run.' Roache and his colleagues turned out to be the actors in a better position. Rothwell says of *Top Secret*, 'We only did one series of that. It was fairly well received and I think it would have gone on to another series or actually struggled on quite happily for a while but the actors' strike killed that.'

For Daran Little, the strike permanently embedded in the public's affections those characters whose actors had been on long-term contracts. He says, 'To keep going was pretty amazing, so the characters that came out of that were your key characters who remained in the show for twenty years or so.'

The fame and riches The Street's major actors enjoyed turned them into the closest thing to Hollywood stars a drizzly backwater like Britain could produce. It created in some of them ostentatious extravagance and/or airs and graces totally and utterly at odds with the humble lives of the characters they played and with whose hardships the public empathised. Recalls Michael Cox, 'Pat [Phoenix] had spent most of her working life before The Street in rep or tours. When she'd been in The Street for a few years, she had a house just outside Manchester that was like something out of *Sunset Boulevard*. She was one who really enjoyed up to the hilt all the money that The Street brought.' Meanwhile, several cast members commuted to Granada from homes along the coast, residency at which in those days was a declaration for a Northern entertainer of having Made It. Cox: 'I remember a colleague of mine saying, "You don't need a camera script to do the show, you need the Blackpool railway timetable", 'cos they insisted on leaving to catch the 5.30 train or whatever it was to St Anne's or Blackpool.'

In 1963, actor Geoff Hinsliff had a bit-part in The Street that was the first of three stints in the programme over the decades. Then in his mid-twenties, Hinsliff came from a working class Leeds background but had gone to RADA. Though he only appeared in one episode, he describes his first stint in The Street as 'quite traumatic really' precisely because of the self-conscious celebrity of some of the cast. He says. 'In the television I had done up to that time, The Street was something right out of left-field. These relatively ordinary actors had such fame as everyone in the world would recognise them when they walked down the street, and their behaviour in rehearsal, in studio, was quite different, largely because of this....' As well as the babbling self-obsession of *Street* green room conversation – devoid of the theatre speak he was used to – Hinsliff was amazed by '…what they came to rehearsals dressed in. I was used to quite famous, celebrated actors being in jeans or whatever. They were there in furs, which was all very shocking to me. At the Old Vic I'd worked with Judi Dench, I'd worked with people with immense stature. They don't behave in that kind of stardom way that [The Street actors] did…. It had a profound effect on me. I couldn't get out quick enough.'

The behaviour to which Hinsliff refers was exactly the type guaranteed not to go down well with Jim Allen, a scriptwriter who wrote for The Street from January 1965 to September 1967. Like Jack Rosenthal, Jim Allen became better known as a writer outside of The Street, but in his case his graduation was from a school he detested. An ex-miner and hard left ideologue, he despised what he thought to be the political pusilla-nimity of *Coronation Street* and would leave it with some relief to pen more didactic material like *Days of Hope, United Kingdom* and *Perdition*. Finch says of Kershaw, 'It's amazing how he used to get on with different types of people. Jim Allen was very left wing and of course Harry wasn't and they got on like a house on fire.' Allen was less fond of The Street's cast than he was of Kershaw. He once scathingly described most of them as 'working class Tories acting like thirty bob millionaires.'

One of Derek Granger's last acts as producer before his departure not long after the end of the strike was to invite in a group of writers to observe the programme, give their thoughts and – it was hoped – agree to write scripts. Granger: 'I was very anxious to get the quality of the writing as good as it could be got.' One of said writers was Stan Barstow, whose acclaimed debut novel *A Kind Of Loving* had been published in the year of The Street's birth and had earlier this year been filmed by John Schlesinger. Yorkshireman Barstow was a writer very much in the Kitchen Sink strain, so his invitation was logical enough. Barstow had watched The Street in the beginning 'with some awe and pleasure because I knew the kind of people.' He recalls the thinking of The Street's production team in 1962 as, '"We've got millions and millions of viewers. What are we going to say to them?" and it became a responsibility.' Barstow recalls that said sense of responsibility didn't torment everyone on the team: 'Harry Kershaw said, "Get on with it – entertain people".' Barstow remembers the whole affair as being somewhat barren in terms of results: 'We spent a day in the building looking at the format and talking to people about what it meant. We just had lunch and a drink and came away. I think I did say something about what it lacked was the smack of evil. Somewhere around the place you should have a little hint of the darker side and it was already a tiny bit too cosy.' Though Barstow's visit came to nothing at this point, the same was not the case with another invited writer, Robert Holles, a novelist whose most famous prose work *Siege At Battersea* (later filmed as – bizarrely – *Guns Of Batasi*) was published that year. Holles wrote the first of his *Coronation Street* episodes in April 1962. However, as if confirming Michael Cox's point that the most skilled prose writers had difficulty with the distinct craft of a *Street* script – and despite the fact that Holles would be very successful as a TV scriptwriter subsequently – he would only provide two more.

With the dispute at an end, the pace of the programme picked up. New faces – under the eye of Harry Kershaw, who formally took up the reins of producer from Granger – could finally be introduced. One was Jerry Booth, Len Fairclough's new apprentice at the yard he had bought behind Martha Longhurst's home in Mawdesley Street. Jerry became a popular new addition to the cast, his wispy good nature and youth providing two ingredients not hitherto in abundance in the show. The introduction of bookie Dave Smith – a peripheral but long-running cast member who made his last appearance in 1976 – was the start of a *Coronation Street* tradition wherein a cockney (as many Northerners erroneously refer to all working class Londoners) was brought in to maintain the programme's appeal to Southerners but was used in a way that almost insulted the South. He was what was still commonly referred to then as a spiv but is more generally known today as a wide boy: a slightly sleazy, money- and bird-obsessed character with a fine line in patter and no sense of self-doubt. Though possessed of a certain roguish charm, Smith was – like Mike Baldwin and Danny Baldwin after him – somewhat of a cliché, something that those Northerners who objected to the alleged flat-caps-and-whippets ambience of The Street would have done well to note. Some familiar faces returned, including factory girls Doreen Lostock and Sheila Birtles, who became flatmates above the Corner Shop, perennially capped Scouse ne'er-do-well Jed Stone, Emily Nugent, Leonard Swindley and Billy Walker.

Ken Barlow romanced and married Albert Tatlock's pleasant niece Valerie and they moved into No.9. Ken would now refer to Tatlock as 'Uncle Albert' for the whole of his life. A couple of story threads involving Barlows provide from today's perspective another shocking reminder of how basic life was for the working class at this time. When Val opened a hair salon ('Valerie's') in the front room of No.9, the cobbles had to be dug up to install her telephone cables: as with many streets in real-life Britain, nobody in Coronation Street had had a phone before. Also in 1962, The Street got its first indoor lavatory, when Ken had one installed at No.9.

In August, Harry and Concepta's son Christopher arrived in the world. With him only two months old, Christopher was involved in a massive drama. On the day of Harry and Concepta's wedding anniversary, Lucille left her half-brother outside a shop in his pram. The baby disappeared and the nation was gripped as he remained missing for a fortnight. Concepta was so distraught she wandered the streets looking for him in a daze, while Len was upset enough to utter The Street's first 'bloody', for which he immediately apologised to Miss Nugent, whose delicate ears he had offended with it. It was Elsie who tracked down the kidnapper, a woman named Joan Akers who she knew as a schoolfriend of Linda's. Recalls Finch, 'Harry and I had a dispute on that. Harry wanted the baby to be found and I wanted the baby to be dead because I wanted people to learn a lesson [from] what brought the thing about. Harry won of course, because he was the producer.' At its peak, the story attracted 21 million viewers, the highest audience recorded thus far in UK television history.

Akers' landlady was played by Jean Alexander, who within two years would be back in The Street as one of its most-loved characters of all-time, Hilda Ogden. This recall of bit-part players for more major roles continues to this day. Though potentially a jarring reminder of artifice, the programme's producers have always felt that small roles serve as a useful audition process.

Despite Granger leaving to produce other programmes, including investigative current affairs show *World In Action* ('I wanted to get on and do as much as I could'), he says *Coronation Street* was probably the most enjoyable gig of his illustrious production career (which also took in *Street* spin-offs *Pardon The Expression* and *Turn Out The Lights*). 'I absolutely loved doing it,' he says. 'You feel this God-like power over people's destinies and it is fun working on storylines, like a rather exciting parlour game.' However, he acknowledges that making Harry Kershaw his successor was a perfect choice by Granada: 'He was born to do it and he loved it. I think he loved it in a more integrated way than I did. It was very much his life in a way that it wasn't quite mine.'

January 1963 saw a daring storyline in The Street.

Len Fairclough caused a black bus conductor to be suspended after denying his allegation he had dodged his fare. Len later confessed he had avoided paying, and the implication was that his attitude stemmed from the conductor's colour. It's difficult to imagine The Street these days running the risk of 'spoiling' a major character in the viewers' eyes by portraying him engaging in this manner. The modern day *modus operandi* of the show is to largely circumvent discussions of race – at least among the main, regular characters – because the clear assumption is that the opinions on this matter of characters like the Battersbys and the Windasses would not be palatable.

In the summer of 1963, The Street got its first female producer in the shape of Margaret Morris, who had of course not only been its first casting director but was the person who had first obtained Tony Warren employment at Granada. Kershaw stepped up into the executive producer role. Though John Finch remembers this as an anxious time because he and his fellow writers feared Morris wanted to axe them, he approved of the appointment in another way: 'Margaret Morris to some extent wanted to take the series the way I conceived of it.' Under Morris the programme acquired a slightly harder edge and was involved in its first big scandal.

Before the harder edge came the debut in July of a character called Walter Potts, played by Chris Sandford. A Scouse window cleaner, he was one of the hapless wannabes managed by the even more hapless nascent pop impresario Dennis Tanner and slept on the unfortunate Elsie's sofa. Though Elsie hated the way the lodger ate her out of house and home, in real life Pat Phoenix was more enamoured of Sandford after an incident that showed that though the show was no longer live, there were also hazards to it being recorded as-live: when a pan caught fire, Sandford had to hop up onto the stove to put it out with his feet, the cameras continuing to roll all the while.

Many years before The Street began attracting criticism for being cynically pitched at a younger demographic, Potts – renamed Brett Falcon by Tanner – seemed a blatant attempt to attract teenagers to the programme in a year in which Beatlemania had swept all before it. Brett made a record, 'Not Too Little, Not Too Much'. In real life, the song (a composition by Tin Pan Alley composer Les Vandyke) was released on the Decca label. Helpfully, Sandford was seen singing it in the 20 November edition of The Street, two days before the record hit the shops. In a rather crass move, the record was played over the closing credits of the programme in place of the theme. It would ultimately climb to a peak of No.17 in what was then called the hit parade.

September saw The Street's first proper scandal. With the contract of Eileen Mayers due to expire, Sheila Birtles was marked down for a suicide. It was to be a pretty harrowing one: traumatised over her treatment by boyfriend Neil Crossley – who had taken her virginity despite being married – and over losing her job at the raincoat factory, she was set to take an overdose of sleeping pills and – when that failed after she vomited – gas herself. However gritty and realistic *Coronation Street* was for television, this was sensational stuff in an era where broadcasting output was mostly inoffensive bordering on bland. When the story leaked to the national press, Granada had to contend not only with shock-horror tabloid headlines and protesting telephone calls – and in those days, there really were switchboards that could get jammed by callers – but the objection of the deputy coroner of Manchester who said, 'Anything that puts into people's minds the idea of suicide is wrong.' Margaret Morris responded, 'We produce *Coronation Street* as a true-to-life story. Everything we put into it really happens in such circumstances.' However, with television as a mass medium still in its infancy and the broadcasters green in the matters of handling outrage – real or manufactured – the Independent Television Authority, the body which regulated the output of ITV, or the Bernsteins, or both, lost their nerve. Morris was instructed to excise the offending five minutes from the broadcast. Following hasty rewrites, Dennis Tanner saved Sheila's life by forcing his way into her room after climbing a ladder to her window (although this wasn't shown) and finding a quasi-catatonic Sheila sitting beside an aspirin bottle that was barely depleted. Morris was humiliated by having to issue a statement saying, 'It was an idea of mine which did not come off,' while Kershaw and Mayers were extremely disappointed that what they felt was a harrowing and powerful scene was wasted, in Mayers' case particularly so because of how emotionally draining the build-up to her fictional death had been. The press who had moralised about the storyline hounded the actress, shouting through her letterbox and hammering on her windows while her terrified young daughter wept upstairs.

Back in 1960 it had been something of a triumph that Granada had persuaded almost all of the other regional franchises to broadcast from its start a drama that was so steeped in the dialect and characteristics of one city. Though the company had ensured within a few months that the show went one better by being fully networked, even Granada can't possibly have imagined that such a parochial affair would have appeal beyond the borders of the United Kingdom. However, after finding themselves with the nation's number one show on their hands within five months of it being fully networked, Granada decided to try to sell The Street abroad. Aiming as high as they possibly could, they attempted to interest America. September 1962 saw the publication in the US showbusiness bible *Variety* of a full-page Granada advertisement extolling the virtues of the programme. 'Our advert is an open invitation to American TV networks to buy the show,' admitted Granada. The advert depicted Ena Sharples in her full hairnetted, bulldog-chewing-a-wasp glory, accompanied by the legend, 'What makes Ena Sharples the second-best known lady in England?' Interestingly, the advert referred to the show as a 'prime-time soap opera', a phrase virtually banned within Granada's offices. No doubt they were employing the phrase as a form of shorthand because they suspected America was not quite ready for a description like 'gritty kitchen sink drama'. However, they did try to convey that latter flavour in the rest of the advertisement's wording, which explained, 'Gone are the cliché characters, the sudsy situations. In their place is a feuding, middle-aged matriarch, an Angry Young Man milieu. A working-class saga with the vinegary bite of reality. People bitch, fight, gossip, are generous-hearted, humorous, delinquent, real.' A pretty accurate and attractive summary, but the networks weren't tempted enough to make an offer, not even when their bigwigs were invited over to watch the programme being made.

Just desserts for Granada's hubris, one might think. However, when the company made its first foreign *Street* sale to Australia in 1963, its totally unexpected level of success there proved a harbinger for the show in many other territories. Broadcast initially to urban areas, and then taken up by rural transmitters, *Coronation Street* was soon running five nights a week Down Under, before inevitably having to be cut back to Britain's twice-weekly frequency as available episodes were depleted. By the time of a March 1966 three-week official visit to Oz by *Street* cast members, the show was so massive that a 20,000 crowd greeted them in Adelaide and one of 50,000 waved them off, crowds bigger than those commanded in the country by the Queen Mother.

It's easy to be cynical about the success of *Coronation Street* in Australia on the twin grounds that there was no language barrier and that Australia was a country at that point starved of quality home-grown television. That scepticism can even be maintained when contemplating the repeat in short order of the success story in New Zealand and Canada, two English-speaking nations whose indigenous TV of the era hardly produced fondly remembered classics. Then again, most countries' TV output at the time paled in comparison to Britain's and The Street was making inroads where a lot of BBC fare, for instance, hadn't. Additionally, the programme's success was not restricted to countries whose first language was English. By the end of the Sixties, The Street was being shown in Greece, Holland, Hong Kong, Nigeria, Singapore and Sierra Leone, at which point one runs out of excuses for the success of the show other than the universality of its dramatic themes, its good writing and its quality acting.

Curiously, Denis Forman dismisses notions of The Street's overseas sales marking a success story, his impressionistic memory of them being that they were patchy, certainly compared to globe-spanning Granada triumphs like *A Family At War*. Perhaps the failure of the programme to make inroads in the United States throws a malign shadow in his mind. Forman states that the show was screened in three separate US states but never caught on. Even today, it can only be seen Stateside through the aegis of cable and the internet, which facilities did not exist when Granada began its selling campaign. Kershaw once said that most of The Street's staff knew in their heart of hearts that the programme was too parochial to succeed across the Atlantic. That's debatable – if Southerners had got used to the Northern idiom through The Street, why not Yanks? – but in any case one of the three networks that then dominated US TV seems to have spurned The Street because it had decided it could do it on its own terms.

In September 1964, ABC television began broadcasting in an evening slot a semi-weekly half-hour drama called *Peyton Place* based around the lives of ordinary people in an American small town as distant from its nation's epicentre as Weatherfield is from London. Though largely bland and sentimental in the way of much American TV of the time, it also dealt in sexual themes and social issues previously alien to the American broadcasting schedules. It was almost as if *Coronation Street* had been put through a washing machine's American Cornball rinse cycle. It was a huge ratings success. Doug Cramer, Director of Programme Planning at ABC when *Peyton Place* was commissioned, admitted the inspiration provided by The Street in *Campaign* magazine in 1969, wherein he said, '…the only comparable serial that had ever been seen at night was *Coronation Street*. Actually it was the success of *Coronation Street* that led us into doing *Peyton Place*. I'd been in England and, after seeing it, came back to ABC and said, "My God, look – it's working and we really ought to do it".' In light of which, a photograph sent to Granada by *Peyton Place*'s cast signed 'To our friends across the water. To the No.1 show from the No.1 show' could be considered a real – to use a phrase you would hear in *Coronation Street* but not in *Peyton Place* – Mickey-take.

The opening titles of The Street changed in 1964, the Archie Street shot replaced by aerial views of Salford terraces. (St Clement's Church, at the end of Archie Street, could be seen in one.) It was followed by a shot of a woman scrubbing the ground in a ginnel, that curiously arcane word for alleyway that most people have only ever heard in *Coronation Street*, which has its own one behind the houses on the terraced side but which was not the one depicted in said shot.

Dennis Tanner continued this year his journey from edgy character to comedy turn. Explains Daran Little, 'Actors by nature want to be loved, so they soften characters.' The writers, he says, then take their cue from their mannerisms and demeanour: 'You start to write what you see on screen.' Kershaw always thought that had Ken Farrington landed the role of Dennis, Warren's original vision of him as a tearaway would have been adhered to. As it is, Dennis was by now more a lovable scamp who had made mistakes in the past than the seething pit of resentment who had sneered at Ken Barlow for not sharing his own ignorance in the first episode of The Street.

That was a relatively trivial development. However, there were seismic changes afoot this year too. What is now a longstanding *Street* tradition was inaugurated in 1964 when it was decided to shake up the programme by clearing out dead wood. Of course, this is a wholly necessary measure vital to keep any long-running drama interesting to successive generations of viewers. The fact that this year BBC – and working class – comedy *Steptoe and Son* gave The Street the unfamiliar experience of being beaten in the ratings demonstrated that. However, because such major shake-ups affect people's livelihoods and have the potential to upset fans of particular characters, they tend to shock. As with subsequent shake-ups, this one coincided with the arrival of a producer determined and/or given a remit to be a new broom. The Great Purge, as it was tagged, occurred when 28-year-old Tim Aspinall took over from Margaret Morris in the middle of the year.

There were shabby circumstances surrounding the cull. Jennifer Moss recalled later that Aspinall walked into the green room and announced that a cancerous growth had to be cut out. The specific details of who would be leaving were broken to the unsuspecting actors on 1 April 1964 – by all accounts not by Aspinall but by the unfortunate Margaret Morris – in a process Lynne Carol (Martha Longhurst) described as: 'You, you, you and you… are all going out!' Martha Longhurst, Frank Barlow, Harry, Concepta and Lucille Hewitt, Jerry Booth, Ken and Val Barlow and Florrie Lindley had all been rumoured to be facing the chop. Some got a reprieve but Frank, Harry and Concepta, Florrie, Jerry (and his wife Myra) and Martha were all dispensed with over a period of months, starting with the last named. Some axed cast members no doubt held out hope that they might eventually be brought back – and indeed Graham Haberfield would return as Jerry Booth and remain there for many years – but no such salvation was available to Carol: on 13 May 1964, Martha Longhurst died quietly of a heart attack in the Snug of the Rovers, slipping away unnoticed as the pub resounded with singing.

Ken Irwin, in his role as showbusiness correspondent, got to know many of The Street's cast and crew, and Aspinall was no exception. 'Tim Aspinall was an ex-journalist,' he says. 'I had a lot of time for Tim Aspinall.' Nonetheless, he also says, 'I think he decided he was going to make a name for himself. He upset an awful lot of people. They were quite cosy, three or four years into the series and suddenly along comes a new young producer, a whippersnapper as far as they were concerned, and starts turning some of them over and ending their contracts.' Adele Rose says of characters being killed off, 'We never liked that. We always tried to fight against it because we all felt the producer was not doing it in the interests of the programme but because they wanted to put their stamp on the show by doing something dramatic, losing sight sometimes of the fact that by doing that you lost a good character with still a lot of potential. That trio in the Snug were absolute gold. That should never have happened.' William Roache feels as strongly as Rose, but is less measured. He sounds veritably angry when asked about Aspinall's alleged plans to kill off his character, and his anger takes in television killing-offs in a wider sense: 'Yeah, but you say this. Producers come in with all sorts of…. He wanted to get rid of Martha Longhurst. He wanted to get rid of a longstanding character. Why did he want to do that? The BBC, every time they got a serial like *Compact* or *United!* that was successful, they took off. And Cecil Bernstein was told time and again, "Take The Street off. Get rid of it, 'cos it's doing well." Why? Why? Anyway, he hung on, we stayed there and that was it.' It's probably best not to mention in Roache's presence a final sick twist to the story: director Mike Newell told Stephen F. Kelly and Judith Jones, authors of *Forty Years Of Coronation Street*, that the whole thing was down to a bet: a producer he didn't name but presumably Aspinall as he employed the pronoun 'he' and Aspinall's predecessor was female told him 'I bet you don't think that I can kill Martha Longhurst in the pub on Christmas Eve.' Only the Christmas Eve part was omitted from the execution of said producer's wager.

Says John Finch of the purge, 'Harry didn't approve. Harry was quite upset about it, but – and this was the kind of bloke he was – he'd say, "Well, he's a producer, if that's what he wants to do, that's it".' This makes Kershaw somewhat different to other executive producers The Street would have: it's difficult to imagine, for instance, Eighties/Nineties exec producer David Liddiment standing idly by and allowing major events with which he disagreed to take place.

There was a true pathos surrounding this death, both because of the much-loved status of the character concerned and its unexpectedness: it occurred in the days before Granada trailed such big events and before newspapers paid money to insiders to leak them. Added to that is the effect it had upon the actress's career, which died the same night that Martha did. Lynne Carol's lifetime in the theatre and her household name status were no defence against the reluctance of casting directors to employ someone they were afraid would simply put viewers in mind of Martha Longhurst and thereby deflect attention from their own product. She would obtain other roles, but very few. Lynne Carol had become the first but by no means last victim of the curse of ex-*Street* actors: a career-high of financial remuneration and professional recognition followed by a lifetime of 'resting'.

Times have changed. Over the last decade or so, having The Street on your CV has evidently turned from a black mark into a plus. Perhaps it's because casting directors are becoming more lazy and simply picking faces they know, or perhaps it's because in an age where television is having to compete more ferociously than ever before for the attention of a now easily distracted public, but many living rooms in recent years have resounded to the shout 'Oh look, it's whatsisname who used to be in *Coronation Street!*' as a face familiar from a certain fictional backstreet turns up in a drama or comedy.

As for the death of Martha, while the consensus is that Aspinall behaved insensitively, there is no way to adjudge his decision empirically wrong. Additionally, that no character is indispensable to *Coronation Street* is proven by the fact that the show has enthralled subsequent generations who mostly have no idea who Martha Longhurst was. It should also be pointed out that no damage was done popularity-wise – the following year was a miracle ratings year for The Street, with only the high-water mark of 1962 beating it for number of episodes making the week's top spot.

27 May saw the farewell of Frank Barlow, as he moved to the Cheshire house he had bought with his £6,000 premium bond win. (Martha had died at his leaving party.) No.3, which was left vacant by Frank's departure, would remain in that state until 1968, the consequence of a reluctance on the part of Granada to give the programme the casting budget it needed. Recalls Ken Irwin, 'They were notorious for being a cheapskate company. Sidney Bernstein would go around and make sure all the lights were turned off in the offices every night. He'd go around looking in the "Out" trays of the letter baskets and make sure that all the post went out second class post.' Such parsimoniousness clearly extended even to their most successful product and this state would continue until the very end of the 1980s. Asked about this, Denis Forman insists that Granada was proud of its asset and that a big budget would have killed the programme. 'Discipline is all important in a show like that and the most difficult discipline was to keep the storylines on the basis of what that particular culture would stand,' he reasons. 'Once you started launching out into murders, mayhem, fast cars, aeroplanes, whatnot – you're gone. You had to keep it in the pub, they had to keep it in the street, and that meant low budget.'

The Hewitt family departed to Ireland in August with the exception of Lucille, whom Cecil Bernstein insisted be retained, as The Street needed some semblance of youth, his insistence no doubt partly motivated by consciousness of the fact that the baby boomers were just coming of age. Lucille, now 14 to 15, stayed behind to finish her exams, living with Jack and Annie Walker.

Though a period of calm followed on The Street after Aspinall's autumn departure – Harry Kershaw coming back in – he would not by any means be the last controversial *Street* producer. As a function of The Street's success and longevity, the tradition that he had established would continue, with a new broom brought in every so often to rejuvenate a programme that was flagging insofar as it had lately not quite reached the astronomical viewing figures to which it was accustomed. Explains Little, 'Some producers want to come in and make their mark. They feel it's the chance to get noticed in the industry and also they feel it's the best thing for the programme to [shake] things up a bit. By the time they've finished doing all of their stuff, which tends to take about two years, the next person who comes in is left with the show that's been changed quite a lot and what they need is a period of stability for everybody involved in the show, so they do that. Then the next people come along and they change it all again.'

One of the purposes of the purge was to make way for fresh blood and on this score Aspinall can't be faulted. This was the year that the Ogdens made their debut. Aspinall was responsible for their characters and casting. Though it wouldn't be for a few years that the Ogdens really began to take centre-stage in the programme, their brilliance and longevity must go some way toward rehabilitating the producer for whatever sins he allegedly committed vis à vis Martha. First to appear was Irma (Sandra Gough), a dopey but decent young woman. She was followed by her dad, lorry driver Stanley (Bernard Youens), who it transpired had come looking for her after she had run away. Stan was a vast bellied, uncultured slob with an incongruously neat Errol Flynn-like moustache.

As with Dennis Tanner before him and as with many *Street* characters in the future, Stan was a much darker figure when he first appeared than the one the writers gradually made him. Those who only recall him as hapless, feckless and henpecked will be surprised to learn that Stan had to swear to his daughter that the drink-fuelled violence that had seen Irma's siblings taken into care was a thing of the past. Stan bought No.13 and Irma moved in with him, her mother Hilda (Jean Alexander) and her 14-year-old brother Trevor (Jonathan Collins). (Incidentally, though the pot-bellied, pop-eyed gentleman who was the selling owner of No.13 was named Wormold, he, strangely, referred to himself as Alfred, not Edward.) Hilda was a prattling, nosey, bird-like woman. Almost always to be seen wearing a pinny, curlers and a headscarf, she universally addressed people as 'Chuck'. She had a strange conviction that 'my Stan', as she referred to him, was some sort of babe magnet, and would frequently become convinced that he was having affairs with various women in the neighbourhood, especially a female at 19 Inkerman Street, who – like Nellie Fairclough, Len's first wife, and Mr Papagopolous – was often referred to but never seen on screen.

Illness on the part of Doris Speed (Annie Walker) proved devastating to the actors cast as the Ogdens' other kids. The episode in which they were shown moving in was written but not broadcast. Explains Little, 'There's about four or five [instances] in the Sixties and Seventies [where] there was no *Coronation Street* transmitted that night because in the days of recording programmes as-live, if say, Violet Carson was ill and she was carrying the story, you couldn't make it.' Of the Ogdens moving in, he says, 'It's a wonderful script. They have a knees-up in the street as they're moving all their stuff in and Hilda has four children.' When the show resumed upon Speed's recovery, the two additional kids were airbrushed out of the picture with the explanation that they had remained in care. By 1976, when Hilda was talking to Stan about their kids, she referred to only two.

Trevor himself was short-lived, fleeing to London within three months of his family's arrival with some stolen money. What was remarkable about the people who played the remaining Ogden trio was that they were among the few *Street* actors who didn't virtually play themselves and were completely different to their characters: Alexander was quiet and modest, Youens cultured enough to have been a Granada continuity announcer and Gough a religious and rather pious person who didn't share the shallowness and materialism of Irma.

There was a coda to The Street's Aspinall era when in 1975 he wrote four episodes of the programme. This took place shortly before the appointment of Bill Podmore, another producer who was a new broom, but who in contrast effected his revolution while causing a minimum of rancour.

ichard Everitt took over from Kershaw as *Coronation Street* producer for the first couple of months of 1965 and was succeeded by first Kershaw, then in the early summer by Howard Baker, who, apart from a short period in the late summer of the year covered by Kershaw, remained in his post through to the summer of 1966.

The first *Coronation Street* episode of 1965 – broadcast on 4 January – was the *Street* directorial debut of 30-year-old Michael Cox. He would direct 20 episodes between then and October 1969. His recollections provide an interesting snapshot of the programme at this juncture in its history. 'There was always a bit of snobbery about it,' he says. 'People said, "Oh it's only a twice-weekly serial" or "soap opera" but from the point of view of people like myself who were building a career and hoping to go on to bigger things it was certainly the place to be. At that time it was shot as if it was a live show in a multi-camera studio. You couldn't stop, you couldn't edit it, so you had to make sure that you'd got your planning right for three or four cameras, two booms. Of course you are dependent on some very skilled people you're working with. You had to release a camera from one set in order to have it in position on another ready to start that scene. It was sometimes amazing to watch. If you looked down on the studio from the gallery above, to see a big pedestal camera going from one end of the studio to the other with the cameraman perhaps riding on the trolley and swinging the lenses as he went, it was exciting. The cast were very reliable. I can never remember anyone forgetting their lines or getting them wrong so that you couldn't continue. They would occasionally improvise a little bit if they were in trouble, but you can generally get back on the [rails]. The writers were very good.... They would distribute the cast around the scenes so they didn't play two consecutive scenes in different sets and so on.

'We used to go into the studio on a Tuesday and start camera rehearsal on a Thursday afternoon and continue it on the Friday morning and then record both episodes on the Friday afternoon. After that, those sets would be struck and some other show would be in the studio the next week. In a normal week, if you didn't have the street exterior you'd have probably six sets in the studio, one of which would be the interior of the Rovers, which took up twice as much space as anything else.

'If there was an exterior scene in the street then the street was built in the studio, and it took up a lot of space obviously, like down all one side of it. That did make life a little more difficult. Very often it was on two levels so someone could look out of an upstairs window onto what was happening in the street below. I remember with great pride doing one of those big argument scenes between Ena Sharples and Elsie Tanner in the street and using a crane – which obviously was setting myself problems because that takes up a lot more room than an ordinary pedestal camera – and I think I finished it off with a Salvation Army band coming through. Youth and ambition for you.' This was one of the few flashy directorial touches Cox was able to execute within the confines of *Coronation Street*. 'I don't recall doing any tricks or giving any challenge to Alfred Hitchcock,' he says. 'It was down-to-earth, straightforward storytelling. That was the important thing.'

In January 1965, Elsie Tanner's worst nightmare came to pass when Ena Sharples became her landlady. Ena had been given No.11 in the will of a member of the Mission's congregation named Elsie Briggs who had moved away several years before but had always enjoyed Ena's harmonium playing. It would have been a bewildering development for those who remembered that as recently as early 1963, during a rent strike storyline, it had seemed clear that, like the other houses in The Street, No.11 was owned by Edward Wormold. Daran Little puts it down to 'continuity error' rather than the storyliners simply ignoring the established facts for the sake of a good plot. 'The Sixties are scattered with stuff like that,' he says. 'I tried to make sense of it when I was doing the archives but some of them you just can't make sense of.' It's a matter of opinion whether sense was brought to this situation by Ena's decision to sell the house to Wormold. Meanwhile, Ena remained a poor pensioner because she used her money to travel to America to stay for a while with her long-lost brother.

There were more understandable reasons for the lack of continuity involved in the revelation this year that Florrie Lindley wasn't – as Ena

Sharples had immortally put it in the first episode – 'a widder woman'. It turned out that she was merely estranged from husband Norman, who was doing engineering work in India. The *volte face* was executed in order to contrive actress Betty Alberge's Great Purge-dictated exit. (Florrie decided to emigrate to Canada with Norman.) The Corner Shop was bought from Florrie by Lionel Petty (Edward Evans), a bald, moustachioed Welshman. Petty had previously been a sergeant major and it showed in his somewhat brisk attitude with customers.

Ironically, another victim of the purge, Jerry Booth, made a return, although minus Myra. He became a partner in Len Fairclough's builders' yard. One of their first jobs together was to demolish No.7, which had collapsed due to a snapped window beam. (Conveniently, and peculiarly, the rest of the terrace was unaffected.) Wormold decided that the £300 it would cost to rebuild wasn't worth it. It would leave a gap in the terrace for 17 years, filled only by a bench installed by the council. The real-world reason for the demolition of No.7 seems simply ridiculous. The house that had been vacant in the programme since the Hewitts' departure was got rid of because the casting budget couldn't stretch to fill it – and this despite the fact that No.3 had been empty since May the previous year (and would be for another three years) and the shop flat remained empty for all of 1966. There was at least a practical benefit to the demolition: with the terrace now split, only half of it needed to be erected in the studio at a time.

Whatever its deep-set corporate parsimoniousness, many would assume that Granada would have an interest in lavishing funds on at least this programme, whose stratospheric viewing figures made advertisers flock to purchase time within its centre-break. In fact, it wasn't quite the money spinner for the franchise that people might imagine, as explained by David Liddiment, not only a future *Street* executive producer but future director of programmes at ITV. 'Granada don't get the advertising revenue from the rest of the country,' he says. 'They only get [it] from the North-West of England. So the financial benefit is shared by all the ITV companies, and if you were the London company – Thames – you were making a lot of money. Granada did well out of its region – and obviously *Coronation Street* did particularly well in the North-West – but actually Granada charged the ITV companies a very small amount of money for the show. The reason it did that was because in those days each of the big five ITV companies basically carved up the network between them and they each made a proportion of the network programmes. That's the way it used to work before there were independents and before there was a network centre and central commissioning, so programmes were kind of exchanged between the companies on a share-out basis that had been pre-agreed. Granada didn't want all of its allocation of network programmes to go on *Coronation Street* because it wanted to make lots of other things like *World In Action* and *Jewel In The Crown* and *Brideshead* and *Sam* and *Disappearing World* and so on and so forth. They didn't want all their network money going on these two episodes of a soap opera. So it was in their interests to keep its costs down, because they weren't going to get any more money from the network for them.' Nonetheless, there were other ways in which The Street was highly lucrative to Granada. 'It was the most enormously powerful card in Granada's hand,' says Derek Granger. He asserts that Cecil Bernstein found it highly useful when Granada was trying to sell some of its programmes to fellow ITV franchises. Granger: '*Coronation Street* was the one card Granada had, and if other companies were being a bit rough with Granada and saying, "Well I don't think we're going to take that, Cecil", Cecil would simply say, "Alright no *Coronation Street*". That's what happened – it was used. When you think of the power of that show…. A rating puller like that was absolutely gigantic. It was used as a bargaining chip the whole time.'

Arthur Lowe made his last *Coronation Street* appearance as Leonard Swindley in the episode of 31 March. However, this did not mean the character disappeared from TV screens. Just over two months later, Lowe was back as Swindley in the first *Street* spin-off series, *Pardon The Expression*. True to Swindley's comic turn properties in The Street, *Pardon The Expression*, was an all-out comedy show that actually had a laughter track. (The show was recorded, to the recollection of Michael Cox, who worked on it, before an audience of around 50 people.) The programme's very title sprang from Swindley's comic properties: he was a man so proper and so unable to cope with the changing mores of society that he would append an embarrassed 'If you'll pardon the expression' to innocuous comments that he was anxious might be interpreted as risqué. First broadcast on 2 June 1965, *Pardon The Expression* saw Swindley take his brand of bustling incompetence into the job of deputy manager of a branch of chain store Dobson and Hawks. Though not fully networked, the show was handily broadcast by some franchises on Wednesdays at 7pm, i.e., directly before *Coronation Street*. The first run of 12 episodes was well-received enough for a second series

– 24 episodes long – to be commissioned. Though there were few direct references to *Coronation Street* in its scripts, those scripts often came from the pens of people whose names were familiar from The Street's end credits, including Harry Driver & Vince Powell, Jack Rosenthal and Geoffrey Lancashire. Additionally, the show's executive producer was Harry Kershaw and its first series' producer Harry Driver.

The second series ended with Swindley being sacked (an event only the surreptitious intervention of his loyal staff had prevented in the preceding episodes) but that still wasn't the end of the character. Swindley returned in 1967 in a spin-off of the spin-off called *Turn Out The Lights*. This show saw him travelling around Britain in his new role of professional speaker on astrology, investigating spooky mysteries he stumbled upon in the process. Its mixture of comedy and drama returned Swindley to the milieu in which he had first appeared in The Street, the difference in tone to its predecessor programme underlined by its 55-minute duration. As with *Pardon The Expression*, there was a significant overlap of *Coronation Street* backroom staff, even to the extent of Kenneth Cope, who played Jed Stone in The Street, contributing script-writing work.

'[It was] one of the worst things I ever wrote,' says John Finch of *Turn Out The Lights*, which recollection chimes with some of the awful notices the programme received, as well as the recollection of Michael Cox, who says, 'That was a disaster. We just didn't get it right. There was a marvellous review of it by Nancy Banks-Smith in *The Guardian*. She said, "Hello, it's only January and here's the worst series of the year already".' 'The funny thing was Arthur loved it,' says Finch. The latter feels that had not Lowe become committed to the Captain Mainwaring role for which he would become immortal – *Dad's Army* began its 11-year run in 1968 – there would have been another series of *Turn Out The Lights*, '…because it was improving.' Sadly, unlike *Pardon The Expression* (which has been released on DVD), tapes of *Turn Out The Lights* no longer survive, at least not in Granada's archives.

Back in The Street, David Barlow got married to Irma Ogden, a union which severely tested the leftist principles of his brother. Ken may have been all for the worker, but he drew the line at having Stan and Hilda as his in-laws. Meanwhile Ken and Val became parents of twins, Peter and Susan.

The Street's 500th episode was broadcast on 29 September but that demonstration of the fact that the programme had become a national institution paled beside the award of the Order of the British Empire to Violet Carson in the Queen's birthday honours list three months earlier. Like the MBEs given The Beatles in the same list, it was interpreted by many as a sign that the Labour government of Harold Wilson was trying to appear trendy. It should be noted though that while Wilson was a somewhat unlikely Fab Four enthusiast, there is no doubt that he was a genuine fan of The Street. Wilson hailed from back-to-back housing not a million miles removed from The Street's milieu, while many are the surviving ministers of the period who can relate stories of how Wilson would get restless if Monday and Wednesday cabinet meetings looked like dragging on past 7.30. When Kershaw met Wilson, he found him genuinely knowledgeable about the show.

The apparent fan status of Wilson's chancellor James Callaghan, though – ostensibly demonstrated at a reception when Callaghan told Pat Phoenix he thought her the 'sexiest thing on television' – was entirely fraudulent. Decades later, Callaghan admitted he had made the comment for the benefit of the press and had never seen the programme.

When Peter Eckersley graduated from *Street* scriptwriter to producer in 1966, he decided that updating was the order of the day.

His strategy included turning Elliston's into a 'PVC welding factory'. The establishment still made raincoats but of the man-made variety, something that it was felt would create better visuals than the employees working with cloth. If this was a rather fatuous piece of modernisation, Eckersley was on firmer ground with his decision to open out the function of the Mission from a narrowly religious one to that of a Community Centre. Not only was the underused Mission set a waste of resources, but Missions were becoming rare in the real life that *Coronation Street* sought to represent. Eckersley also introduced storylines more in tune with an increasingly permissive artistic landscape. The results of this were mixed. While the attempted rape of Lucille Hewitt got high viewing figures, some reacted with distaste to this. Ditto for storylines that saw Ken Barlow embark on an affair with *Weatherfield Gazette* reporter Jackie Marsh and Sheila Birtles (brought back for more controversy) reveal that she was an unmarried mother: she explained to Neil Crossley that she had given birth to his illegitimate baby in 1963.

Though her – for the time – shameful pregnancy retroactively provided a more plausible reason for her suicidal feelings three years previously than simply being dumped and losing her job, that the storyline did not go down well with the viewers demonstrated the limits of both television and *Coronation Street*. Fans of The Street liked its realism but they were not as broad-minded as the people who fully four years before had paid to see the movie *A Kind Of Loving*, which was also concerned with premarital sex. When Harry Kershaw took back over from Eckersley later in the year, the programme was toned down a little and its focus switched back to the remaining original characters. However, a significant legacy of Eckersley's tenure was new scriptwriter Leslie Duxbury, gifted at both social comment and humour. He would become one of the long-term titans of The Street's scriptwriting staff and would even serve two terms as producer.

In January, David and Irma Barlow bought the Corner Shop off Lionel Petty. Meanwhile, a new and important face would first be seen on 21 February, when teenager Ray Langton (Neville Buswell) was taken on by Jerry Booth at the yard. Though this ex-Borstal (juvenile prison) boy was hounded from the street within a couple of months over a mini-campaign of petty theft as well as maltreatment of Lucille, he would return and become a major, longstanding character and notable heartthrob. Another new face briefly seen this year but destined for *Street* legend status was Bet Lynch (Julie Goodyear). The brassy blonde made her entrée as a machinist at the raincoat factory, quickly alienating both Lucille (whom she gave a black eye) and Mrs Walker (who thought her common, though as she had whacked her ward, this might have been down to more than merely her usual snobbery).

Unusually, Elsie Tanner found she could occupy the moral high ground over Ena when the latter was caught shoplifting in a supermarket and fined £2, a state of affairs caused by the fact that Ena had given her savings to her daughter Vera, who had been abandoned by her abusive husband. John Stevenson, later a *Street* scriptwriter but then a *Daily Mail* journalist, heard of the story thread in advance. He recalls, 'It's a terrible blow to her reputation as a righteous woman who's very keen on [pronouncing] on other people's sins. With the photographer on the *Mail* at the time, I organised an exclusive picture story and he got a very atmospheric photograph of Ena Sharples on about the fourth floor balcony of a rather grim Salford tower block looking out over a rather grim Salford street. She's all in black and she's thinking whether to top herself. They've got pictures of it here and there in Granada 'cos it's so atmospheric.' Said picture can also be seen on the back cover of the hardback edition of Harry Kershaw's autobiography *The Street Where I Live*.

In 1967, the threat of death hung over *Coronation Street*.

Such a state of affairs must have seemed as ridiculous to many then as it does now: with both episodes of the programme consistently high in the ratings, what could there possibly be for the Granada top brass to be unhappy about? But the end of 1966, a year of controversy over The Street's racy – some thought grubby – storylines, saw Granada seriously discussing cancelling the show. Reveals Daran Little, 'Coronation Street was to finish in 1968. The actors were told the contracts weren't going to be renewed the following year. The show was going to finish because it was outdated because all Coronation Streets were being knocked down and they were putting up all these tower blocks. And the viewing figures were down at that point. Drastically down.' The two occasions in July 1966 that The Street had only been switched on by an estimated 9.79 million viewers/4.45 million homes was a nadir for the programme since it had first made the ratings in early 1961 (and that's only for editions of the show that made the top 20 – stats for ones below that were not compiled at that time). Additionally, 'only' 22 episodes of The Street had reached number one in 1966, hardly failure for most programmes but a stark contrast to the previous year, when more episodes than there were weeks in the year – 56 – scaled the ratings summit because in some weeks both *Street* episodes tied for first place. Mentioning an ill-fated BBC continuing drama serial that ended in a bloodbath two decades hence, Little continues, 'So it was like the end of *Eldorado*: "Come on, let's just get rid of it".' Perhaps prompted by the success of *Pardon The Expression*, Granada were contemplating moving some residents of The Street into new shows. 'Save the key characters that people like,' says Little of the rationale. 'There were three [proposed] spin-offs. There was one taking Jack and Annie Walker and Lucille Hewitt to a Derbyshire guest house with Ena Sharples as their housekeeper. There was a drama series set in Australia which featured Ken and Val Barlow. And there was a romantic comedy with Len Fairclough and Elsie Tanner and their lodger Jerry Booth.'

John Finch lays the blame for such ideas at the feet of people at Granada who he says, 'Got a bit blasé about being top of the ratings all the time. They got the feeling that, "Oh well, if we can get to the top with this, we can get to the top with something else" and they were probably slightly worried that people would think that all Granada could do was *Coronation Street*. Later on, this feeling resulted in *Brideshead* and *Jewel In The Crown*. It was a feeling that they needed to be seen to be doing something different.' He adds, 'There was a feeling that they'd carried it to its limit. Nothing else at that time had run that length of time. And to some extent they felt it was not necessarily a good thing to run forever. That one should keep changing and doing new things.'

Additionally, 3 April 1967 saw the advent of a new serial drama with a working class milieu that not only looked like becoming a rival to The Street, but had production values that were in danger of making *Coronation Street* look tatty. *Market In Honey Lane* was created by Louis Marks for ATV. It focused on the lives of a dozen or so market traders in London's East End. Personality-wise, they ran the gamut from the rough, tough and wonderfully named fruit-and-veg seller Billy Bush to the dapper, gentlemanly flower stallholder Harry Jolson. ATV poured money into the new show, constructing the roads in which the market was located plus the shell of an adjacent pub and shops at a cost of £20,000 and importing a regular, costly supply of street rubbish and market detritus. The programme was initially weekly and an hour long, with each episode focusing on a single character. It was transmitted on Mondays at 8pm, i.e., directly after that evening's *Coronation Street*. Though it was awkwardly titled (why not *Honey Lane Market?*), it must have seemed to many at Granada to be The Street only more so, especially as it began picking up excellent ratings. Its first episode attracted no fewer than 19.47 million viewers.

Against this backdrop of possible cancellation, The Street mounted a fight back, with a pair of huge storylines.

In the episode of 10 May, a train fell off the Viaduct. The scene of devastation of five goods train carriages jack-knifed beside the Corner Shop with a flattened Mini beneath them, dust and debris strewn everywhere, led everyone to believe the worst, especially when Ena Sharples, Jack Walker, Elsie Tanner and Lucille Hewitt couldn't be found. The latter three were in fact discovered to be elsewhere by their relieved loved ones. Ena was buried alive but rescued by David Barlow. A local girl named Sonia Booth was not so lucky.

The other big story was the marriage of Elsie Tanner. American serviceman Steve Tanner (the same surname a deliberate ploy as we'll see), an old wartime boyfriend of Elsie's played by Canadian actor Paul Maxwell, had fetched up in The Street in May and proposed. Elsie's ceremony (for that's what it was – who remembers Steve Tanner now?) marked a milestone in *Street* history and the inauguration of a *Coronation Street* tradition: the nation-stopping wedding. Celebrity chef Tony Stoppani, famous for providing the cake for the wedding of Princess Alexandra, was commissioned to make a two-tier affair for the Tanners. Though it was to be filmed in No.6 studio, a press release announced that the wedding was to take place in St Stephen's Road Methodist Chapel, Warrington. Dennis would be giving away his mother, who – it was explained for those watching in black and white, i.e. everyone – would be wearing a coffee-coloured French ribbon-lace dress chosen by Pat Phoenix. It was even announced what hymns would be sung at the service: O God of Love and O Perfect Love. The reception would be at a Cheshire country club and the honeymoon in Lisbon. This pretence of realism was playful, but calls poured in to Granada from people who wanted to throw confetti, as did more than a thousand good luck letters and telegrams. Phoenix was the not-displeased recipient through the post of sundry wedding gifts from complete strangers. She – and other crew – were not so pleased to be the recipient of death threats from a fan outraged that she was going to marry a Yank. All of this was one of the first significant examples in Britain of the slightly disturbing propensity of some TV fans to conflate reality and fiction. It is a phenomenon that seems to afflict continuing serials more than most dramas, presumably because their realism makes them seem less like a manufactured narrative and more a window on other people's lives. Such a confusion of fiction and reality probably afflicted more the generation who had not grown up with television, many of whom on some level couldn't quite grasp the artifice of what they were seeing. In any case, Pat Phoenix seemed no less confused about the dividing line, asking a famous jeweller to bring a selection of wedding rings to the studios when she must have known full well that props could supply one for nothing with nobody noticing the difference. She also initially refused to come out of her dressing room to film the vows on the grounds that she actually felt the turmoil of a bride on her wedding day.

That the wedding was treated by Granada, and perceived by the public, as akin to a Royal Union was appropriate, for Elsie's alter ego was now increasingly taking on regal airs. Stories abound of Phoenix pulling rank on staff at Granada. She also bore grudges on an epic level, refusing to speak to Philip Lowrie when he decided to permanently give up the role of Dennis Tanner and managing to go through two years of rehearsals with William Roache without once speaking to him (as opposed to his character) after a row about her scene-hogging (itself another imperious trait that raised her colleagues' hackles).

The glitz of the Tanner wedding was of course at odds with the dowdiness that was supposed to be *Coronation Street*'s trademark (as was the edition shot entirely on location that preceded the wedding episode wherein The Street's men went off on a canal trip while the women visited a stately home, with the two parties' paths improbably bisecting). However, the nation waved that inconvenient fact aside as it got behind Elsie, who had had a love life as energetic and trauma-filled as a 21st century teenager's in the previous six years. On 6 September 1967, around 20.79 million Britons sat down to watch the slice off a cut loaf become a respectable married woman (or as respectable as a second-time bride could be at that juncture in history). By popular demand, the programme was repeated, becoming on 20 September the first *Coronation Street* to be broadcast twice, even if not in every ITV region. A million people bought a wedding souvenir special edition of the *TV Times*. One wonders if such public excitement would have occurred had the public known that they were being cold-bloodedly manipulated by the programme makers. Highly unusually for a drama, the husband had the same surname as his bride. This was so that when Steve was shortly killed off, Elsie could – as would be expected – keep her husband's name and at the same time retain her familiar handle.

However cynical their motivations – Jack Rosenthal, who took over from Harry Kershaw as producer in the middle of the year, hated the marriage storyline, considering it unrealistic for a woman of Elsie's age – Granada had stumbled upon something that the public were ready to lap up and weddings would henceforth feature regularly in *Street* storylines, with an inevitable spike in viewing figures.

That wedding repeat did not herald a new trend. Though disruption of transmission of a 1968 episode saw ITV cave in to demands for a repeat shortly afterwards and a 1970 episode was re-transmitted after a strike to remind the public of the storylines, there were no further *Coronation Street* repeats until Granada's 25th anniversary celebrations of May 1981, which occasioned the broadcast of six landmark shows over the course of a week. (One of these was the first ever episode – because of the late take-up of The Street of some franchises, some regions were seeing that episode for the first time.) Even after that, the nation's most popular programme continued to be rationed carefully, with only a handful of past episodes being exhumed and only to mark programme anniversaries or deaths of major former *Street* stars. Not until the invention of domestic satellite and cable television did the policy about repeating vintage episodes change, while it took the competition of *EastEnders* in the late Eighties to force ITV's hand with regard to retransmission of more recent *Street* editions.

The 15 March edition saw the brief return of an old face: Ken's father Frank. Those who detected that Frank Pemberton seemed rather fragile would be right. Bill Roache later recalled that the man playing his screen father could hardly walk, let alone act. In the last three years, Pemberton had not only been afflicted by *Coronation Street*'s typecasting curse – his only work since he had left the programme in 1964 had been a theatre tour and one TV series – but he had suffered a stroke less than a year after being written out. Symbolically, his stroke had occurred when he was on his way back from the Labour Exchange: though his role in The Street had enabled him to buy his first car and his first house, he had very quickly been reduced to claming the dole. The stroke robbed him of the use of his left arm and the ability to walk unaided. He was still only 50.

It was early enough in the course of *Coronation Street*'s history for the programme to still be possessed of a sense of family. When The Street's production team heard of Pemberton's plight, they made a gesture of compassion by inviting him back for an episode to see if he was fit to make a long-term return. This action was of course made all the easier by the fact that Tim Aspinall, the man ultimately responsible for his original departure, had long moved on. Perhaps Pemberton would have been able to continue in The Street – he remembered his lines and his voice was as strong as ever – had it not been for another example of fate seeming to kick him in the teeth. Upon his return from filming in

Manchester to his Surrey home, he was informed by his wife that she wanted a divorce. He returned to hospital while his wife moved away, taking their daughter with her. In June 1968, he found a sliver of solace in his increasingly precarious lot when he married one of his nurses, but the turn of the decade found him living in a bungalow especially adapted for invalids and pining for the appearance of an acting role 'where I could sit down all the time and not have to move about....'

Pemberton got another episode of The Street on 3 February 1971, four years after his previous compassion-dictated recall. The episode in question marked a Barlow family funeral, so it was logical for his character to make an appearance. However, it was Pemberton's 277th and last appearance in The Street. He passed away in 1975.

The last years of Pemberton's life had been as filled with pathos as any *Coronation Street* storyline and his tragedy could be posited as being caused by its first cull. Of course, that doesn't make Tim Aspinall a murderer, any more than the career doldrums experienced by Lynne Carol make him a villain. A TV producer is perfectly entitled – indeed obligated – to put sentimentality second to the long-term good of a programme. But one wonders whether Aspinall – who himself died in 2000 – felt the occasional pang of conscience about the far-reaching effects of his Great Purge.

Though over the course of the decade, the hair of The Street's male characters had grown longer and the skirts of its female ones shorter, it seems safe to assume that these reflections of changing times were down more to fashion-conscious performers than on-the-ball scriptwriters. In this year of the Summer of Love, of all times, preventing The Street looking like soot-covered ancient history was imperative, hence the transformation of Gamma Garments from a clothing emporium to a psychedelic boutique. For a while boutique manageress Miss Nugent was (to use the argot of the day) a groovy chick. Nonetheless, Michael Cox makes a valid point when he reflects of the Summer of Love, 'I think it was a London phenomenon rather than one in the North-West of England.... I don't think society changed quite as rapidly as history seems to suggest it did.'

At the end of the year, *Coronation Street* was still perceived by Granada to be in the doldrums. That a fifth of the population rated it their favourite programme in an opinion poll, that it still generally rode high in the ratings and that it continued to rack up valuable overseas sales were deemed less important to the Granada bigwigs. Instead they were concerned that, rather alarmingly and paradoxically, the show was far more popular in the South than the North, that even despite the Tanner wedding viewing figures had drifted back down to 'only' 18.75 million and that pretty soon – it was believed by many – nobody would live in terraced housing in working class districts.

Michael Cox took over from Rosenthal as producer in late 1967 and was there to the early months of the following year. Granada's policy at this point was to keep *Street* jobs in the family and a pattern had been established whereby The Street was usually produced by *Street* directors or *Street* writers. In the latter camp were Peter Eckersley, Jack Rosenthal and Kershaw. In the former were Howard Baker and Cox. Cox was simply holding the fort. Cecil Bernstein had asked Richard Everitt – another director, as well as floor manager on The Street's first episode and producer for a brief period in 1965 – to become an executive producer with a difference. Recalls Cox, 'It was a planned strategy by the powers that be that I would be, as it were, the line producer for six months while Dick Everitt who was a little senior to me went away into an office with Stan Barstow and they planned the future of The Street.'

'A new producer came in in 1968 and it was decided to save *Coronation Street*,' says Daran Little. 'To build an outside set and to actually invest in it, bring new characters into it, and that's what they did and that saved it.'

Market In Honey Lane had finished the previous year as the fifth most watched television programme, one place behind The Street – which had the benefit of an extra episode per week. Granada must have been thanking their lucky stars that *Market In Honey Lane* was not a year-round proposition like The Street and that it came off the air after its first 13-week run. Nonetheless, it was due a new series. Actor Bill Kenwright, who joined The Street in April 1968, recalls a feeling of doom hanging over the cast because of it. Kenwright: 'I remember certainly in the first two or three weeks they were all thinking, "Ah, it's coming off because *Market In Honey Lane*'s gonna be the success." I absolutely remember there was a worry about whether contracts were gonna be extended.'

Stan Barstow's involvement in the rejuvenation of The Street came by a curious route. In late 1967, his agent informed him of an approach by Everitt. Barstow: 'Dick Everitt had thought of me as somebody who might do this big novel. He said, "They want you to write a sort of *Coronation Street* novel, projecting into the future because it's all getting a bit bitty and short-term and they're losing storylines. They'd like a long novel which they can pick from and dramatise from for several years".' Barstow agreed to meet Everitt but found his notion 'impossible'. He explains, 'You can't take into account any development, any eventualities that come along. They'd pick up on topical issues and I didn't know what was going to happen. Characters want to leave, actors die and so on. Dick and I met and got on quite amiably. I said, "If you like, I'll take a three-months' contract to come in and out and talk to you about The Street and see what we can do about extending storylines rather than letting them go." They were very wasteful. Storylines were being used up, situations were being used in a very wasteful way. Which is no reflection of the people involved. It was just the style at that time and Dick wanted to change it. So we projected certain things that were happening, made them last a bit longer.'

Michael Cox recalls an objective of Everitt as 'reflecting a wider life than The Street did at that time. I can remember a conversation with Dick where he said, "What happens when Elsie Tanner goes through the menopause? We're never going to know are we?" Both Everitt and Barstow insist that Everitt did not harbour the contempt for The Street that some producers – past and future – seemed to but that he approached the job from genuine respect.

Barstow says 'I couldn't have actually written for The Street myself because it was far too stylised by that time and I didn't want to do it anyway', but in his formal role of 'special consultant' he went into Granada regularly to follow up his suggestion memos to Everitt. Barstow also attended story conferences. 'It was a bit of a nerve-wracking experience because some of the writers were rather resentful,' he recalls. 'And I got blamed for certain cast changes which were not my doing. Most of them were extremely amiable. I just felt a certain coolness coming off one or two of the people. Not the best ones. I won't name names. One or two just had flashes of resentment about one or two of the things that I suggested. I suggested they let Emily Bishop [sic] have some kind of a sexual fling with somebody, a foreign visitor. It did happen but it was thrown back at me that I'd spent the time getting their character into bed.'

Some of Everitt's and/or Barstow's more radical ideas were nixed, presumably by Granada top brass. This included a homosexual storyline involving Jerry Booth that would have been extremely topical considering the decriminalisation of gay love in 1967 but which certainly wouldn't have done much for The Street's ailing fortunes in the North, which was socially conservative in such matters. Proposals to make Emily an unmarried expectant mother, Lucille a drug user and to put Elsie and Len in bed together were also dropped, as was the introduction of The Street's first black family. The latter objective bumped up against the same issue that had stymied John Finch in this regard before. Says Barstow, 'Dick said, "Cecil says The Street is not real for these days. We ought to have a coloured family in it." So we talked around this. I said, "You can't just put a coloured family in a street and expect everybody to say, 'How do? How lovely to see you.' Somebody's going to resent them. Somebody's got to dislike them." And the minute you get somebody like, say, Len Fairclough saying, "I'm not living next door to those black so-and-sos" you put another nail in the coffin of racial tolerance. And so we skated round that one. You see, there's no closure on a soap like that. With a single play, you can set out the problems and work through the conflict and then come out at the end with some kind of resolution, but you can't on a soap, which just goes on and on and on. We found it just too difficult to think about that kind of potentially controversial situation.'

Though changing mores would have probably made The Street more permissive anyway, it seems safe to assume that it can be put at the door of Everitt and/or Barstow that sex was suddenly everywhere in The Street in 1968: Dennis Tanner arguing with Elsie about his right to share a bed with fiancée Jenny Sutton under his mother's roof; Elsie in a low-cut nightie; David Barlow leeringly showing a girlie magazine to Ken; a fleetingly returning Myra patently naked beneath the covers in bed…. However, if including the virginal Emily Nugent in the racy storylines via her dirty weekend with her Hungarian boyfriend might seem like shoehorning, The Street's production team were going to the opposite extreme by implausibly preserving Lucille Hewitt's maidenhead when her peers were drowning in free love. Their motivation for the latter was probably the same as Cox's publicly stated reason for not tackling the drugs issue when all the rest of the media were discussing pot and acid: the worry of imitation by the young.

There were profound physical alternations to The Street. It got its first outside set, located at an old railway yard about 200 yards from Granada on the junction of Walter and Grape Streets. When Harry Kershaw was invited to have a look at said railway yard by a Granada general manager, he clearly felt that fate was not just smiling but positively beaming on him. As he later wrote, 'There in front of me was a large cobblestoned area bounded on two sides by a high brick wall, on a third by a bonded warehouse and on the fourth by – and I could scarcely believe my eyes – a railway viaduct.' The railway yard was duly rented and Denis Park supervised the transfer of the old studio set there. (About 18 months after that, he was given the budget to build the back yards. The wooden interior sets were totally replaced by real brick at around the same time: rain was eroding them.) The actors were disinclined to work at what became colloquially known as the Grape Street Set because of the extreme cold caused by lack of sunlight at the location, so initially exterior scenes were kept to a minimum. Additionally, by necessity the cobbles no longer ran parallel to the house fronts but were at an angle. However, when outside scenes did occur, Coronation Street suddenly seemed more authentic, with laughable pieces of visual shorthand like the painted backdrop of the viaduct now history and the acoustics clearly those of the genuine outdoors. The only real problem was that the road vehicles that could now occasionally be seen in The Street exposed the fact that the houses were out of proportion: the transplanted set had, back in 1960, been built slightly smaller than real scale to fit in the studio and the new lot was too restrictive to allow for correcting those proportions.

Finch admits that the production team had become ever more self-conscious about the terraced side of the street as their real-life counterparts had disappeared. 'It was a very tearing thing really,' he says. However, though Finch says demolishing the terraced side of Coronation Street was discussed, it miraculously continued to seem immune to the slum clearances currently decimating real life counterparts in Salford and Manchester. In 1968, though, the existing architecture of the non-terraced houses was completely dispensed with in the first of what would transpire to be several face-lifts of that side of Coronation Street. It was decided to get rid of that featureless vista that was the backs of the raincoat factory and the Mission Hall via a plot development that saw them replaced by a row of seven maisonettes: three pensioner's bungalows, four two-storey family homes. Though this was probably the closest, for dramatic reasons, The Street could come to the tower blocks by which streets like Coronation Street were being supplanted, these new buildings were certainly in the modernistic-but-grim tower block architectural style.

Ena, of course, was made homeless as the Vestry disappeared along with the Mission in January. She was allocated the ground floor of a maisonette (No.6) by the council. Ken and Val moved into No.14, a two-storey modernist pad directly above Ena's place. A pensioner called Effie Spicer – a lofty woman fallen on hard times and an old flame of Jack Walker's – occupied No.4. However, the plans stated in a memo by Everitt to populate the redeveloped side of The Street with characters whose lifestyles would constitute a young and modern counterpoint to those of the inhabitants of the terraced side were never properly realised. Partly this was because plans to people the redeveloped side with *anyone* were barely realised. It became a running joke among viewers and critics how ghost-town-like were the new properties. The reality behind this was once again the stinginess of Granada with the programme's casting budget, a problem that Little points out got worse the longer The Street lasted. 'If you have a casting budget, that casting budget doesn't go up every year,' he explains. 'It stays the same. Now if you have cast [members] within it who have their contract renewed every year, then most years you tend to give them a little bit more to keep them there. So the problem over the years is you have actors who've been in it for [several] years and they're on a quite hefty sum compared to actors who are only in it for two or three years. You can't necessarily bring in that many new people. You have to wait until you get one of them that's been there for about five years and from their salary you can get two or three new ones. So sometimes you get a big culling and you get an injection of cash.'

An additional problem with the redevelopment was that the raincoat factory and even to an extent the Vestry had enabled multiple character interaction, but the maisonettes offered no such communal situations. By 1971, it had been decided by the show's makers to simply start all over again and execute another full bulldoze operation.

In March, the Queen of The Street made her return, minus her husband. The marriage was over, a mirage resulting from her dashed dreams of youth. All of this was explained by a devastated Elsie to Len Fairclough in a single continuous scene of over 13 minutes in the 4 March episode. Though there had been extended scenes before, such as the one lasting seven minutes in a 1964 edition in which Jerry Booth had argued with Myra over the debts she had racked up on hire purchase, because this one took up all of part two it felt like the first proper two-hander in the programme. It was a culmination of several weeks' worth of mystery as to the reason for the marriage breakdown, itself the result of Barstow's attempts to help tame the voracious storyline beast. He recalls the original plan was for Elsie Tanner 'Coming back with her tail between her legs, just another failed thing.' He says, 'I just thought that was awful 'cos I knew people who watched the programme who wanted more from it than that. We spun that one out, or got somebody else to spin it.' Episode writer Adele Rose was delighted to be the 'somebody else' offered this groundbreaking job. 'It was a huge challenge,' she says. 'It was wonderful to be able to really explore those characters in depth. In those days the scenes were much longer, but to have a whole half-episode was a real treat.' In the episode of 25 September, Steve Tanner was found dead off-screen and the mystery left dangling.

David and Irma Barlow decided to emigrate when David got offered a job as a professional footballer in Australia, a somewhat unlikely plot development considering it involved the injured knee that had caused his recent retirement to suddenly get better and considering the modest remuneration offered by soccer Down Under. It was made necessary by the decision of Alan Rothwell – a *Street* regular again since April 1965 – to once more pursue other roles.

In April the Corner Shop came under new ownership for the third time in eight years when local family the Cleggs bought it. Maggie Clegg (Irene Sutcliffe) brought a New Age ambience to the staid old Corner Shop with her belief in homeopathic products. Husband Les (John Sharp) was more interested in the contents of another sort of bottle. The Cleggs were used to inject some social issues – alcoholism, domestic violence – into the programme. Barstow was instrumental in their introduction. 'The Corner Shop at that time was a bit moribund and I put that onto a character I read about in the newspaper, a sort of recovering alcoholic who came in and took over a shop,' he says.

The Cleggs' 17-year-old son Gordon was played by heartthrob-in-the-making Bill Kenwright (actually 23). While filming at Granada, he was invited to lunch by Everitt. Kenwright recalls, 'They'd never had until that time – which is amazing to think of it now – any real youngster in there to appeal to the girls or the teenagers. They'd written in this family who had a son. I said no instantly. Because then much more than now, if you're typecast that was your career gone. I wanted to play *Hamlet* and *West Side Story* and all of those kind of things. They were pretty persistent.' Not long afterwards, Kenwright was at his parents' house in Liverpool. His mother asked him if he had any forthcoming acting work. Kenwright: 'I said "I've got nothing lined up. Funnily enough, they've asked me to do something but I don't want to do it. They've asked me to go into *Coronation Street*." She was doing the drying or the washing and she dropped all the plates on the floor. She said, "What? Oh, son." She put her arm in mine and we had a little room where the telephone was and she took me without saying a word to the room and she sat me down and rang my auntie Beth, my uncle George, my uncle Phil, my gran, and she said, "Just tell him. Tell him what it would mean to us to have my son in *Coronation Street*." And an hour later I came out of that little room and I thought, "I love my mum more than anyone else in the world" and the next morning I said yes.'

Kenwright had no audition and didn't meet his screen parents until they were brought together to pose for photographs for the *TV Times*. 'You could tell the way they dressed me, the whole thing was a little bit Liverpool rock 'n' roll,' Kenwright says. 'I always got the impression the plan was to give it a bit of youth, and I was the first. And then Dickie Fleming and Audrey Fleming were the second two. And they brought in soon after me Ray Langton.' Like Chris Sandford before him, Kenwright was another young *Street* actor with pop star ambitions, with the difference that he had actually released his first record before joining the programme. He would release four further singles over the next couple of years, one of which – 'Love's Black And White' – he sang on-screen to Minnie Caldwell's cat after the producers found out about the disc's existence.

From Kenwright's recollection, The Street's production methods had changed a little again. Kenwright: 'It was two-and-half days' rehearsal. Technical run through for all the technicians on the Wednesday afternoon. One episode [filmed] on the Thursday. Another episode on the Friday.' He says, 'On the first day, my first line I think was with Pat Phoenix. I wouldn't say I was nervous because I didn't quite know what to expect but I'll never forget she took me to the side of the room and she said, "Listen son, you're a good-looking boy. We know why they've brought you into this show. Can I just remind you that the graveyards are full of people who thought they were indispensable." I had no idea what she meant. The week my first episode came out, I got the train on the Friday night. I was sort of mobbed. I thought, "Oh my God, that's what she means." That it's very easy to be in that show and think you are the be-all and the end-all.'

Les Clegg left The Street almost as soon as he had arrived, disappearing in June when he admitted himself to a psychiatric hospital over his drinking and violence. Says Barstow, 'I don't think he could become permanent really. It was a finite situation but it was good for a few months and you never know what these things will kick off in other directions.'

After standing vacant since May 1964, No.3 finally got some new residents in the form of engineering apprentice Dickie Fleming and petrol pump attendant Audrey, who arrived in June. Played by Nigel Humphreys and Gillian McCann, they were an underage married couple of runaways. That plans to put them on the new and supposedly trendy side of the street were abandoned was a harbinger: the potential of these characters was squandered. Far from being depicted as kindred spirits of the real-world stone-throwing, campus wrecking class of '68, they were given storylines that a couple of almost any age could have plausibly acted out.

In August, there was a siege at No.6 wherein an escaped violent convict held Val prisoner. Ena raised the alarm when Val tapped out a message on the pipes. Though parts of this drama – spread across two episodes – were powerful, other aspects of it were idiotic, particularly the way the whole neighbourhood was depicted as being paralysed by the fear of one loose criminal and the preposterous pseudo police procedural stuff (drinkers at the Rovers being told to go home to make things look normal, a senior police officer solemnly telling residents that his men are stationed around the street but that they won't see them).

The end of the year saw the first ever *Coronation Street* special with the 28 December broadcast of *Christmas on Coronation Street*. Christmas episodes in which the residents were depicted organising and performing in Yuletide pantomimes and concerts was by now a tradition in *Coronation Street* and this programme was a 50-minute look-back by Jack and Annie Walker at some scenes from such shows. Those Yuletide events would cease to be part of The Street, but programmes providing an excuse for clips of past episodes would themselves become ever more prevalent, even when the public's appetite for half-remembered old scenes was apparently catered for by commercially available videos and DVDs.

Stan Barstow moved on after his three-month stint, although would continue to be on the scene at Granada, adapting his novels for screen. Though the 'tele-novel' he had been asked to devise was not one that would have been available commercially, within what he estimates was a couple of years he found himself sounded out about a *Street* narrative that would be for public consumption. Barstow: 'They wanted to start off a series of *Coronation Street* novels and would I be interested in doing one.' He turned the offer down and suspects that the Harry Kershaw novel *The Early Years* was the one for which he had been earmarked. *Street* director Richard Doubleday succeeded Everitt as producer halfway through 1968 for a brief period, before handing over the reins to a *Street* writer in the form of John Finch.

Cox says of the regime of Everitt and Barstow and their plans for widening and deepening the programme, 'I don't know that the result ever showed very clearly. I think it went on being what it was and depended upon the everyday crises of ordinary people's lives.' Perhaps so, but the modernisation process can be adjudged a limited success. Though Granada could not have foreseen this when they appointed Everitt, 1968 was a year in which the Western world was in flames. Keeping The Street in a sleepy bubble while youth rioted from Chicago to Paris to London would have made it look ridiculous. The new element of sensuality may have been self-conscious but at least ensured that the programme wasn't going to be the recipient of contemptuous disinterest by a generation weaned on The Beatles, The Rolling Stones and Bob Dylan. Meanwhile, the maisonettes had, by making half of the show's titular street look modern, removed that patina of age from it, and it's not Everitt's fault that Granada would not provide the budget to populate it.

inch confesses, 'I was a lousy producer.' Things got off to a bad start during the usual chat with an incoming producer to sound him out on his ideas for the programme. Finch: 'I said, "Well, really, I'd like to write it out and bring it to an end and do something else, 'cos I think it's had its time." They were quite upset about that.' Somewhat surprisingly, Finch wasn't sacked and continued in the role – as far as he was able. 'I depended totally on the directors,' he says. 'I had a certain amount of managerial experience but the whole business of television production was completely new to me and I didn't think I contributed anything. I was never very good at things like budget meetings and so on. I was better at dealing with the writers. What I did was try to retain the tradition of The Street but not to do anything frantically new.

A producer's job is pretty exhausting and I hit The Street at a bad time when Peter Adamson was having problems with drink and Pat was being a bit difficult and Jennifer Moss was being very difficult. Coping with the day-to-day stuff was quite enough for me really. I suppose the exec producer [should] have taken a lot of this off me but I think he was a bit punch drunk at the time too.'

Finch says he 'nearly dropped Peter Adamson because the studio staff were getting fed up of the drink problem because of the way it was affecting the schedules.' Adamson had taken to the drink partly because his wife was suffering from a degenerative disease. Compassion for him had caused colleagues to try to cover for him. After a *Street* shoot in which Adamson was so inebriated that for the first time ever – other than for a technical breakdown – the cast and crew had to reconvene to do it again on another day, it was decided to suspend the actor. Finch: 'I was deputed to break the news to Peter. It was a very emotional moment. I was told by someone later that a camera in the studio was live and recorded the interview, but I don't know if this was true. We hoped that the threat of action would persuade Peter to alter his ways, but I suggested to Harry that it was no good making the threat unless we were prepared to go through with it, and he agreed.' In fact, Adamson later revealed to Kershaw that he had been cognisant of the production team's fear of three months' worth of storylines involving Len Fairclough being ruined by any suspension and had always banked on that. Kershaw and Finch got round this potential disruption to a programme written well in advance by informing him of his suspension in July but delaying its start until early October. According to Kershaw's memoirs, Adamson beat the bottle at the first attempt.

Moss, it would transpire, was hurtling toward problems that would prove even worse than Adamson's. Finch: 'I remember once she was in the hospital, pregnant. She'd been rushed in. I think it was a miscarriage. Two episodes were coming up the following week in which she was the main character and I went to the hospital to see if she would be fit enough to come back, but she said her doctor had said that she couldn't. We got the Granada doctor to investigate and she came up with the opposite opinion. So I had a brainwave and I decided to rewrite the story slightly so that she would be in a wheelchair all the way through, and that's what we did. She didn't stay in the wheelchair all the way through though. It was a cry for help, I think.'

Most traumatic of all for Finch, though, was the spiritual deterioration of Tony Warren, whose return to the programme following his period of estrangement and public sniping had come to a dead end. Finch: 'I was always very friendly with Tony and Jack Rosenthal was a close friend of Tony…. Jack Rosenthal came to me and said, "Tony's in a bit of a state because he feels that the way The Street's gone, he can't write it. That it's gone away from his conception. But he wants somebody to tell him that he ought to pack up…." I didn't think it had gone that far away. There were writers like Jack Rosenthal and Peter Eckersley particularly who were very close to the characters as Tony originated them. He just felt I think – and we all felt from time to time – he wanted to move on…. Tony came in and we had a chat and I said to him, "If you want to pack up, that's up to you. But don't forget there are dozens and dozens of other people who've been kept in work because of what you did originally and you need never be ashamed of anything." We finished up actually nearly in tears.'

The final year of the 1960s – in the early part of which Harry Kershaw stepped back into the breach as producer following Finch's unhappy stint in that role – saw *Coronation Street* fairly free from cast, character or set upheaval. However there was a huge development in the programme, albeit one it shared with the rest of British television: colour.

Over the course of late 1968 to late 1969, black and white pictures had begun getting sharper and richer, losing their washed out look of hitherto. However, it was still a quantum leap from that to colour. Though many Americans had had colour images flickering from their television sets since the Fifties (though 1966 was the point where significant market penetration really began occurring in the US), Britain lagged well behind. BBC2 had begun colour broadcasts to selected regions in summer 1967, but it was an arty channel watched by very few. It wasn't until 15 November 1969 that the more populist BBC1 and ITV began to dispense with monochrome images. Naturally, this switchover included the nation's most watched programme.

Or, perhaps, not so naturally. A colour television set in 1969 cost the equivalent of £3,000-plus in today's money. Even with hire purchase (the equivalent of today's credit cards) and rentals, it was an item well beyond the means of two-thirds of the population, a disproportionate part of which made up The Street's demographic. Fewer than 1 per cent of homes had colour TVs in 1969, and that figure hadn't reached 10 per cent even by two years later (thus making it an irrelevance for most that several of the ITV franchises didn't start colour broadcasts until 1970, and some not until 1971). Then there were other considerations. Says John Finch, 'I was dead against colour for The Street.... I do have this strong feeling that there are some things that are suited to black and white.' William Roache observes, 'In the late Sixties, even though colour had been in films for years, certain films like *Room At The Top* and one or two others were deliberately made in black and white.' However, these objections that The Street's black and white was spiritually appropriate to the non-glamorous lives it depicted cut no ice in the face of the relentless march of technological progress. Denis Forman: 'In the end, it had to be colour. The world is colour. The convention of keeping it in black and white was a very attractive idea. It wouldn't have worked, but it was an attractive idea.' Michael Cox, meanwhile, had a director's practical concerns for this show with a short turnaround: 'We all worried about it a lot. We all said, "Is it going to take longer? Is it going to be more difficult to get the lighting right?"'

Almost as if to reflect the uncertainty many production team staff, cast members, critics and viewers felt about the change, The Street's transition to colour was a rather stuttering and error-prone affair. This was despite some meticulous planning involving an episode containing a day trip to Lake Windermere which deployed as many cast members as possible. Unfortunately, and almost pathetically, the episode – broadcast on 29 October – ended up being shot in the usual black and white. Daran Little reveals, 'It should have been the first colour episode but they hadn't ordered the colour stock for the film cameras. The whole point of taking them away to the Lake District was to show it off in colour. For the first colour to be, "Look at us, look at the North of England, it's wonderful".' Farcically, the first episode containing any colour was the next one – broadcast on 3 November – which took place in the visually sterile environs of a hospital following a coach crash after aforesaid day trip. Unfortunately, as flashbacks to the day trip were scattered throughout the 3 November episode, the programme veered from black and white (including the opening titles) to colour and back again.

Not that any of this mattered. Completing the farce is the fact that the production team would seem to have got their dates mixed up: ITV didn't start colour broadcasts until 12 days after the 3 November episode.

There is an alternative theory about these colour recordings made prior to the ability to broadcast them. Cox says, 'We made some episodes which were shown in black and white but shot in colour as an experiment.' Though Cox says this is 'definitely' the case, without wishing to be patronising to him this idea of a sort of grand tone-test seems implausible for the Windermere episode at least, considering the costs involved in a two-day location shoot. There is another theory that black and white facilities simply weren't available at Granada at that point because of the impending switchover, but Cox says, 'I think the black and white facility always remained.' Little himself is adamant about the Windermere episode being intended to be seen by the wider public in colour because he interviewed 'everybody who worked on it' – including Harry Kershaw and director Howard Baker – for his various books about the show. For the record, the first episode broadcast in colour was that of Monday 17 November 1969. Because the new colour titles were not yet ready, the opening music played over a still photograph of a generic backstreet.

One can understand some of the misgivings of The Street staff who wanted to remain in monochrome when looking at the Public Bar of the Rovers in colour: it suddenly seemed very small without the shadows and gloom in which its corners had been draped previously. Additionally, Cox says, 'We did learn one very important thing – that colour glamorises things enormously. So the interiors of those houses looked impossibly smart and a lot of things had to be toned down.' Before long, The Street got the contrasts right, the shock of being able to see Ena's tresses clearly beneath her hairnet faded, Elsie Tanner's flaming locks were recognised as a positive benefit and the days of monochrome gradually turned from the definitive visuals of the programme to just the way it used to be in the olden days. By the second half of the Seventies, the majority of British homes had colour sets, long before which all newly-made British television shows were shot in colour.

Additionally, the age of colour ushered in the end of the era of shot-as-live and a corresponding new slickness for The Street. Crew struggled to cope with the new colour technology. Camera floods and technicians' mistakes necessitated much more splicing of different parts or even complete scene retakes. This in turn did away with the culture of uninterrupted half-episode shooting. This was a gradual process: scenes were still recorded in sequential order and editing was broadly discouraged, but the programme inevitably got more streamlined and the sight of actors stumbling over their lines less common.

There were new opening titles and closing credits to go with colour transmissions. The new opening titles even seemed to direct an 'Up Yours' at those who sneered at The Street's increasing datedness: they started with a shot of a tower block before panning to rows of the Coronation Street-type terraced houses that tower blocks were supposedly supplanting.

Of course, colour was merely a technical advancement and there was the usual plethora of drama in The Street in 1969. The Windermere episode may not have been in colour but it was a superb edition with a great script by Harry Kershaw and excellent cinematic direction by Baker. It was just a pity that the episode that followed it was so poor, the accident's aftermath portrayed in absurdly melodramatic terms by scriptwriter Malcolm Lynch in a dreary, flat episode with pedestrian direction by Joe Boyer.

Following a period away, Billy Walker returned to The Street with Chinese girlfriend Jasmine, but the smile of welcome on Annie's face froze when it was announced the two planned to get hitched. As with the storyline of 1963 when Len's prejudices caused an innocent black bus conductor to be sacked, it was notable that the producers did not hive off the racial bigotry to an expendable supporting character.

Len's marriage proposal to one Janet Reid was rejected. Len blamed what he thought was an interfering Elsie and slapped her. Though such an event being depicted in The Street was rare, Sixties *Coronation Street* scripts are littered with what are now quite shocking quotes that virtually imply that violence toward women was socially acceptable – some of those scripts written by females.

The Street's history shows that bringing a family into the programme is risky because as often as not constituent parts of it soon get written out, thus almost besmirching the very concept of the family that was the *raison d'etre* of that unit's presence in The Street. A case in point is the Cleggs. When Bill Kenwright decided not to renew his contract as Gordon Clegg for another 12 months this year, suddenly there was only one remnant of the family that had arrived in a blaze of publicity the previous April. Recalls Kenwright of his decision to leave The Street, 'I didn't enjoy it. They weren't nasty in any way whatsoever but I don't think many people had said that to them.'

The woman this year whom Hilda inexplicably thought Stan was having it away with was forceful new character Betty Turpin (Betty Driver), sister of Maggie Clegg. Betty became a barmaid at the Rovers and, now in her 10th decade on this earth, is still in the show, even though storylines involving her that don't relate to the hotpots she provides the Rovers' customers are almost non-existent. Another new character was mild-mannered photographer Ernest Bishop.

A conversation between Emily Nugent and Ena Sharples in one episode demonstrated that The Street's production staff knew times were a-changin': Ena was surprised Emily had left Elsie's door open. When Emily responded she thought that's what people did in the North, Ena informed her that that North was dying. Nonetheless, for reasons of plot expediency, people kept bursting through strangely unsecured Coronation Street front doors for many years to come.

By March 1969 *Market In Honey Lane* – the programme that had inspired dreadful intimations of mortality among the *Coronation Street* cast – was no more. In September 1968, it had been transformed by ATV from a weekly, hour-long serial into a semi-weekly affair of 30 minutes duration. It had also had its name shortened to *Honey Lane*, at a stroke broadening its potential character set and becoming redolent of the title of *Coronation Street*. Yet combined with this audacious throwing down of the gauntlet to The Street was a manoeuvre that marked its death knell, for the ITV network fatally failed to adopt the transmission uniformity that did so much to seal The Street's success. Some franchises broadcast the programme not in its logical early evening slot but in the afternoons or late at night. It was an insane tossing away of an audience. Inevitably, ratings tumbled and the show was cancelled. The programme may now have disappeared into the cracks of history but for a while the threat it posed to The Street was genuine. Its inaugural episode transpired to be the 15th most watched British television broadcast of the decade. *Coronation Street* had seen off the first of what would be many rivals.

Part Three

The Seventies

The opening year of the new decade saw yet another layer added to the culture of conscientiousness at The Street that had helped make it such a high quality programme. It was in 1970 that a *Street* fan in his mid-forties named Eric Rosser submitted an episode of *Coronation Street* to the production team. Although no *Street* script by Rosser was ever broadcast, Harry Kershaw was astounded by Rosser's detailed knowledge of the show and its characters. Rosser – a civil servant by trade – had been an avid watcher ever since catching the first episode during a lengthy hospital stay. As a hobby, he had kept notes about every event and established fact in the programme. Rosser was offered the role of archivist. 'He was quite a belated thought,' recalls Stan Barstow. 'Somebody realised that "God, we've got no record of this. We need to know all about these people, keep it on record that somebody doesn't like sugar in their tea or something like that".' Once Rosser took up his post, lapses like Stan Ogden being served a plate of bacon and eggs by Hilda when it had already been established he was allergic to eggs tended only to happen when Rosser was on holiday, especially when he began vetting scripts. Naturally, Rosser sometimes had to rely on more than just his encyclopaedic knowledge, but in an age before computers he could utilise no system more sophisticated, easily accessible or centralised than files, a card index and bound story volumes. Rosser continued his role well into the Eighties, despite being disabled.

Fate and *Coronation Street*'s transmission pace ensured that the programme reached two landmarks in 1970. The first was the 1,000th episode, which was due to be broadcast in the summer, the second was its 10th anniversary, which would be occurring in December.

It's absolutely symptomatic of the times, however, that these milestones were threatened by industrial action. Firstly, a strike at Granada in the middle of the year meant that only two episodes of The Street were broadcast that month. This achievement of wrenching The Street off of TV screens that even the 1961/62 Equity strike hadn't managed thus pushed back the point at which the show would have been broadcast a thousand times. Things got even worse, though, towards the end of the year with a dispute that centred around the unions' insistence that cameramen working with more complicated colour technology deserved higher remuneration. In the end, the disaster of The Street not being broadcast during the month of its 10th anniversary was averted: an edition went out on 9 December, a decade to the day since the first episode. However, the broadcast was in black and white. Colour episodes of The Street would not be resumed until the following February. The unions had an arguable point – as anyone who can remember the 'flaring' on their screen in the early days of colour TV can attest – but many will be inclined to assert that The Street reverting to black and white on 16 November 1970 (almost exactly a year since ITV had begun colour transmissions) was a backward step that gave ammunition to accusations of Luddite organised labour behaviour.

Unlike anniversary episodes of later years, there was no particular sense of occasion about the 10th anniversary broadcast in its format or storyline, though the fact of the milestone was widely publicised by Granada. Nor, in fact, was there anything particularly special about the 1,000th episode. Which was just as well: Granada managed to make a mess-up of that without any help from a union. The episode broadcast on Wednesday 19 August was advertised as the one that had achieved that millennial milestone and was marked by the appearance of a special souvenir edition of the *TV Times*. In fact, it was the 999th episode. The real number 1,000 was that broadcast on 24 August. The excellent website coronationstreet.wikia.com has posited the theory that this mix-up occurred because of a change in the format of Granada's production codes, but the idea seems unconvincing: the site itself admits that the 999th episode was clearly catalogued as such. Since then, incidentally, meaningful identification of episode numbers has become increasingly more difficult because two *Streets* broadcast on one night (as opposed to hour-long specials) are treated as one episode for cataloguing purposes. Thus numerical anniversary – as opposed to decade anniversary – *Coronation Streets* should be treated with caution, if not completely dismissed.

The 10th anniversary year saw the publication of the first book about the programme. Entitled *The Real Coronation Street*, it was written by, of all people, Ken Irwin, the reporter who back in 1960 had said the show was doomed from the outset. As a showbusiness correspondent, Irwin had had cause over the subsequent years to interview just about every actor who had ever passed through the show, so was steeped in it. Though he hadn't changed his mind about his early criticisms, he had also come to the conclusion that the programme had improved. 'Maybe two years,' is his estimate now of when it turned the corner. 'It did have a good team of scriptwriters on it, it was quite an amusing programme. It became much better. I'm not knocking Tony Warren, but when they had the scriptwriting team together and they got rid of Tony Warren it became much more professional. While Tony was handling it, it was all sort of one man's experience and one man's whim.'

Regarding his book, Irwin explains, 'It was based on all the stuff I had written about it over ten years, plus I then went and interviewed most of the actors who'd left because I didn't want to go to Granada and say, "Can I do a book on it?" because I knew that they would want copy approval, et cetera. I wasn't aiming for a PR book. Bernstein wanted to know how a writer from the *Daily Mirror* could have managed to write a book without Granada's permission. I pointed out to the press officer, "Norman, I don't have to ask your permission to write a book." Corgi commissioned it. It was serialised in one of the national papers. It did very well and went into second print within a few weeks.'

June Howson, a former director, was appointed *Street* producer in March. Howson decided to let the vignettes in the programme breathe, telling a journalist, 'Women don't go for... short, jumpy scenes.' The decisions not to renew the contracts of the actors who played Dickie and Audrey Fleming and Bernard and Sandra Butler – the latter pair Elsie Tanner's geeky nephew and more outgoing niece – would seem to be ones Howson implemented rather than made, as the bad news was broken in her first week.

One departure was sadly made necessary by the fatal heart attack of Arthur Leslie in July, a man as genial and loved as his Jack Walker alter ego. Another death was done for dramatic and logistical reasons. Both Granada and Sandra Gough were keen on Irma Barlow née Ogden returning to the show. Alan Rothwell was sounded out about coming back as her husband but, busy with theatre work, he declined, so the decision was made to kill off David Barlow. 'I was a bit surprised and a bit sad,' says Rothwell. 'Not too much. I saw what the reason was and I thought, "That's fair enough".' He admits that part of his sadness was in the fact that his comfort zone had been taken away: 'I'd always been able to run back if things got tight.' When the death storyline was broadcast, the fact that the man at the centre of the pathos could not be seen made for a potentially ludicrous scenario, but scriptwriter Malcolm Lynch utilised Rothwell's absence as a virtue. In the episode of 13 April 1970, Ken waited for a telephone call on the progress of David after hearing in the previous episode that he had been involved in a car crash in Australia. The episode was so full of pregnant pauses and significant silences as to be positively Pinter-esque, culminating in a devastating call in which Ken was told that his brother hadn't made it.

Though 16.28 million people tuned in, Rothwell wasn't one of them: he was on stage at the time. He had returned to the show several times since asking to be written out in 1961 to appear in *Top Secret* but he had always been somewhat ambivalent about both the privileges The Street afforded him and about the virtues of the programme itself. Rothwell: 'I was a bit snooty about it really. I used to say I could have walked down the street with Laurence Olivier and everybody would have said, "Who's that grey-haired fellow with David Barlow?" I felt uneasy about it. Now the situation's changed absolutely totally. Television's now king in terms of work for actors. I was doing quite well before *Coronation Street* as an actor in the theatre and on radio and this television was alright but I loved the camaraderie of the theatre and the excitement of it.' Has he changed his opinion regarding the Olivier situation? 'Not really, no.'

Another thing that made him uneasy was what he felt was an unrealistic depiction of a matriarchal society. 'The programme became woman-dominated,' he says. 'All the relationships in The Street had a strong woman and a weaker male. That's always been something that the theatre has used quite a lot for a bit of fun. I think unconsciously *Coronation Street* picked it up from writers like Walter Greenwood and carried on with it. Whether there were more women watching it than there were men, I think that might have been part of the reason. To a large extent that was why I lost faith in it and wanted to leave it for good. We weren't exploiting other areas of relationships.'

Elsie was involved in another big storyline this year, when she got wed to Alan Howard, played by Alan Browning. Alan had vied for her affection with her old boyfriend Bill Gregory (Jack Watson), the latter returning after having last been seen in 1961 when he had hurriedly been written out because of the Equity strike. The 18 February episode in which Bill returned featured a flashback in the form of a clip from an October 1961 episode, jarringly but necessarily in black and white. The wedding to Alan on 22 July was – in contrast to the 1967 extravaganza – this time only a registry office affair. However, it was preceded by a very flowery set of scenes wherein Elsie and her intended took a romantic walk that was remarkable for the fact that it was accompanied by an exceedingly rare instance of The Street employing incidental music, albeit of public domain authorship and therefore not expensive to use. This time the producers had no option but to change Elsie's surname, although the people who compiled the credits roll apparently had as much trouble as the public in getting used to it and continued to refer to the character as Elsie Tanner for the better part of a year. Something that could not be changed was Elsie's Everywoman role, so the previously apparently well-to-do Howard was transformed into a bankrupt. Phoenix had personally chosen her screen husband as a way to overcome her resistance to her character being married. In a publicist's dream development, Phoenix and Browning fell in love off-screen too.

New arrivals to The Street included Bet Lynch, brought back after four years because Howson had been impressed by Julie Goodyear in *A Family At War*, which she had produced (and which John Finch had created and written). When Billy Walker took her on, the Rovers suddenly had two Bets behind the bar. Another arrival was an American serviceman named Joe Donnelli (Shane Rimmer), who lodged with Minnie Caldwell at No.5. At close to year's end, Donnelli drunkenly confessed to Irma that he had murdered Steve Tanner over a gambling debt. He then told her she wasn't going to live to blab his secret in a storyline that was played out over a fortnight and culminated in a siege at No.5. In the 21 December episode, Donnelli killed himself, with no street resident harmed.

Though he had gone on to pastures new, John Finch wrote this episode as a favour to a desperate Harry Kershaw, who had received a substandard script. It was to be Finch's 137th and final episode, following which he took his classy writing hallmark to TV series almost as titanic as his *A Family At War* blockbuster such as *Sam* and *The Spoils Of War*. After an altercation with Granada in the Seventies, he couldn't bring himself to ask to return to The Street despite the fact that he knew the then producer Bill Podmore would have welcomed him.

In 1970 *Coronation Street* acquired a brand spanking new recording of its theme tune, one that would last for 40 years. According to Granada musician David Browning, 'They weren't very happy with the original recording for whatever reasons. They dragged their heels on it for a little while.' It doesn't seem that the end-of-year celebrations surrounding the programme's 10th anniversary provided the impetus for the re-recording, as it made its first appearance in the early part of the year.

Times had changed since the theme had first been laid down on tape. Though stereo TV sound was still a couple of decades away, the public now expected higher audio fidelity from the box in the room that was now more than ever a staple of their lives. Says Browning, 'If you heard the original recording, it was very bad to be quite frank. Let's face it, it was the early days of television. Producers used to say, "It's the picture that matters, not the sound in terms of the public", so there wasn't that much attention paid to it.' A second difference was the fact that no longer did the franchises genuflect towards London; this re-recording was, unlike the original, not done in the capital but at Granada's Manchester studios. Therefore, the musicians conducted by Granada musical director Derek Hilton on the rearrangement of the 1960 original were all locals: Browning on trumpet cornet, Jimmy Lonie on clarinet, Frank Ingham on lead trombone, Bram Fisher, Frank Brierley and Harry Simons on supporting trombones, Bill Nickson on drums, Les Beavers on amplified acoustic guitar and Dave Lyane on stand-up bass. Browning: 'Most people think it's trumpet and maybe a rhythm section. It's a much bigger band than you would imagine. When it was done for the second time they used exactly the same instrumentation that they had on the first recording. The trombones were all playing in cup mutes, so that's why it sounds subdued.' From what Browning remembers, Hilton wanted a certain sleepy ambience: 'We managed to sort of re-create the feel but with a much better recording and I have to say better playing as well.'

Browning's job was to replicate the trumpet that was the dominant part of the original recording. 'What I did was play a more modern style in terms of the trumpet playing,' he says. He also used a trumpet cornet rather than standard trumpet on the session, an instrument that – appropriately – is generally only heard in brass bands. Though the sound he made with the trumpet cornet is utterly distinctive and has been enjoyed, hummed and whistled by millions, Browning is almost ashamed of it. 'Normally I don't play with that much vibrato,' he is anxious to point out. 'I was deliberately turning on the brass band vibrato which is a very shallow, quick vibrato which sounds a bit corny now…. I wouldn't want to play like that – it's bloody awful.'

Only a fraction of what was recorded made the air. Browning: 'You probably hear eight bars of it. The actual full recording that I did was 32 bars. You record the tune as composed by Eric Spear and then Granada use whatever they wish to use from that.' Snippets from the same places as before were lopped from the master recording for the break bumpers.

The re-recording on which Browning played was used on *Coronation Street* up until 31 May 2010 and will therefore forever remain the definitive version to millions. Browning's subsequent *curriculum vitae* takes in massive television shows like *Opportunity Knocks*, *New Faces* and *Jewel In The Crown*, but the *Coronation Street* theme remains by far the most famous piece of music on which he has played. The show is not Browning's cup of tea. However, such is its predominance in our culture (and in his own living room – his wife is an avid viewer) that it would have been difficult for him to escape the piece of music he laid down so long ago. Asked if the strains of his trumpet cornet drifting across the aural background made him resentful of the fact that he enjoyed no remuneration for it beyond his initial one-off session fee of £36, he says, 'You could say yes, but I don't lose any sleep over it. From that [entry on my] CV, work tends to come in. I was paid the official union rate for the job…. Thirty-six pounds was a week's wage and I got it for a three-hour session on the Monday morning.' Actually, it's not quite accurate to say that the £36 was his only reward, because he has usually been first choice for the multitudinous recordings of the theme that have graced LP compilations of TV signature tunes down the years. Nonetheless, a

Mancunian by the name of Johnny Roadhouse in whose music shop Browning gave trumpet lessons took up the supposed injustice done to Browning via the media in 2004, leading to Browning hitting the press. 'It was getting a real pain in the backside too, I can tell you,' Browning says. 'It was just getting silly here. The papers, the TV were here. There were vans on the drive, radio stations and that. I was even getting phone calls from Spanish television, 'cos of all the expats out there.' Unbeknown to Browning, things got even sillier when some of the newspapers got their facts wrong, stating that Browning was claiming to have played on the original 1960 recording of the theme, leading some *Coronation Street* fans to denounce Browning as a liar and fraud on the internet.

The exits from *Coronation Street* of Barlow women bookended 1971. The reasons for the departures of the actresses playing Val and Irma were very different. Anne Reid had informed the producers that 10 years as Val was enough and wouldn't be talked round. They considered falling back on the groan-inducing *Street* cliché of an emigration – as hackneyed by now as the *EastEnders* exit in a taxi would become – but then decided to just kill Val off. The charmed life that had kept Bill Roache in employment for a decade (and would do for another four) was at work both there and in the fact that the producers abandoned the notion of having the traumatised widower fleeing the neighbourhood – they thought that depicting a young father bringing up young children alone would be dramatically interesting.

In the episode broadcast on 27 January, Val got electrocuted by a faulty hairdryer on the eve of the couple's departure for a new life in Montego Bay. As she fell unconscious, she knocked an electric fire into a packing case, resulting in a blaze that burnt the maisonette down. As far as the viewers were concerned, the death of popular ordinary mum Val was probably a bigger deal than the much trumpeted death of Martha Longhurst, who had more of a niche appeal. Says William Roache, 'Val was a young wife, mother of two children, so it had quite an impact.' Including on him: 'I had some great scenes there. I had to cry at the end when I walked round the flat that had been burnt and that was the first time I realised I was quite good at crying, so I got a lot of crying scenes later. It was a very dramatic moment and a good one.' Care for the kids was eventually ceded to Val's mother, who took them to live with her and her husband in Scotland, where Ken acknowledged they would be better off. Anne Reid remains a successful actress to this day. She is the widow of *Street* scriptwriter and producer Peter Eckersley.

No such sense of occasion surrounded Irma Barlow's departure: she abruptly disappeared after 8 December. The scriptwriters were doing the best they could in difficult circumstances, for the alter ego of Irma had been sacked. That Sandra Gough was ambivalent about what some would consider the privilege of being in The Street had been obvious as far back as 1968 when she voluntarily left the programme. A devout Catholic, she had always appeared to find TV stardom inconsistent with her spirituality. She said she was leaving The Street 'to make myself into a better person for God when I die…. It is a false life and all it offers is a false sense of security….' These sentiments were a stark contrast to the vacuity of the girl she had portrayed. Gough went further than a general denunciation of fame though, criticising her fellow cast members as people who 'just don't care for each other.' One would have thought that she had burnt her bridges, but after working behind a bar in her adopted Spain and a period of desultory employment back in Manchester, she met Harry Kershaw by chance in a pub and, offered the chance to rejoin The Street, she accepted. It has been alleged in some quarters that on her return Gough was blanked by some of the colleagues she had criticised in the media, and one wonders whether this was part of the reason behind her continuing disillusion with her role. She later said, 'I was taking more and more time off, hoping that they would sack me. I was sick of being Irma.' She got her wish for dismissal. Perhaps surprisingly, she was able to sustain an acting career after that and even returned to soapland in 1995 when she took up the role of Nellie Dingle in *Emmerdale*.

The storyliners cannily exploited Val's death: the fire revealed structural faults so severe that the whole set of buildings on the non-terraced side of the street needed to be demolished, thus conveniently getting rid of the much ridiculed maisonette ghost-town. 'I don't remember them ever feeling an integral part of the street the way the rest of it did,' says Adele Rose of the maisonettes. 'It felt a bit grafted on. The street was always the star and when you moved outside it, it lost something.' William Roache seems to share Rose's slightly illogical geographical perspective on the issue. He says, 'They weren't the street, were they? The street was meant to be a little backwater street, terraced houses – that was the sort of essence and heart of Coronation Street. They were a bit different. But you've still got it: you've still the contrast of the houses opposite being that little bit more upmarket. I don't think they quite used them properly then.'

The maisonettes disappeared in February and by the middle of the year had been replaced by a Community Centre and a warehouse owned by mail order firm Mark Brittain. The potential for the new workplace to introduce compelling characters was instantly proven when diminutive firebrand Ivy Tilsley (initially Ivy Tyldesley, played by Lynne Perrie) and simpering Mavis Riley (Thelma Barlow) turned up as members of its staff.

The Street's producers – Brian Armstrong took over from Howson this year – had the kind of audience that could break a product or even topple a government and it was no surprise that they were constantly being badgered by charities and pressure groups who wanted to exploit the access they had to the nation. Such approaches – however good the cause – were always rebuffed. As Rose explains, 'We never wanted stories that were grafted on.' The first exception to The Street's policy of resisting such entreaties came in 1971. It was the year when Britain's currency was decimalised, switching from the £-s-d system to one in which there was an easily calculable 100 pennies in the pound. Because Kershaw could see no harm and some good in helping get the public familiarised with their new coinage, in the episode of 15 February – the day of the switchover – the executive producer allowed a scene wherein Len Fairclough pays for his pint with a new 50 pence piece and has to explain to an indignant Jack Walker that it wasn't 'foreign rubbish.' The new coin was by coincidence unexpectedly seen in glorious colour as a result of the end of the dispute that had kept the programme in black and white since November (although there would be a couple of programmes in the near future with monochrome inserts).

December saw an early real-life celebrity appearance in The Street when Bernard Manning did a turn at the Licensed Victuallers Boxing Day Ball attended by Annie Walker. Frost formed on Mrs Walker when she heard the near-the-knuckle shtick of the rotund Mancunian comic. However, Manning's material was actually in keeping with a certain self-conscious earthiness that began informing The Street at around this juncture, and which in truth informed a lot of culture at the time,

William Roache as Ken Barlow. Roache has played the character – the only one remaining from *Coronation Street*'s first episode – for fifty years.

Alan Rothwell, who played David Barlow. Rothwell was once one of the UK's most famous faces but many modern-day *Street* fans are unaware Ken Barlow once had a little brother.

Elsie Tanner (Patricia Phoenix), Leonard Swindley (Arthur Lowe) and Emily Nugent (Eileen Derbyshire), 1965.

The cast outside the Rovers Return, 1970. FRONT CHARACTERS L-R: Albert Tatlock, Jack Walker, Emily Nugent, Ena Sharples, Elsie Tanner. CENTRE L-R: Annie Walker, Hilda Ogden, Stan Ogden, Len Fairclough. BACK L-R: Betty Turpin, Cyril Turpin, Ray Langton, Valerie and Ken Barlow. Though this is not the entire cast, it's striking how few young characters there are.

SINGALONG AT THE ROVER'S RETURN

Singalong At The Rovers Return was a 1969 effort by the *Coronation Street* cast – credited as 'Coronation Street' – consisting of a pair of medleys involving songs as varied as 'Show Me The Way To Go Home' and 'Yellow Submarine'. It failed to set the charts alight.

Elsie Tanner Fights Back was one of a trio of seventies novels by *Street* scriptwriter and producer Harry Kershaw. Before repeats and videos, such products were the only way for long-term fans to revisit The Street's past.

The Street's ballooning popularity quickly brought about merchandise like this early sixties jigsaw. Depicted on the box's bottom right is Archie Street, real life Ordsall, Greater Manchester location that was the physical basis for *Coronation Street*.

Julie Goodyear, who played Bet Lynch, displaying her large collection of earrings. Goodyear returned to The Street after a long absence but departed again in acrimony.

Jennifer Moss. The woman who played Lucille Hewitt had a tragic life.

Hilda Ogden, played by Jean Alexander, was often unbearable, but everybody missed her when she was gone from the programme.

Brian and Gail Tilsley, newly married in 1979. Brian was played by Christopher Quentin, Gail by Helen Worth. They were love's young dream for a while, but the necessities of drama makes a quotient of *Street* split-ups inevitable.

Eighties producer Mervyn Watson. He is standing in Salford's Pendlebury Church, whose gravestones provided the names of many of the original *Coronation Street* characters.

The Street's creator Tony Warren (left) with television presenter Melvyn Bragg in the year of The Street's 25th anniversary. Note Warren's famed animation.

Mike Baldwin (Johnny Briggs) and Maggie Redman, (Jill Kerman). Maggie was the mother of just one of several sons by different women Mike didn't know he had.

Mavis and Derek Wilton (Thelma Barlow and Peter Baldwin), The Street's beloved pair of ditherers.

A terrified Rita Fairclough (Barbara Knox) fleeing Alan Bradley (Mark Eden), 1989. Bradley is just about to expire beneath a tram.

The day that Hayley Patterson (Julie Hesmondhalgh) never thought would come when she was growing up as a little boy: she becomes a bride, marrying Roy Cropper (David Neilson), 1999.

Julie Goodyear with her sometime screen husband Roy Barraclough, who played Alec Gilroy.

Tony Blair with Vera Duckworth (Elizabeth Dawn), Jack Duckworth (William Tarmey) and Raquel Wolstenhulme (Sarah Lancashire), 1996. He was neither the first nor the last politician to exploit the popularity of The Street.

Geoff Hinsliff. This RADA-trained actor had three stints in The Street as three different characters, most famously as the tortured Don Brennan.

Two people you wouldn't like as your neighbours: Blanche Hunt (Maggie Jones) and Norris Cole (Malcolm Hebden), 2002.

Tracy Barlow (Kate Ford) on trial for murder, 2007. Behind her, left to right, are mother Deirdre Barlow and stepfather Ken Barlow (Anne Kirkbride and William Roache) and Gail's son David Platt (Jack P. Shepherd).

Bill Kenwright. He once played Gordon Clegg in The Street but is now better known as a theatre impresario who employs more people per year than the BBC.

Brian Capron sweeps the boards at the 2003 British Soap Awards for his menacing performance as Richard Hillman.

Michelle Connor, played by ex Hear'Say pop star Kym Marsh.

Tina McIntryre, played by Michelle Keegan, an example of the increasing youth of The Street's cast.

The *Coronation Street* cast attend the National Television Awards at the O2 Arena, 20 January 2010. Though its average age is now much younger, the cast still includes first episode survivor William Roache (back, centre).

manifested in the likes of needlessly titillating paperback book covers. Says Daran Little, 'In the early Seventies it attempted to get gritty: it was very sexist, it was very racist, it was very yobs running down the streets smashing windows, it was very kidnap babies and murders and things. Looking back, it's quite tame but at the time people were going, "This isn't *Coronation Street*. What's going on?"'

In mid-1972, ex-director Eric Prytherch started what was by *Street* standards a lengthy two-year stretch as producer.

He decided to rejuvenate the formula with younger characters. He was particularly interested in a fresh influx on the female side, and to this end Corner Shop assistant (and shop flat resident) Norma Ford (Diana Davies, another veteran of *A Family At War*) and teenage secretary Deirdre Hunt (Anne Kirkbride) made their debuts. Of the two, the former was only around until the following year as a regular and, though endearing, is largely forgotten. The latter has endured in the public's affections and in the programme, albeit under a variety of different surnames, but mostly as Deirdre Barlow. Deirdre's ever-changing parade of spectacles unintentionally provide the television equivalent of a tree trunk growth ring, with viewers able to make a guess about what year an episode originates by the period-reflective glasses style, which started with huge, brown face furniture and culminated in sleek, rimless affairs.

Another female, of slightly less recent vintage, also staked her long-term future in The Street this year. Barbara Mullaney (who became Knox in 1977) was supposed to be playing one last role before retiring from showbusiness, but the character brought in for a couple of episodes – and given the name Rita Littlewood when the writers found out Mullaney had played a character named Rita in the show before – became another decades-spanning queen of The Street, albeit another with marriage-dictated changes of surname along the way. Some suspected that flame-haired Rita was the producers' solution to the growing respectability of Elsie Tanner, but Rita quite quickly lost her early edge. Originally a short-tempered singer, she ended up a perennially bemused counter assistant.

Emily Nugent became Emily Bishop with her wedding to the mild-mannered photographer Ernest. The 5 April episode in which the wedding took place included a bizarre couple of scenes in which Ray

Langton walked through a park with short-lived character Vicki Bright. These scenes (which culminated in Ray's marriage proposal being turned down by Vicki on the grounds that she was pregnant) featured some more rare *Street* incidental music. In an echo of the flowery signature tune rearrangement that accompanied the edition featuring the Hewitts' marriage back in 1961, the Bishops' wedding episode closed on a bizarre jazzy/calypso version of the theme, with fluttering flute and a saccharine strings finale. This is the last time to date that the theme tune has been featured in a different arrangement.

Billy Walker returned to the show after another sojourn and took over the running of the pub for Annie. The following few years were the peak ones for Billy's alter ego Ken Farrington in The Street. Broad-shouldered and fashionably sideburned, Billy became a heartthrob figure to rival Ray Langton. Ena's grandson Colin Lomax came to visit with wife and baby, and – rather too soon after the Hewitt baby kidnap, let alone the 1966 Paul Cheveski canal scare or the disappearance of Peter and Susan Barlow at the zoo in 1969 – their baby temporarily went missing and the canal was dragged before it turned up safe. It would have been a nice touch if Davy Jones had reprised the role of Colin he had played in 1961: with The Monkees recently disbanded, the actor-turned-singer might have said yes if asked. Instead Alec Sabin played the part. (On a similar theme, Herman's Hermits singer Peter Noone could have reoccupied his role of Len Fairclough's son Stanley when the character made a return appearance in 1977.) There was another instant feeling of mortality created in viewers when Paul Cheveski (Nigel Greaves) came to stay with his Nan Elsie Howard. The Street's first baby was now 11 years old.

Down the years, Stan Ogden interspersed his periods of bone-idleness with stints as, among other things, a labourer, a would-be waste paper business magnate, a milkman (he liked the noon finish), an ice cream salesman, a builder's yard worker, an assistant night watchman, a lorry driver and a window cleaner. He was useless at all of them. One thing Stan was good at, though, was what he called 'supping', and in 1972 he won a beer drinking contest against a patron of the Flying Horse, the oft-mentioned but only occasionally seen rival pub to the Rovers located in Jubilee Terrace on the other side of the viaduct.

Rest Assured almost followed *Pardon The Expression/Turn Out The Lights* as a comedy-oriented *Street* spin-off this year. A pilot of the show, which featured the exploits of Ray Langton and Jerry Booth, was written by Harry Kershaw. Though the pilot was filmed, it was never screened and the intriguing concept went no further.

1972 also saw the first and only Christmas Day *Coronation Street* broadcast of the decade. There wouldn't be another until 1985, even when the 25th was a Monday or Wednesday. Though Christmas itself had always been a big deal in *Coronation Street* storylines, and though there were four Xmas Day broadcasts before 1972, it became obvious to Granada that they should avoid 25 December editions of the programme because The Street died a ratings death on Bank Holidays. In time, the Christmas Day edition of The Street would become one of the most crucial of the year, and watching it became a tradition almost on a par with settling down for the Queen's speech.

In 1972, not a single episode of The Street had made number one in the ratings charts, the first time this had happened since the programme had first attracted enough viewers to qualify for inclusion. The year before that, 21 episodes had hit the top spot. The 'crisis' was relative of course: all but two of The Street's 104 broadcasts in 1972 made the top 20. However, The Street was used to far loftier heights than that, and it didn't help that in recent years, almost as a function of The Street's longevity, it had found itself having to fend off 'End-of-the-road?' conjecture from the papers.

It can't have done The Street's self-confidence a lot of good, then, that throughout much of 1973, they had to deal with the fact that three larger-than-life female members of The Street's original cast were absent for long stretches. Violet Carson was suffering from poor health and Ena Sharples was temporarily written out to accommodate her recovery. Meanwhile, Elsie Howard was despatched to train for a job in Newcastle for three months because Pat Phoenix was missing the boards and went touring with the play *Subway In The Sky*. Doris Speed decided to take a two-month sabbatical, so Annie Walker was portrayed as retired, if temporarily. Some might assert that the female heart of the programme being absent is what caused viewing figures to continue their downward drift: though in 1973, seven of the episodes made the top slot, three of the episodes didn't make the top 20 – the highest number since 1968.

Carson's illness and age must have brought home to Granada that no character lasts forever, no matter how much a part of the furniture, leading in turn to agonising about whether they would be able to find a replacement as powerful when the day finally dawned that, for whatever reason, she would not return. Similar thoughts must have occurred to them regarding Speed. Phoenix was younger than Carson and Speed but arguably more important in the set-up and her apparently itchy feet must have given them a case of – to use a Northern expression sometimes heard in The Street – the collywobbles. Today, it has became clear that *Coronation Street* endures across generations regardless of the departures of characters whose absence once seemed unthinkable. In the early Seventies, though, the hindsight provided by decades of comings and goings wasn't available and, to some, an impression of decay hung over the programme.

The storyliners and scriptwriters did their best to maintain interest in the goings-on in Weatherfield. Ken Barlow became a merry widower, first of all via an affair with a character played by Joanna Lumley and then by a patently unsuitable marriage to Janet Reid (Judith Barker), a minx who had once broken Len Fairclough's heart and who had lately been having it away with married Alan Howard. The fact that Janet slightly confusingly had the same surname as the actress who had played Ken's first wife somehow seemed to underline how awkward and unconvincing was the marriage, which itself wasn't even shown – Ken just arrived back from Scotland with her, having decided to marry not for love but to provide his kids a mother. The plan was scuppered when young Peter didn't get on with Janet, and the twins went back to Scotland.

Peter this time around was played by Roache's real-life son Linus, who was handily only a year older than the character. 'It was quite fun,' says Roache Snr. 'We sort of ran the lines at home and he enjoyed it. On the set there's a photograph of Peter when he was nine with Ken, and that's actually one of Linus.' Though Peter has been a recurring character since, Linus Roache stopped playing him in 1975. However, he did continue acting. Unlike his father, he has consciously spurned the idea of playing one role most of his life and gone on to a varied career that has taken in Shakespeare, Hollywood (including *Batman Begins*) and Emmy-award-winning American NBC drama *Law and Order*.

Len Fairclough bought Biddulph's newsagents on Rosamund Street. He decided to call it The Kabin and to employ Rita as the manageress. Rita appointed Mavis Riley as her assistant, thus starting another of The Street's great double acts, in this case a sort of genteel Laurel and Hardy.

Many would be the discussion between them in which Mavis would complete an exhibition of her unworldliness and dithering manner with a cry of, 'Well, I don't really knooow…', followed by a rolling of Rita's heavily mascaraed eyes.

3 October marked Elsie's farewell. The production team's worst nightmares were realised when Pat Phoenix – apparently having come to understand the decisions behind Philip Lowrie's departure six years before – announced she was leaving the programme. She later said she was 'Bored out of my mind' with playing Elsie. Says close friend Adele Rose, 'She wanted to do stage work too and to be honest I think she thought she could make a lot of money outside. She was offered all kinds of deals for advertising she couldn't do while she was in The Street. I think she slightly miscalculated, but it wasn't so much she wanted to leave The Street as she wanted to find out before it was too late what else she could do.' The Street couldn't even gain a ratings spike by giving Elsie a big send-off: Phoenix sent word that she would not be returning from her break, so Elsie Howard simply transpired to have made her job in Newcastle permanent, with Alan Browning's character going with her.

The Street prepared to face an uncertain future.

1974 saw Coronation Street and the surrounding area in the sights of a rapacious developer, no less than Douglas Wormold (Michael Elphick), son of Edward. Though the plan was scuppered by a canny Rita, who realised that the deeds of The Kabin were in her name not Len's, there was a metaphor to be perceived in a story about Coronation Street being under threat.

Those who predicted that the programme would be nothing without Elsie Tanner/Howard seemed to be shown as at least partly right as the ratings continued to be disappointing. As ever, it was all relative, with most of the year's episodes achieving figures for which most other programme makers would kill. However, two episodes fewer made number one in the ratings than in 1973 and one more than last year failed to crack the top 20. The figures became far more alarming when viewed with a long-term perspective: what had happened to the days when The Street achieved ratings like 1962, when in all but two weeks one of the week's episodes hit number one? Moreover, the time that another *Street* icon delivered her last line on the programme seemed to be getting ominously closer when Violet Carson had a stroke, ensuring her appearances were restricted to just 13 episodes all year.

Meanwhile, a hellhound called *Crossroads* was on The Street's trail. Launched by ATV in November 1964, the show was quite blatantly the Midlands' answer to The Street, albeit one that spurned its grittiness for a more glossy milieu, if that is not talking up too much the trappings of a motel in a village near Birmingham. The intrigues of the Crossroads Motel's staff and guests were originally shown five evenings a week. It's a sign of just what different values operated back then that in 1967 the Independent Television Authority ordered ATV to reduce its output by one episode a week for the sake of quality. London franchise holder Thames also had its doubts about the programme, dropping it from its schedules in 1968, though six months later, viewer outrage forced it to reinstate it. Many might find it fatuous to bracket the melodramatic storylines, rushed acting, frequently absurd characters and habitually wobbling sets of *Crossroads* with a thoughtful programme with relatively high production values like The Street, but there is no question that the two shows had a significant crossover of demographic. *Crossroads* was making the top 10 even before Granada belatedly started to broadcast it in 1972 and despite the fact that it never had the advantage of being shown at a uniform time across the country. Denis Forman denies Granada's tardiness was informed by feeling threatened. However, when *Crossroads* did make it to Granadaland, it certainly seemed to have an adverse effect on The Street. While the two programmes were not an either/or proposition – both being broadcast on ITV, they weren't scheduled against each other – it was painfully obvious from the steadily climbing ratings of *Crossroads* and the gently declining viewing figures of The Street that much of the public felt the ATV programme was doing something right that Granada was doing wrong.

In May 1974, Susi Hush was appointed The Street's producer and, in light of all the above, it was inevitable that she would be a new broom-type. Hush started by asking some of the cast to de-glam by making their on-screen jewellery and hairstyles more appropriate to a backstreet. Hush was also another producer who decided to bring more social issues to the scripts.

'Susi was quite innovative,' says Adele Rose. 'She wanted to [have] an episode set on location abroad. For practical reasons actually she made it just the women and to cap it all she had me – the only woman writer – to write it, so that caused a few raised eyebrows. But Susi was afraid of nothing and if she felt it was right, she'd go ahead and do it…. I liked working with Susi. She had a nice, deep insight into the programme and of course connected well with the women characters….'

The story to which Rose refers – actually spread across two sun-kissed episodes in October 1974 – saw the women of The Street holidaying in the glamorous location of Majorca after winning a Spot the Ball competition. Kershaw later claimed that the female-only Spanish sojourn proved a man-hating agenda on Hush's part but Rose laughs at the suggestion. Bill Kenwright also denies he saw such an antipathy and invokes an act of kindness to him on Hush's part when he returned to his role of Gordon Clegg this year. With his mind on problems in his other career as producer, he '…had a terrible, terrible technical day. Susi Hush came to me and said, "Are you okay?" I said, "Yeah I just got a few problems in London." Just before we started shooting she came to me. I was standing at the bar of the Rovers Return and she gave me a package. I walked to one side and she'd gone out and bought for me *War And Peace* and she'd inscribed in it, "Just to help you and to let you know other people have problems too. Love, Susi." I think that was a fantastic thing for her to do. I thought she was a great producer, Susi.'

Kenwright's encomium is not motivated by overt gratitude at being given a recall to the programme. Kenwright says that by now he was 'a very different human being' to the man who had first appeared in The Street in 1968. Acting was taking up less and less of his time in favour of theatre production, which he had branched into with fellow *Street* actor Reg Marsh (Dave Smith). Of Hush's overture, he says, 'Because I was no longer that ambitious young actor I thought, "Why not? Be great for a few weeks." I went back for a three-week storyline with Jennifer Moss. I think that the idea was that they'd try and get me back to be a regular.' Hush got a shock when Kenwright turned up for work: 'My hair had gone silver-grey. She walked up to me to say hello and looked at my hair and went "Haaah!" and they had to darken it down for those episodes.'

The planned revitalisation of the romance between Lucille Hewitt and Gordon Clegg was scuppered by the deterioration of Jennifer Moss. Following 14 years (off and on) of playing Lucille Hewitt in more than a thousand episodes, she made her last appearance on 3 July 1974 after being dismissed by Hush. Kenwright says, 'It was inevitable and I think Susi waited and waited and waited. The storyline just had to be totally turned round. She came to me in the dressing room and she said, "Listen, I'm so sorry about this but I've got to do something".' Moss had been spiralling out of control for some time. She had on the surface had a dream career, entering what became the nation's favourite programme just weeks away from her 16th birthday, making pop records for the legendary Joe Meek and even appearing in a feature film, *Live It Up* (1963). She had also for a long time been a *de facto* Voice of Youth. But behind the scenes life had often been difficult. Being a 16-year-old playing 11 had impelled her to prove her maturity to her colleagues, while at the same time she was pressurised not to be seen doing adult things in public because of the nation's perception of her as a child. Kenwright: 'Apart from *The Appleyards* and *The Grove Family*, I think Jenny really was the first kid to become a television star. She was a major part of *Coronation Street* and I think coping with that, it wasn't good for her.' Says Adele Rose, 'Jennifer was sad really. She was a child when she came into The Street and in those days people didn't realise that they needed looking after and mentoring and it all went to her head. She was fifteen, sixteen, going out for dinner and saying "I'll have a Hine's brandy please." I remember being quite shocked at this.'

Moss had the trauma of a miscarriage in the late Sixties (although later gave birth to a healthy daughter). She became depressed when her father died. When a heroin addict lover forged cheques in her name, she stood by him at his trial, but he then committed suicide. Heavy drinking during pregnancy caused a daughter from her second marriage to be born handicapped. The girl was subsequently taken into care. Moss's worsening drinking problem made her increasingly unreliable. It was at this point that Moss was sacked by Hush. Rose: 'I think in the end the producer had to do what they had to do.' Kenwright: 'She was a smashing kid. It was tragic and the change was colossal in her from the first time. I'd heard rumours she was drinking very heavily and she was unactable with. Funnily enough, she ended up living – isn't this odd? – in the house where I was born in Liverpool. Total coincidence she ended up there.'

Moss's life got even worse upon her dismissal. She had a son the following year who died when a few weeks old. An existence performing menial jobs followed, the cushioned lifestyle conferred by her £60 early Sixties weekly wage (£1,000 today – not bad for a teenager) a thing of the distant past. By 1988, Moss was reduced to applying for a job as a tour guide on the *Coronation Street* set. Her alcoholism understandably continued and her 12-year-old daughter was taken into care. In 1980, Moss and her third husband gained criminal convictions after breaking into a club to steal drink. A later allegation of shoplifting resulted in an acquittal, by which time she was on her fourth marriage.

Eventually Moss turned her life around as much as was now possible. She overcame her alcoholism, was reconciled with her daughter and seemed to find some contentment with her fifth husband. Though she picked up various TV and radio roles, she ended her days running an internet stamp collecting business in Dunfermline. She died in October 2006 after several years of failing health. In a latter-day interview, she said she had never forgiven her late mother for pushing her into showbusiness when she had wanted to be a barrister, a tacit admission of unsuitability for fame that suggests Hush's decision was not completely unreasonable.

It's possible that the writing crisis that Moss's sudden departure left is what created the impetus for the storyline in which Gordon discovered his mother was not Maggie Clegg but her recently widowed sister Betty Turpin. The turn of events struck some as preposterous and a naked attempt at sensationalism (illegitimate babies being still just about scandalous in 1974). It certainly left a bad taste in the mouth of Irene Sutcliffe as she prepared to take her leave of The Street after six years of playing Maggie. Of Sutcliffe's upset, Kenwright says, 'It wasn't only that it was artificial. We really were close and she wanted to remain my mother in it. We had this scene where the pair of them sat down with me and said, "We've got something to tell you. I'm not your mother." And of course the first instinct that goes through your head is, "Well of course you're not – me mother's in Liverpool." So within thirty seconds I had three mothers. That started a new phase in my life, not just my career, where Betty Driver became hugely important to me. Still is.' To this day, Kenwright sends Driver a yearly Mother's Day card signed 'Gordon'.

Viewing figures failed to pick up under Hush (or her temporary fill-in late in the year, scriptwriting stalwart Leslie Duxbury). A feeling of being cursed must have afflicted The Street in 1974 when Kathy Staff had to give notice that she was leaving the programme for several months to appear in oldies sitcom *Last Of The Summer Wine* after having only just made her debut as Vera, daughter-in-law of Granny (Megan) Hopkins, whose family were renting from Maggie with a view to purchase the Corner Shop. Additionally, the viewers never really took to Granny Hopkins: whereas Ena Sharples was the type of neighbourhood curmudgeon to whom most could relate, there was just something a bit too sinister in Granny's piercing stare and gravelly delivery.

Even worse for the programme was the fate of Patricia Cutts. The woman who was the original Blanche Hunt – straight-talking mother of Deirdre – had appeared in two episodes but was found dead in September after having taken a massive barbiturate overdose. Because there was no time to rewrite scripts, for the first time the programme recast an adult character. Maggie Jones got the role (and, admittedly, would make it her own). It might seem fanciful to extrapolate from Cutts' personal tragedy a crisis about the programme, but it was yet more bad press for a show that currently seemed to be stricken with every form of bad luck possible.

The marriage of Ken and Janet Barlow broke up this year over Janet's fury with his lack of ambition. Not only had Ken refused to look for a headmaster's job, he had sabotaged her ambitions to move out of The Street. The man who had so often derided The Street – in 1964 he fulminated of it: 'You should use houses like these like boxes of matches: use them and chuck them away' – had now grown fond of the place. There was at least one person who loved Coronation Street in 1974.

Ken Barlow found out in 1975 that his father had died of natural causes, a nod by the storyliners to the fact that Frank Pemberton had passed away. The marriage of Billy Walker to Deirdre Hunt that was due to take place this year – a prospect that dismayed Annie – did not happen. The reason was nothing to do with the writers: the producers had taken little notice of actor Kenneth Farrington when he told them he wanted to leave and were shocked when he pointed out that he was entitled to depart immediately because of his holiday entitlement. A rather contrived marriage on the rebound to Ray Langton – who had only shown much interest in Deirdre previously when he'd subjected her to bullying in her job at the builder's yard – resulted. Ray moved out of No.9, which he had shared with Len Fairclough and Jerry Booth, for a converted flat above Blanche Hunt's house in Victoria Street. Come November, Len was rattling around an empty house: actor Graham Haberfield had died at the shockingly young age of 34 from liver condition-related heart failure and of course lovable, unworldly Jerry Booth had to die with him. The two untransmitted episodes he had recorded before his death were broadcast uncut at the insistence of his widow.

The drawbacks of a programme like The Street lasting as long as it had – this year it was celebrating 15 years on the air – were illustrated in April when Bet Lynch contemplated suicide. She was found in a distraught state sitting on her bed psyching herself up to take some aspirins. The pathos was undermined for those with long enough memories to realise that it was Sheila Birtles and Dennis Tanner all over again. The cause of Bet's state was partly the fact that she had been messed around by Len – with whom she had been going out, as much as Len ever went out with a woman – but more importantly that she had received bad news about an illegitimate son named Martin whom she had been forced to give up for adoption. The Street viewers had seen Martin tracking down his mum the year before but leaving without telling her who he was because he was appalled by her tartiness. Martin had just died in a road accident.

It was by no means only decay and *déjà vu* in The Street, though. Ironically, amid all the turmoil of 1974, a couple of characters made their debuts who would transpire to be long-running, powerful *Coronation Street* characters.

The other members of the Hopkins family were dad Idris (Richard Davies) and chirpy teenage daughter Tricia. Kathy Jones, the actress who played the latter, was a pretty woman with a slight peculiarity in the way she pronounced the letter 'r' that was almost a speech impediment but was also winning. She had been identified as a star-in-the-making by Granada, who were also no doubt conscious of the possibility of her appealing to the youth of the nation as Lucille Hewitt had once done. It wasn't any of the above who would endure though. The Hopkins family did a moonlit flit after Megan decided to use blackmail to get a lower price for the purchase of the shop, unaware that Gordon Clegg had already been told of the dark secret surrounding his parentage. Only Tricia remained behind, and her not for long. Rather, it was Tricia's friend and colleague Gail Potter (Helen Worth) who remained. She is still in The Street today. Eddie Yeats (pronounced Yates) arrived in The Street at Christmas 1974, too late to have much of an effect on that miserable year for the programme, but it soon became clear that this chirpy, tubby, tousle-headed Scouse ex-cellmate of Jed Stone was a great character. Another excellent new character who made her debut in 1974 was Vera Duckworth (Elizabeth Dawn).

More of Hush's favoured social issues were addressed in 1975. Three 'boot boys' (to use a then common phrase) terrorised the neighbourhood, culminating in them setting the warehouse alight, albeit accidentally, in October. Two people died in the accident. This episode had an aftermath episode that was written by Tony Warren, his first broadcast *Street* script for six years. It saw the entire cast evacuated to Bessie Street School and a rival pub. It was nicely written and – assuming his work was not unduly touched up by a script editor – indicated the programme creator's talent was still intact. Domestic violence was explored via the character of abused wife Lynn Johnson, who approached Len for help in his capacity as councillor but was later murdered in No.9 by her husband. (Her husband effecting entry couldn't even be explained by the usual *Street* get-out of an open-door community: Len's then-housemates Ray and Jerry were shown using a key when they came home to find her dead body.)

Despite the good new characters and the harder edge, ratings for *Coronation Street* continued to be – by the programme's standards – mediocre. There was a feeling that the BBC – which for so many years had chickened out of taking on *Coronation Street* – was now spoiling for a fight. When Bryan Cowgill had graduated from the Corporation's head of sport to controller of BBC1 in 1974, he had spurned the defeatism of previous incumbents of his job regarding 7.30 on Mondays and Wednesdays and pitched first runs of popular comedies like *Till Death Us Do Part* and *Steptoe and Son* against The Street (sometimes twisting the knife by starting them 10 minutes earlier than the ITV show). With video recorders not yet a mainstream consumer good, this meant that people were confronted with an either-or scenario, and a further dent was made in The Street's viewing figures. Only two *Street* episodes made number one all year and, rather symbolically, five of its episodes failed to make the top 20, which meant that the number failing to make the top 20 had increased by one each year over the last five years, a poetically symmetrical encapsulation of an incremental decline in popularity.

Unsurprisingly, Granada decided it was time for another new broom. Enter Bill Podmore. A producer mainly known for comedy series, as well a director with a couple of episodes of The Street under his belt, he was not pleased at the end of 1975 to be offered the poisoned chalice of production of the most famous show on British TV but he reluctantly agreed to try it for a year. He later wrote of Susi Hush, 'She handed me the reins without the slightest hint of animosity, or regret for that matter. In fact, Susi gave me the distinct impression that she was very relieved to unload the burden.'

John Stevenson provides this anecdote about Bill Podmore: 'I remember being near the Granada bar one day and there was a director standing just along the bar and somebody said to him, "What are you doing?" He said, "Oh it's only *Coronation Street*." Bill heard this and never used him again. Bill Podmore, although he didn't want to do the job, whatever he did, he did to the best of his ability.'

That ability was significant. Just as the period from 1960 to 1972 was The Street's Harry Kershaw epoch, so the span of 1976 to 1989 was *Coronation Street*'s Podmore era. The man who reluctantly agreed to take on the show's producer role on the condition it was only for a year stamped his mark on it over 13 years as either producer or executive producer. This period saw the programme's reinvigoration, some of its greatest dramatic successes and so sharp a revival in ratings that they nudged even those long-ago mid-Sixties figures which it had been assumed sociological changes had put forever beyond reach.

One of the more minor changes Podmore made was to revamp the opening titles, which had only recently been changed. Though the 1975 titles featured the Grape Street set for the first time, Podmore was dissatisfied with the quick intercutting between the Salford rooftops they also showed because the pace worked against Eric Spear's leisurely theme tune. He asked to see the entirety of the relevant footage and to his delight found a sequence where a cat came into shot and curled up – as if settling down to watch the programme. Though he didn't say this himself, it was also a tidy complement to the dog that had been seen in the early Seventies opening titles (running free, as dogs commonly were in those days). The 1976 credits incorporating said moggy were used virtually unchanged right up until 1990.

Podmore imported actress Madge Hindle from his production *Nearest And Dearest* to portray the character Renee Bradshaw in The Street. Although ultimately Renee – who bought the Corner Shop – would not be a hit with *Street* viewers and would be gone within four years, another import from *Nearest And Dearest* would be with The Street long-term, albeit not in front of the camera: John Stevenson's last script for *Coronation Street* wouldn't be until 2006. As with Podmore, The Street had never been a programme on which Stevenson aspired to work. 'In the Seventies, nobody wanted to do *Coronation Street*,' he reveals. 'I'd been asked to write for it several times and always politely said, "Oh, I can't take it on at the moment".' As well as it then not being very well-paid, he says The Street, '…was at the time just thought of as an elderly soap, and I don't think most people thought it would live much longer….' It was Podmore who changed his mind: 'Because he'd directed nearly all of the sitcoms I'd been writing for seven years and he was a very good friend, I couldn't refuse. He said, "We're only doing it for a year".' Significantly, most of Stevenson's scriptwriting hitherto had – like *Nearest And Dearest* – been comedy. Laughter was something Granada felt the programme needed after the sometimes dour Hush reign.

A conclusion that Podmore drew was that the Corner Shop needed a matriarchal figure running it again in preference to the youthful combination of Gail Potter and Tricia Hopkins who had lately been behind the till, hence the introduction of Renee. Tricia herself was axed, Kathy Jones being told of her exit in one of the tearful meetings that is the lot of the new producer of any show. Podmore's views on the gender balance at the Rovers was the reverse. He made peripheral character Fred Gee (Fred Feast) live-in potman at the pub to negate the implausible female-only atmosphere that had prevailed there since Jack Walker had passed away. The balding, bespectacled, red-faced, pot-bellied Fred was rather mean-spirited, but he illustrated that The Street's characters do not need to be likeable to be compelling.

Though Ena Sharples was still a reasonably permanent presence despite the fact that Violet Carson was not getting any younger or healthier – she appeared in 42 programmes in 1976, more than double her tally of last year – the show unavoidably lost her companion when Margot Bryant's poor health and inability to remember her lines became painfully apparent. Minnie Caldwell – adorable in her lack of malice – had been in the programme just under a quarter of a century.

Derek Wilton made his first appearance this year. Graham Haberfield's death had put paid to the writers' plan to pair off Jerry Booth and Mavis Riley and salesman Derek was brought in as a suitably quasi-innocent replacement. Though initially a minor character and not too sympathetic (he messed Mavis around for years), he would become one of the longer-running and most endearing of *Street* people.

Endearing is not a word that could be applied to Mike Baldwin, who turned up in October as the new owner of the warehouse, which had been closed since the fire and which he restyled as denim factory Baldwin's Casuals. Baldwin was a Londoner. The Street's history shows that a female

Londoner will be portrayed as good-natured (barmaid Nona Willis; Jenny Sutton, who married Dennis Tanner in 1968) but a male Londoner will be anything but. Lo and behold, Baldwin began behaving in the ruthless, exploitative way to be expected of any rag trade boss. Daran Little: 'That's done on purpose. It's the mill-owner. It's the them-and-the-us. If you're bringing in a character who employs people, they have to be seen to be significantly different to the denizens of Coronation Street.' Actor Johnny Briggs – who had previously appeared in the programme as a lorry driver, although was better known for a role in *Crossroads*, which indicates Podmore didn't consider the latter show a threat – was handsome and the writers gave Baldwin a patter and a confidence that made his character riveting even if it not anyone's choice of drinking pal.

Minnie had inhabited No.5 since 1962. When Mike Baldwin bought the vacant property, he ushered in a new era on several counts. In modernising, he rid the house of its status of last house in the street without an inside toilet. He also gave the street its first through-lounge when he knocked down the wall between the front parlour and sitting room, thus making No.5 the first Street house to no longer play host to that antiquated situation of people mysteriously inhabiting the back room and not the one where people keep their televisions. Finally, the landlord whose name had once struck fear into residents would never be a presence on The Street again: over the years, Edward Wormold had sold off his houses and No.5 had been the last in his possession.

The most important arrival, though, was not a new character. Pat Phoenix returned as Elsie Tanner. When she had left, pleading boredom, Phoenix had commented, 'I should be happy to think that some time in the future – maybe years from now – I may return.' It had taken her just three years to come to the conclusion that she wanted to make that comeback, of which decision she said, 'Somebody caught me on a very cold night in a dressing room in Morecambe and I was fed up and I said, "I want to go home".' She might well have been fed up, but the impression given by that quote that The Street sought her out was denied by Podmore, who later claimed that it was Phoenix who approached him. Stevenson: 'She was begging him. Whether Susi Hush or any other predecessors would have taken her back I don't know.' The films that Phoenix had spoken of making with her husband had not come to pass and if the advertising offers Rose refers to had rolled in when she was in The Street, by definition they would have been fewer if she no longer had the exposure granted by her presence in the programme.

However, Bill Kenwright – a close friend of Phoenix's as well as sometime employer in his capacity as theatre producer – says the reality was a little more complicated. 'She was by far and away the biggest star in the theatre in the provinces,' he insists. Though Kenwright laughs off the suggestion that Phoenix wasn't fulfilled by her stage work ('She loved it'), he says she became unhappy because she 'missed' The Street. 'She was doing *Random Harvest* for me,' he recalls. 'Pat and I were really, really close and I knew she was unhappy. We went out to dinner. She'd been touring for four years and she said, "Chuck I think I made a mistake. I shouldn't have left".' Kenwright says, 'She went back because of me.... I knew she'd left quite acrimoniously.... I think she found it difficult to say, "Please can I come back?".... I made the odd phone call and certainly the word was, "Over my dead body." But then I finally got a chink and had a meeting.' Said meeting was with Bill Podmore, although it's unclear whether it took place before or after the 'letter appealing for a second chance' Podmore mentioned receiving from Phoenix in his auto-biography. Kenwright: 'I wasn't [her] agent but I loved her, I adored her and she was the most loyal star to me. I arranged a situation where they met up again. I told Pat, "You've got to be a wee bit less demanding than you were" and it all worked out.'

Up to a point. The imperiousness implicit in Phoenix attempting to give the impression that The Street needed her rather than vice versa was the type of behaviour that Podmore – though he was in favour in principle of the return of such a much-loved character – wanted to stamp out. He made it a condition of her return that it stop. Also at issue was the way her vanity had been in danger of making a mockery of the supposedly ordinary lifestyle of the woman she played. Podmore told Phoenix that dressing in ways patently beyond the means of her character was now *verboten*, as was Phoenix's disregard for script specifications that required her hair to look less than immaculate. Phoenix agreed to all these stipulations, then reneged on them once she had her feet back under the table. Her regal manner around the set was not appreciated by her colleagues, especially the perennially courtly Jean Alexander, but once again it was tolerated by the production team. Perhaps at the back of their minds they did not think it a coincidence that there was a rise in ratings not long after Elsie made her reappearance (minus husband Alan) in the episode broadcast on 5 April 1976.

Ken began an affair with married Wendy Nightingale. She moved in with him and, though this arrangement lasted for only a brief while, it was a milestone – The Street's first example of a cohabiting unmarried couple as we would say now, but which back then would have been described as a common law marriage. In the summer, Eddie Yeats decorated for the Ogdens, but ran out of wallpaper. He filled the gap with a huge, strangely evocative mural of a mountain range. Hilda loved her new 'Muriel', as she called it. In 1978, water damage would see it replaced by a seascape mural, which would become (with the augmentation of a row of three flying plaster ducks, the centre one of which was always crooked) one of the iconic images of *Coronation Street*'s history.

1976 saw the last *Street* scriptwriting credit for Tony Warren: Ena Sharples' 'father' bowed out with the 8 March edition. It was a fairly humdrum episode in that nothing spectacular or violent happened – but, then, that depiction of everyday life was the whole point behind *Coronation Street* in the first place. Though he would never write for The Street again, Warren would finally receive more than a 'From an idea by…' (or a variation thereof) credit as reward for his fatherhood. In his first year in his job, Podmore – feeling that it was plain wrong that Warren did not profit from the programme he had created – sought and achieved for Warren an annual, index-linked financial acknowledgment of the debt Granada owed him.

In 1977, Ken Barlow's estranged wife Janet returned to The Street to beg him to take her back. Ken insisted they had never been right for each other but let her stay the night. The next morning, Ken found her dead: she had taken an overdose. In the 14 years since Sheila Birtles' suicide bid, the offices of the deputy coroner of Manchester seemed to have altered its corporate position and there was no particular fuss surrounding the storyline. Ken was understandably distraught – although the bewilderment he expressed to Rita about why he seemed cursed may have been more to do with storyliners and scriptwriters nervous about plausibility issues: death had claimed this character's mother, father, brother and two wives in the space of just 16 years.

Suzie Birchall (Cheryl Murray) was a new character. A somewhat calculating peroxided blonde girl, she became Gail's room-mate at Elsie's house. In an example of the adage that you can't manufacture magic in a bottle, the aim of the producers (which included Leslie Duxbury for a short spell again this year) to make Suzie a successor to Elsie never really took with the viewers and Suzie was destined soon to become another one of those *Street* characters whose names now make people furrow their brow as they attempt to remember them.

The Street – like much of Britain – celebrated the Queen's quarter-century on the throne in 1977. One didn't have to be a republican to find the Silver Jubilee edition of the programme on 8 June a very silly affair. It saw Stan Ogden put on trial in the Rovers for ruining everybody's day by letting the battery go flat on The Street's *Britain Through The Ages* carnival float. Found guilty, he was sentenced to buy everybody a drink. Far more successful, for one notable personage anyway, was The Street's part in a Silver Jubilee variety show at the Palace Theatre in Manchester. All but a handful of the main cast appeared in a skit in which keen royalist Hilda Ogden waited in vain for a rumoured Royal visit to Coronation Street. The climax saw a dead drunk Stan wheeled on in a pushcart by Eddie Yeats. Stevenson, who wrote the sketch, recalls, 'They say, "Well you've missed the Queen, Hilda." And she says, "Yes, I'd better get him home. I'd like to have seen her." She's covering him up with the Union Jack I'd given her to carry, saying, "And after all, I'm only doing what she'd have done if her husband was taken tired and emotional." I was watching the Royal Box just to see how this went down and the Queen never cracked a smile. Nothing. Poker-face. Whereas the Duke of Edinburgh fell off his chair, practically, laughing.'

Other 'triumphs' of Stan this year included becoming a washerwoman when Hilda bought a new washing machine – his plans for her to do the work came asunder when she refused and he had to get to grips with an alien object called an iron – and, along with Eddie Yeats, taking advantage of a drayman's strike that left the Rovers dry: they brewed beer in the bath. Hilda pulled the plug – literally.

By now it had been proven that a wedding was always good for The Street. The nuptials of Len Fairclough and Rita Littlewood on 20 April were no exception. Some felt the whole thing a bit *ersatz* and that Len had been paired off with Rita in lieu of a certain other redhead with whom he had also been on-again, off-again and to whom he seemed far better suited. However, that the footloose and fancy free Len was finally settling down was itself a big deal, justifying its own *TV Times* commemorative supplement. That other redhead, Elsie Tanner, didn't attend the wedding because, the scripts said, she was too 'upset'. In fact it was, according to Podmore, Pat Phoenix who was upset. So convinced was the actress that a single Len was an integral part of her own character's image that she couldn't handle the scenario and pulled a sickie, necessitating hasty rewrites. She missed a real ratings milestone: the 20.9 million audience was The Street's highest since January 1965, making it not only the most watched *Coronation Street* of the Seventies, but the 15th most watched television broadcast in the UK of the decade.

It might have been to the chagrin of Alan Rothwell that his recognisability factor was greater than that of Laurence Olivier, but it's doubtful that said ennobled thesp shared his views. A huge fan of The Street, he was due to appear in the episode of 4 January 1978 as Ozzie, a vagrant who insisted on joining Hilda Ogden in an all-night vigil outside a shop where a colour television was on special offer. Unfortunately, the filming schedule of a movie prevented this stellar cameo taking place.

Neville Buswell shocked Podmore by telling him he was leaving the character of Ray Langton behind. It was initially decided that Deirdre and the Langtons' daughter Tracy should depart the show too but Buswell was unhappy that his decision would adversely affect Anne Kirkbride and the eventual storyline devised was that the Langtons' plans to start a new life together in Holland were scuppered when Deirdre changed her mind at the last minute, creating the memorable image of Ray stalking off over a long bridge while the credits rolled.

Ernest Bishop's exit was far bloodier. Actor Stephen Hancock had taken umbrage over a rather arcane issue involving cast payments whereby some of the star names received guaranteed levels of income regardless of the number of episodes in which they happened to appear. When Podmore refused to change this policy, Hancock told him he would not be renewing his contract. Considering that Podmore claims Hancock told him that he was happy with the money he himself was receiving for his role, it's difficult to argue with Podmore's assessment that Hancock was cutting his nose off to spite his face. At least Hancock was the recipient of a memorable departure. Explains John Stevenson, 'Generally speaking, characters are only killed when every other possibility was a worst option. He was married to Emily Bishop, and they were God-fearing Christians, very upright. You could not believe that if he left the show, she would not go with him. You couldn't believe they would split up over any sort of infidelity, so if he was going, well she would have to go. Well this didn't seem terribly fair to Eileen Derbyshire who played Emily Bishop, and so we brooded and brooded about this and I said to Bill, "Well, he'll have to die." And Bill said, "Yeah, he'll have to die. It's the only way." So he was killed off in a bungled robbery at the denim factory.' Stevenson wrote the relevant edition. 'Whoever came up with the key idea most times would get to write the key episodes,' he explains. Ernest had been taken on as wages clerk at Baldwin's Casuals in 1976. He caught a shotgun blast in the chest there in the episode broadcast on 11 January 1978. Stevenson: 'What was a bit new about that was taking things to a reasonably realistic conclusion. Some of the older writers wanted the killers of Ernie Bishop to drive away and in their panic crash the getaway car and die in the flames. Most of the younger writers thought that was a cop-out, so they wanted to stay with it and see the snot and the tears and the grief and the misery and eventually hear of trials and convictions and so forth.'

The greatest irony to come from a death that was never wanted by the production team and was really completely unnecessary was that it marked a critical watershed for *Coronation Street*, one which rescued it forever from the ghetto of soapland and established it in the public mind as a serious and gritty drama. As Stevenson says of the elevated critical standing that The Street now enjoys, 'It wasn't thought of in that way until really mid-to-late Seventies when suddenly the higher culture noticed it more.' Though it may not be fashionable to say so, whatever its previous critical plaudits and commercial successes, in 1978 The Street had still not achieved a gravitas in the wider public's mind. It continued to be dismissed by surprisingly large parts of both the media and the populace as a women's programme and to be bracketed with the utterly lightweight *Crossroads* simply because the two were both half-hour dramas broadcast more than once a week. All this changed with the Ernest Bishop murder, or rather the aftermath of it. The first violent death of a major *Street* character created a large amount of media commentary, and not just the column inches predictable in an era where the debate about violence on TV was gaining in volume. The whole affair seemed to kick off a process of evaluation, partly helped by the (rather arbitrary) marking of The Street's 18th anniversary at the end of the year, and partly by a Thames Television documentary called *Death On The Street* broadcast fully 18 months after Ernest's death, in which fans of the show were filmed weeping as they watched the death scene and other actors whose characters had been killed off in the programme – Noel Dyson and Lynne Carol – were interviewed about the experience.

During this protracted period in the spotlight for *Coronation Street*, newspapers were running articles and opinion pieces remarking on its revolutionary nature when it started, what a cut above the usual soap fare The Street was and how it constituted a window on the real world of the Northern working class.

All of this crucial acclaim, of course, didn't do any harm to the ratings. Though the Podmore regime had not effected an immediate improvement in viewing figures, by now a corner had visibly been turned. Nine episodes had made number one in 1977, as opposed to the solitary one the previous year. In 1978, eight episodes made number one. Only three episodes failed to make the ratings top 20 in 1978 – the lowest figure since 1973. Those who might sniff at the improvement would do well to take heed of *Blake's 7*, which made its debut in 1978 and which demonstrated the continuance of the BBC's refusal to be intimidated by The Street. A classy, big-budget (for the Beeb) science fiction series, all but the second of its four seasons were transmitted directly against The Street on Monday nights. The show proved curiously sturdy competition to *Coronation Street*. Or perhaps not so curious. Sci-fi expert and *Blake's 7* fan Kim Newman once opined that the tone of *Blake's 7* was 'absolutely bloody miserable.' How reminiscent that description is of *EastEnders*, a future BBC drama serial that would become The Street's great nemesis.

In May 1979, Margaret Thatcher became the new Prime Minister of Britain.

The main plank of her mandate was to reduce the amount of strike action in the country. How ironic then that two months after her party's election to government, industrial action did something that had happened only rarely since *Coronation Street*'s inception: take it off the air. The 8 August episode of *Coronation Street* was the last seen until 24 October as a consequence of industrial action over a pay dispute by ITV technicians which blacked out screens. When the channel's programmes reappeared following the resolution of the dispute, the first post-strike *Coronation Street* had a filmed prologue in which Len Fairclough and Bet Lynch walked along the outside lot reminding the viewers of the now distant storylines via a gossipy chat.

The Tilsley family were given a home in the Street, Ivy joined at No.5 by her mild-mannered husband Bert (Peter Dudley) and son Brian

Tilsley, a heartthrob albeit in 6/8 scale played by Chris Quentin. Bert had actually been known as Jack when previously seen in two 1975 appearances, but Vera's husband was also named Jack and was soon to feature prominently. This coincidence of Christian names, though common in real life, would be confusing in a drama. Jack Duckworth (William Tarmey) was initially a minor figure. John Stevenson: 'We might have seen Jack playing darts in a pub and all that but we never linked them up as husband and wife until the wedding of Brian Tilsley [to Gail Potter]. We knew that Vera Duckworth was a friend of Ivy Tilsley so we thought, "We'll see her husband." I wrote him in as a rather miserable mother who didn't get his hand in his pocket to pay his round and Vera didn't like him and they had a row. But when we saw him on screen, we all said, "This fella's got something" so we thought we'll have a look at their marriage and found in fact he was a good comedy player.'

It was almost as though Tarmey and Dawn were destined to be together: not only had they both been *Street* extras, but both had had professional singing careers. The double-act Jack constituted with Vera – he a work-shy, pigeon-racing cellar-man, she a harridan with a heart, both of them intellectually uncomplicated to say the least – would provide as many comic moments as the similarly uncultured team of Stan and Hilda Ogden. Unlike the bedrock of affection underlying the Ogdens' marriage, Jack and Vera harboured mainly contempt for each other. In fact, their marriage marked the passing of an era to some extent: a couple a generation younger than the Duckworths who stuck together despite fighting like cat and dog would simply not be believable in a society where the loosening of social constraints and the fact of women's lack of dependency on men has meant that warring partners routinely give up the ghost of a decaying relationship. Jack, incidentally, was a far more nuanced character than he might at first appear, and down the years he would show great sensitivity in crucial moments.

Audrey Potter, mother of Gail, made her first appearance in April. Meant to be in the show for two episodes only, she was given a contract after the potential of this man-hungry and often rather brittle woman was recognised. So much so that she ended up as the character with most appearances all year. She was played brilliantly by Sue Nicholls, whose long, thin face was already familiar to television viewers from programmes as varied as *Crossroads,* the children's comedy *Rentaghost* and the adult satire *The Fall and Rise of Reginald Perrin.*

This was the year that Elsie changed her name back from the Howard that had never seemed right to the Tanner that people felt most comfortable referring to her as. Sadly, it constituted a synchronicity of art and life, as the man who had played Alan Howard – her real-life husband Alan Browning – died of a liver complaint in September. Phoenix didn't attend the funeral because she was bruised from her latest face-lift. In November, Gail Potter also changed her name when she became the wife of Brian Tilsley.

The critical respectability for The Street that had been building since the publicity surrounding the Ernest Bishop murder continued apace this year. At a Variety Club of Great Britain dinner at which Doris Speed was granted a Lifetime Achievement Award, the poet laureate John Betjeman compared the programme favourably to Dickens. 'Manchester produces what to me is *The Pickwick Papers*,' he said. 'That is to say, *Coronation Street*. Mondays and Wednesdays, I live for them. Thank God, half past seven tonight and I shall be in paradise…. Not a word too many. Not a gesture needless. It is the best writing and acting I could wish to see….'

Part Four
The Eighties

With the Betjeman endorsement to add to all the other celebrities' nods of approval it had acquired in previous years and with the ratings continuing to climb, *Coronation Street* entered the year of its 20th anniversary (and 2,000th episode) with confidence. It never really looked back.

Though after 1980 there would be the mountains and valleys inevitable in any long life, it was still difficult not to view the programme as unassailable. Who now – Granada, the ITA or anyone else – would dare take away from the nation this deeply embedded part of its fabric? At the end of the following year, even the achingly trendy *New Musical Express* put The Street on its front cover. Inside was an effusive piece written by the high priest of cool (and impenetrable prose) Ian Penman. Features editor Tony Stewart was a big fan of The Street and seems to have commissioned the article on a personal whim: there were almost no young people in the programme at a time when few over the age of 30 read the *NME*.

It is the *NME* that may be responsible for the entry into the language of the diminutive 'Corrie'. Julian Cope, lead singer of alternative pop act The Teardrop Explodes, had used the word in a recent interview and it was highlighted in the paper via a pull-quote that almost became a catchphrase: 'You do call it Corrie, don't you?' Cope's comment was probably a reference to his surprise that the Southern interviewer was not familiar with a word already in wide circulation in the North-West. 'Corrie' was in line with the habit of people in that region to confer playful pet names on institutions of various types. While North-West diminutives like 'leccy' (electricity) have not spread, the self-consciously fond irreverence of 'Corrie' was more in tune with increasingly informal times than the previously prevalent abbreviation for the programme, 'The Street', and in the intervening years has taken hold nationwide and all but supplanted it.

The public didn't take to Renee Bradshaw and she was dispensed with in 1980. John Stevenson: 'You'd get feedback from among the people who watch the show 'cos whoever you meet, if they know you work on the show, they'll always tell you what they think and who they like and who they can't be doing with and "she's not good and I like him" and all that…. Madge Hindle, she herself didn't think she was quite right in that part. I don't think she was too bothered when Bill said, "I think we're going to write this character out".' Hindle was at least given a significant and memorable farewell. Renee was killed in the episode broadcast on 30 July 1980 when a lorry ploughed into her stationary car. She and her husband of two years Alf Roberts had recently decided to sell up and open a Post Office in Grange-Over-Sands, but the grieving Alf decided to keep the Corner Shop.

On the lighter side of things, Albert Tatlock refused to ride in Ken's new Volkswagen because it was German, Stan Ogden nearly had a heart attack when he was told he was allergic to beer (it was a misdiagnosis) and Hilda Ogden won a dinner date with Mike Baldwin that Baldwin failed to buy himself out of.

Eddie Yeats became the Ogdens' lodger this year. It was primarily to reduce the workload for Bernard Youens following a stroke that had left him – and Stan Ogden – with slurred speech but for John Stevenson it was a good move dramatically. 'With Geoff Hughes [Eddie Yeats] coming in, it became a tremendous three-way act,' he recalls. 'There were stories to wring your heart occasionally in that house but they were basically comedy characters.' It added to the joy he already got from writing for Hilda: 'She had this wonderful resilience. However many times the dustbin of life was tipped on her, she'd eventually brush herself off and carry on with it, even though Stan Ogden was always pissing the money up against a wall and Geoff Hughes was no better. She was nice to write for, Jean. It's a mannered performance but a very effective performance.'

Violet Carson's increasingly failing health had seen her regularly take lengthy sabbaticals from The Street in recent years and in the episode broadcast on 4 April, she started another. The story – as it often did with elderly characters leaving the picture for a while – had her character going to St Anne's (just up the coast from Blackpool), in her case because the council decided to rebuild the front of the Community Centre where her flat was located. What was in effect the end of an era went unmarked. Though the intention of all parties was for the character to come back when possible, Ena Sharples' hairnet was never to be seen again, possibly the result of the fact that Carson had sometimes been reduced to tears in recent times by her increasing inability to retain her lines. Carson passed away in 1983.

As a grim but fondly thought-of face departed, a fresh one arrived – though it never felt quite right. When it was announced that Elsie Tanner's grandson Martin Cheveski was coming to stay with her, many were the long-term *Street* fans who cried, 'Paul, surely?' But no, this was an offspring of Ivan and Linda three years younger than Paul and never previously mentioned, let alone seen, in all the times the Cheveskis had visited Elsie as Paul was growing up. While viewers might have been able to swallow this if they really tried, what was not so easily digestible was the fact that actor Jonathan Caplan seemed exactly the 19 years of age that Paul would now be, rather than the 16 Martin was presented as. Martin was around for six months, got a juicy-ish storyline involving a spurned marriage proposal, and was never seen again. It was the first major example of the show truly twisting itself into knots in order to introduce a character for artificial reasons – in this case apparently to attract the kind of demographic that lapped up the likes of girls' weekly magazine *Jackie* – but it would not be the last. Having successfully navigated two decades, The Street was now showing signs of becoming slightly cynical and calculating in its story development – even if such cynicism was perfectly in keeping with the *zeitgeist* of the Eighties.

1981 saw a Summer of Love. The wedding in *Coronation Street* on 27 July between Ken Barlow and Deirdre Langton occurred – purely by coincidence – within two days of the nuptials of HRH the Prince of Wales and Lady Diana Spencer, the biggest Royal Wedding since that of the Queen herself back in 1947.

The *Coronation Street* wedding episode was reputed to have attracted more viewers than watched the real-life wedding, providing a wonderfully symmetrical confirmation of just how important *Coronation Street* was to the Queen's subjects. Though it was a nice story, and though it is believed by many to this day, it was in fact not quite accurate. Through The Street attracted 15.35 million viewers, the Royal Wedding ceremony itself (as opposed to the much longer programmes it was contained within, which were officially the competing broadcasts) attracted 19 million on BBC1 alone. Additionally, the real-life ceremony was broadcast across all three existing television channels, so another 1.2 million watched it, cumulatively, on ITV and BBC2. It should also be pointed out that viewing figures for Ken and Deirdre's ceremony were actually well short of previous *Street* weddings: both Elsie and Steve Tanner's wedding in 1967 and the nuptials of Len Fairclough and Rita Littlewood in 1977 garnered 5.5 million more.

Nonetheless, many were moved by the culmination of the frequently stuttering relationship between Ken and Deirdre: Deirdre had been game since they had struck up a friendship after Ray Langton's flit to Holland, but 42-year-old Ken had worried both about the age gap between he and 26-year-old Deirdre and about the wisdom of embarking on marriage number three. Deirdre herself had shown ambivalence of late too, flirting with Mike Baldwin, who was miffed when she ultimately chose Ken over him. On the happy day, the glasses – then still of a vaguely comical size – were for once missing from Deirdre's visage.

A character at the other end of the evolutionary scale from Ken also got hitched this year: Fred Gee wed new character Eunice Nuttall (Meg Johnson). Typical of Fred's nature, he had popped the question because brewery rules said he could only manage a pub if he was married. Another new face – and one that would be seen for a far longer period than Eunice's – was that of Alma Sedgwick (Amanda Barrie), wife of the owner of Jim's Café in Victoria Street. In time, her heart would prove to be as preternaturally big as her dark eyes, but her early appearances were as an overbearing boss to Elsie Tanner.

Albert Tatlock asked the police to remove Ken Barlow's new car, ostensibly because it was an obstruction but in reality because it had been manufactured by the enemy. However, he showed the vulnerability behind those famous dewlaps and grouchy demeanour when he privately shed tears after being told by Ken and Deirdre that they were moving away. The newlyweds changed their minds when Albert explained to them he couldn't leave the street and all its memories.

In 1982, *Coronation Street* gained a new exterior set to replace the Grape Street lot, the relative distance and coldness of which had always made it unpopular with the cast but which, more importantly, had in recent years begun to show distinct signs of age.

The commissioning of the new set gave The Street the impetus finally to resurrect No.7, which had remained an empty space since its collapse in 1965. Len Fairclough bought the relevant plot of land and built a house on it – although this construction took place entirely off-screen. His plan to sell the property was scuppered by Rita, who fancied the more modern new house, the first on the terraced side of The Street to have central heating. Len also built a living room that, as with Baldwin's modernisation, was recognisable as something from the modern age instead of an Edwardian, TV-less family room most today would consider a kitchen. The Faircloughs moved into No.7 and Len sold No.9.

New characters included Sharon Gaskell, played by Tracie Bennett, the 16-year-old foster daughter of Len and Rita Fairclough, who had also fostered a 13-year-old boy the previous year. September saw the first appearance of Phyllis Pearce (Jill Summer). It was unclear which was the more disturbing: her rasping baritone or intact sex drive.

Phyllis was actually the unlikely sole survivor of a planned new *Street* family. Chalkie Whitely was a binman colleague of Eddie Yeats who bought No.9 from Len for £10,000 and moved in with his young grandson Craig. However, by December Craig had been taken off to Australia by his father and by the following summer Chalkie followed him Down Under after conveniently winning the fare via an accumulator bet. Only Craig's maternal grandmother Phyllis would be seen again, perhaps because she satisfied those with hag-pangs created by the absence of Ena Sharples, even if she acquired a good nature as she got older alien to the hairnetted one.

Brian Tilsley disappeared for the first half of the year as a punishment for Chris Quentin accepting a panto role: such extra-curricular activity was banned on the grounds that, were it not, The Street could find itself badly depleted each Christmas. Quentin was written out by the device of Brian taking a job in Qatar.

This year the public were able to see some of their favourite *Street* episodes again for the very first time via the recent invention of the video cassette. The success of *The Magic of Coronation Street – Distant Memories 1960–1964* showed there was a market for nostalgia for the programme to which ITV – then restricted to one channel and with the public forever bemoaning the amount of repeats even on that – had not previously been able to cater. Its success led to the commercial release of several other VHS *Street* compilations, such as those chosen by Daran Little in 1990 for 30th anniversary celebration videos and character-orientated clip videos hosted by Judy Finnigan for a Time-Life subscription-only series. The format also enabled 'non-canon' returns of departed characters, such as in *The Lives of Loves of Elsie Tanner* (1987), which saw Anne Cunningham reprise the role of Linda Cheveski as she reminisced about her screen mother with Emily Bishop and Mike Baldwin, and *The Women of Coronation Street* (1998), in which a retired Hilda Ogden was visited in Derbyshire by Betty Williams (previously Turpin) to get nostalgic. Fond dreamy looks segued into clips of the relevant events.

Considering all the brickbats directed at *Coronation Street* for depicting the type of terraced street increasingly rare in Manchester and Salford, it's the richest irony that a demolition of rows of terraced housing in Bury, Greater Manchester in the early 1980s was exploited by The Street to erect... a facsimile of a row of terraced housing. Granada purchased land left vacant when three rows of terraces adjacent to Liverpool Street Station in Castlefield were bulldozed and on it set about finally providing a truly realistic version of the street in the title of their biggest asset. Though still not full-size, the houses on the new outdoor set were bigger than the houses on the Grape Street set (which was located about 200 yards away). The houses, pub and shop exteriors were realised via 49,000 bricks and 6,500 roofing slates, all genuinely weathered from their previous existence: many local *Coronation Street* fans will be seeing, without knowing it, parts of their former homes every time they watch the programme. The viaduct required 29,000 bricks and an authentic Victorian black mortar mix. The new set also coloured in parts of The Street's background: Rosamund Street at the Rovers' end was for the first time three-dimensional instead of the painted backdrop it had been in the Sixties or the verbal reference it had been reduced to in recent years. Meanwhile, a small alleyway – sorry, ginnel – with door was established between the Rovers and No.1 to appease the pedants writing in to point out that those visiting the gents' in the Rovers would end up peeing over whoever was currently inhabiting said house. Because open-sided studio sets enable greater camera movement and easier audio set-ups than enclosed rooms, habitable houses were not necessary. However, the new set's houses were not the completely inhospitable Grape Street shells. Reveals Daran Little, 'They use them for storage and things. We used to have storyline conferences above 9, 11, 13 and the Corner Shop.'

The Queen and Prince Philip accepted an invitation to tour the renovated local area in May. When the Lord Lieutenant of Lancashire noticed that the new *Coronation Street* set was adjacent to the proposed royal route, he suggested a detour. The Street were delighted when Her Majesty agreed: having the royal couple officially open the new set would constitute a huge publicity coup for the programme. Accordingly, on 5 May, the cast of the programme stood in the doorways of their fictional homes while their majesties wandered down the cobbles to the accompaniment of the furiously working shutters of the cameras of invited photographers. The event was broadcast live on ITV. (The first the new set would be seen in the programme itself would be in the 7 June episode.) Naturally, the newspapers the next day carried pictures of the likes of Julie Goodyear curtseying to the Queen and the regeneration of the local area was barely mentioned.

The autumn of 1982 had seen Bill Podmore take a step upwards into the role of executive producer. Pauline Shaw succeeded him for six months, before being replaced by Mervyn Watson at the end of the year. At the start of his tenure of over two years, Watson was thrown straight into the deep end, for 1983 was possibly the most tumultuous year in The Street's history so far, with a sensational, nation-stopping storyline, stratospheric ratings and incredible off-screen scandal. Additionally, the tumult would continue into 1984: over the period, the programme lost 13 major characters in often headline-grabbing situations.

Several new characters were introduced. Percy Sugden (Bill Waddington) was the new caretaker at the Community Centre. An upstanding if curmudgeonly man fast approaching his pension, he had an obsession with all things military, despite having only served as a cook in the forces. ('An army marches on its stomach', apparently.) Curly Watts (Kevin Kennedy), a fellow with John Lennon spectacles who was surprisingly cultured considering he was a dustbin round colleague of Eddie Yeats, became Emily's lodger. Kevin Webster (Michael Le Vell) was a teenage car mechanic taken on by Brian Tilsley at the garage he had recently opened in Albert Street. Both Curly and Kevin were generally benign young men, but the same could not be said for Terry Duckworth, the 19-year-old son of Jack and Vera. Though good-looking, Terry was never going to be the nation's pin-up. His villainy was profoundly more harmful than the cheeky-chappie scheming of the likes of Jed Stone, Stan Ogden and Eddie Yeats. If it seemed somewhat implausible that Jack and Vera – essentially decent-hearted, whatever their vulgarity – could have raised such a character, credibility doubts were dispelled by the heavy-lidded menace brought to the role by Nigel Pivaro. Jack and Vera themselves moved from the margins to the centre when their home at 20 Inkerman Street (presumably adjacent to the house of Stan Ogden's legendary 'fancy piece') was the subject of a compulsory purchase order. With the help of their compensation, they bought No.9 off the departing Chalkie Whitely.

Those saying goodbye to The Street in 1983 included Geoffrey Hughes. Eddie Yeats departed to Bury with his lady love Marion, whom he decided to wed when the latter announced she was pregnant. In a sign of how times had changed since Sheila Birtles' unwed-and-pregnant status in 1966, this fact created no particular frisson.

The disappearances from the storylines of first episode veteran Annie Walker, nearly as longstanding Len Fairclough and more recent resident Bert Tilsley were somewhat less tidy and involved somewhat more difficult circumstances. Doris Speed, ill in hospital, was devastated when a newspaper decided to dig up her birth certificate and revealed that she was, at 84, a full 15 years older than she claimed (or, indeed, looked). She was also traumatised when robbers broke into her home and she had to seclude herself upstairs while they ransacked the place. Such was Speed's upset that she never returned. 'She was possibly the only character the show has ever had who was just about irreplaceable,' says John Stevenson. Referring to Annie's habit of grandly announcing that she was a Beaumont (her maiden name) of Clitheroe (an upmarket part of Lancashire), he explains, 'No doubt just from a backstreet in Clitheroe, but she gave herself tremendous airs and graces and [was] always trying to up her prestige in terms of class, and it doesn't quite work today. You could do it then, given her background and her pretensions and the way society was, but you couldn't do that equivalent of a character now.'

Bert Tilsley departed after slowly losing his mind following a mini-stroke and ending up in a psychiatric hospital in Southport. Actor Peter Dudley had suffered a stroke himself, so his immobile left arm needed to be explained. He also needed time off for his forthcoming retrial for 'importuning'. Essentially an allegation of seeking sex with men in public toilets, Dudley had pleaded guilty to a previous accusation in 1980 and Granada, to their credit, had stuck by him. He had pleaded not guilty when later accused in a separate incident but Podmore made clear to Dudley that he didn't believe him, while the jury had been deadlocked. Dudley suffered a fatal heart attack in October 1983 before his retrial could occur. Bert would die off-screen the next January.

During 1983, Peter Adamson stood trial on charges of indecently assaulting two little girls at a public swimming bath and was found not guilty. In a puzzling development – for British convention is that acquitted defendants receive their defence fees back from the state – and despite a £10,000 loan from Granada, Adamson felt compelled to sell his story to a newspaper. Adamson knew that was a breach of contract because he had got into trouble for selling unauthorised interviews before. He ultimately lost far more than he gained because when he staggered Podmore by refusing to give an undertaking that he would not sell any more stories after this, Podmore had no option but to dismiss him, though waited until after the trial to do so. Says John Stevenson, 'That was clear, absolute breach of contract, so they did have a reason to sack him which wasn't tantamount to saying, "We know you got off but you did it".' Some who had their doubts about Adamson felt their misgivings were proven by a subsequent Adamson *Sun* interview which, though it contained no smoking gun, did feature a couple of curious quotes, one of which was that he was 'fascinated' by the relationship between schoolteachers and pupils, the other: 'I am totally guilty of everything the police said. But what I hope you will print – there was no sexual intent.' That interview caused him to lose his current role in a stage production of *Dial M For Murder*. Adamson's disabled wife died in 1984, and the rest of his life up to his death of stomach cancer in 2002 seems to have been a pitiful one marked by reclusion, a return to alcoholism, bankruptcy and an almost complete absence of acting roles. His character was written out of The Street via a car accident in

December 1983 (his last appearance having been in May). Some, including Adamson, interpreted as spiteful the twist inserted by the writers wherein it was revealed that Len had been cheating on Rita. Podmore denied it was motivated by anything more than the objective of maximum drama, and John Stevenson and Adele Rose both concur on this.

Perhaps the feeling of distaste left in some of the public's mouths by the Dudley and Adamson cases might have affected The Street negatively had it not been for the fact that 1983 contained one of its most compelling storylines of all time when a frustrated Deirdre embarked on an affair with Mike Baldwin. The latter was genuinely in love with Deirdre and Mrs Barlow was torn between the two men. Stevenson: 'That made an extremely effective story because it wasn't so commonplace at all. There weren't that many infidelities, and when they were done and done well, as that one was, it was a real gripper.' The nation was spellbound, columnists pontificated and celebrity fans and religious figures proffered advice to the fictional protagonists as the intrigue played out over the first couple of months of the year. 'That was the time when all the tabloids realised the power of the soap,' notes William Roache. The story reached its climax in the episode broadcast on 23 February when Mike tried to barge his way into No.1 to claim Deirdre after refusing to believe that she'd gone back on her plan to leave Ken. The latter slammed the door in his face before infuriatedly turning on Deirdre. Roache, an actor accused by some of being wooden, turned in a performance so incendiary that Anne Kirkbride – who was unaware that Roache and Johnny Briggs had decided to play the scene by ear – thought it was for real and that Roache had lost his mind. Roache: 'It was a good performance because it was well-written and there was a lot of my energy. I put a lot of feeling into that and Anne and myself are pretty good at that and we can still keep going. Anne was crying, I was shouting and slamming her against the door, but we still carried on. It did have a colossal emotional impact.' Despite the show being watched by a year-best 18.45 million, there were tens of thousands of Mancunians unable to tune in because Manchester United were playing Arsenal at home that night. Obligingly the *Daily Mail* hired the electronic scoreboard at United's Old Trafford ground and flashed up on it the other result in which those present were interested: 'DEIRDRE AND KEN UNITED AGAIN!' The 56,635 present erupted into approving cheers.

Great storylines and characters and brilliant acting had seen The Street ride out storms in 1983 that could have badly damaged it. Not a single one of the year's 104 episodes failed to make the week's top 20. The number of episodes that were the most watched broadcasts of the week of any channel was 48, the highest number since the heady days of 1962 and 1965, and indeed not far off those years' respective totals of 57 and 56. It should also be noted that the 1983 stats were achieved against stiffer competition than had existed in the Sixties: there was now an additional UK channel following the launch the previous year of Channel 4. Moreover, Channel 4 had its own continuing drama serial in the form of the Liverpool-based *Brookside*, which self-consciously attempted to be a grittier, more modern version of The Street. *Coronation Street* had this year triumphantly proven that it was still relevant to the nation even as it approached its Silver Jubilee.

January 1984 saw the final departure from the programme of the woman who had played Elsie Tanner for 21 cumulative years.

Says Adele Rose of Patricia Phoenix, 'I think she got restless and I do know she was ill but I don't think she knew it at the time. I think she felt undervalued.' (Though Rose doesn't mention this, Phoenix had publicly unfavourably compared the £500 per week she was paid to the stratospheric remuneration enjoyed by actors on vaguely comparable American shows like *Dallas*.) Phoenix would explain of her decision in 1985 to Smiths singer Morrissey (a huge fan) in *Blitz* magazine, 'We only have five basic stories in the whole of the world.... So, in *Coronation Street*, stories were repeated with different variations on theme. I had had enough. While I was bored I was not doing my best.' As with a lot of Phoenix's statements, it can be disputed – and is by John Stevenson. 'She didn't get the stories she wanted,' he says. 'She was a bit of a headache for the writers in some ways. Even when she was in her fifties, she wanted to be involved in love stories with men who were very attractive – not her own age – and we wouldn't really oblige her and so she wasn't very keen on some of the men we did give her because they were about her own age.' Both Stevenson and Adele Rose cite another headache Phoenix caused the show: the fact that she continued to insist on an expensive wardrobe. Rose: 'God, we had a lot of fights over that. Constantly, we were sending messages down to wardrobe, "Please, *please* dress down." We once very wickedly contrived a storyline where her house caught fire and all the clothes were burned. But she managed to revive her wardrobe again very quickly.' Stevenson adds, 'She was a good enough actress, but if you ever saw her on stage, she couldn't walk across the stage in a realistic way to save her life. But she was fine for the show. There was no way she'd ever metamorphose into Annie Walker or Ena Sharples. She would grow old a little more desperately.' Of her departure, Stevenson says, 'I don't think anybody was too bothered about it. Because of the way the character had aged and because of the way she didn't want to go with the flow at all, I think it was probably best for both parties.'

Unlike her previous exit, Phoenix gave sufficient notice to enable a good send-off for Elsie Tanner. The episode broadcast on the fourth day of the New Year culminated in virtually a lap of honour. Elsie had decided to leave for the Algarve with her old 1961 boyfriend Bill Gregory and as she walked down the pavement, memories – in the form of overdubbed dialogue – resounded in her head. 'How long are you away?' asked her cab driver. 'Ah – now there's a question' came the reply. Fittingly, the episode was written by Harry Kershaw, one of the few people on The Street's team whose history with the programme went back as far as Phoenix's.

Phoenix appeared in a play and a sitcom after her final *Street* appearance but the illness to which Rose alludes – lung cancer – claimed her in 1986. It would be unfair to leave Phoenix without acknowledging that she had a nice side just as considerable as her previously mentioned imperiousness. Testimony to this abounds but is summed up by Bill Kenwright when he says, 'If you'd said, "Oh, I like your coat" or your missus liked it, she would have taken it off her back and given it to you. She was a fantastic person. Difficult at times, but heart of gold.'

Two other much-loved stalwarts were unavoidably lost in 1984 in the shapes of Albert Tatlock and Stan Ogden. Jack Howarth died in April, aged 88. Bernard Youens – after a horrific decline which saw him have a leg amputated – followed him in August, aged 69. What with Doris Speed's departure the previous year, and the fact of Ena Sharples' return being made impossible by Violet Carson's death the previous December, this left Bill Roache as the last man standing from the original cast as a permanent *Street* character. Though Len Fairclough had not quite been an original cast member, Peter Adamson's recent removal only added to the sense of an end of an era. Perhaps for the first time though, this feeling of the changes being rung was not one accompanied by the whiff of decay: the aforementioned year of great viewing figures and favourable notices and the influx of new characters that had occurred at the same time indicated that a That Was Then, This Is Now attitude was more appropriate than one of Those Were the Days.

There was a half-hearted – or perhaps half-baked – attempt to create a sense of dynasty in 1984 with Billy Walker (five years absent) taking over the Rovers in May and the same month Anne Cunningham making a comeback as Elsie's daughter Linda Cheveski (last seen in 1968, so being witnessed by the viewers in colour for the first time). Linda's husband, last seen in 1967, did not fetch up with her. Ernst Walder states he was not approached to reprise the role of Ivan. 'I probably would have gone back,' he says. Because of the disinterest of the production team in having her husband accompany her, Linda was presented as an embittered divorcee, an inevitable plot device in the circumstances but one which unfortunately rather undermined their previous pledges of devotion, not to mention the emotions such had induced in the viewers. Linda wanted to hang onto the house she had grown up in but the off-screen Elsie wanted to sell it. Cunningham left after only two months and later claimed that she hated her return because the sense of camaraderie once enjoyed by the cast had evaporated. Ken Farrington did not stay long as Billy Walker either, but he had a different grievance. Farrington found himself playing what might as well have been a different person – a nasty operator cast apparently deliberately in the vein of TV's reigning bad guy JR Ewing of *Dallas*.

Bill Webster, a builder and father of Kevin, bought No.11 from Elsie, causing a disgusted Linda to go back to Birmingham. We also met Kevin's gobby sister Debbie. Derek Wilton and Mavis Riley finally decided to get together permanently – and then, with mutual doubts, jilted each other. Fred Gee also disappeared. According to Bill Podmore, Fred Feast ungraciously refused to extend his contract to enable a tidy exit storyline.

The trio of Terry Duckworth, Kevin Webster and Curly Watts began gathering in the Snug. They were quite a contrast to the triumvirate of Ena, Minnie and Martha that had reigned in that area of the Rovers back when a doorframe separated it from the Public Bar but it was perhaps a measure of changing times: in the 1980s, the concerns of these three thrusting young men were in tune with the *zeitgeist*. The bickering and whimsy of the three old ladies that the viewers had so loved in the more innocent Sixties was not the flavour of the day – and perhaps never would be again.

O f all the people who might plausibly fill the vacancy at the Rovers Return, brassy, immature Bet Lynch did not seem one of them. In 1985, though, The Street's production team decided to take a chance with her – and magicked away Newton & Ridley's policy that only married couples could be licensees at their pubs to do so. Before long, few could remember a time when it did not seem natural that Bet was bossing around cellar-men and bar staff while, as ever, cheerfully calling them 'cock'.

When Peter Armitage declined to sign on as Bill Webster for another 12 months, it meant the destruction of the carefully constructed Webster family. Bill married Percy Sugden's niece and moved away, along with Debbie. Only Kevin Webster stayed, becoming Hilda Ogden's lodger. The replacement family was the Claytons, who bought No.11 in January. They were invented with a somewhat calculating eye, because the BBC's latest prospective rival/answer to The Street – *EastEnders* – was launched in February. In response it was decided by new producer John G. Temple (who clocked on in the first quarter) to invent a domestic set-up which would emphasise why people had always loved The Street: its celebration of the strength of family. But as had already been proven with the Hopkins, and as would be demonstrated in the future with the likes of the Mortons, audiences don't respond to the mathematical and demographical formulae behind the way a new family is devised, but to compelling and/or appealing characters. Who now remembers milkman dad Harry Clayton (Johnny Leeze), dressmaker mum Connie (Susan Brown) and teenage daughters Andrea (Caroline O'Neill) and Sue (Jane Hazelgrove)? The family simply seemed bland and uninteresting. Ironically, their only juicy storyline – Andrea being made pregnant by Terry Duckworth – provided the means by which to write them out: the family fled the interference of Vera in August.

While it is not the case that entire families had never been introduced to The Street in one go – the Tanners had of course all made their entrance back in the very first episode – the tendency had been to ease them in gradually, and this is where The Street may have gone wrong on this occasion. John Stevenson: 'You're more or less bound to get at least one badly miscast, so the favourite way to do it is to bring in a forerunner: the father or the mother who's come looking for work and we hear about the rest of the family but we don't see them. Then if that first character's working, you bring in the spouse and you find they're moving into the street and we'll meet their kids as well…. And with this business of bringing them in in a dribble rather than a rush, you get a chance to observe the actors and see what sorts of situations and stories they seem best able to do, and you then begin to write for their strengths and avoid writing for their weaknesses.' For Stevenson, this dribble method has become all but impossible as The Street's output has increased over the years: 'When you get to three and four [episodes] a week, these things do tend to get rushed a bit. It was much easier when it was two a week to bring people on slowly, see what they could do. If they were working, develop them. If they weren't working, ease them out.'

At least one new character turned out to be a stayer. Martin Platt (Sean Wilson) was introduced as a college kid working in Jim's Café. The Street's viewers would see him grow up and mature over the course of fully 20 years. Meanwhile, Susan Barlow, last seen in 1981, moved in at No.1 – and then to Ken's horror began going out with Mike Baldwin, the man whose ruthless capitalism always had and always would infuriate this staunch socialist.

Audrey Potter decided to marry her way into Alf Roberts' 'fortune'. Alf – who had just been rebuffed by Rita Fairclough, the woman he would always really love – accepted. Said fortune, the Corner Shop, began to look very different in 1985. Following a refurbishment, it became a self-service mini-mart. True to The Street's slight time-lag, in the real world the days of customers needing to ask the counter assistant to reach behind them for the provisions they required had long been a thing of history. In fact, Alf and Maggie Clegg had discussed the possibility of going self-service in an episode way back in 1974. The enlarged floorspace created by the refurbishment meant that the living quarters to the rear of the shop were gone. Alf and Audrey moved upstairs to the flat that had been left vacant by Bet's promotion in January.

September 1985 saw the arrival of a Granada comedy called *The Brothers McGregor* which was sufficiently well-received to last four series. Few realised that it was a *Coronation Street* spin-off. Its genesis lay in a 1982 *Street* episode written by John Stevenson, who recalls, 'I invented them for Eddie Yeats' engagement party. We heard that these two pals of Eddie were coming over, the McGregor brothers. Everybody expected them to be Scots lads or Scottish forefathers, but I made one of them black and one of them white and we got a bit of fun out of them, especially the scenes with Annie, 'cos the black lad kept telling her she put him in mind of his own mum and all that, and it really got up her nose, her being what she was. It was a good episode and worked very well, so I did a memo to David Plowright saying, "I reckon there's a sitcom in these two".' Stevenson collaborated with Julian Roach on the spin-off series. The programme's success came despite the fact that the *Coronation Street* connection was not played up in publicity, although it would have been hard to wring much out of said connection considering the passage of time, the fleeting nature of the principals' *Street* appearance and the fact that the two roles had subsequently been recast.

The rising star that was *EastEnders* dogged The Street throughout 1985. In August, Granada launched *Albion Market*. Twice-weekly (Friday and Sunday evenings) and lasting half-an-hour, it was set in Salford and was devised by long-term *Street* writer Peter Whalley with Andy Lynch, a key writer on *Brookside*. The executive producer was Bill Podmore. Because, like *EastEnders*, much of it took place in and around a street market, and because the BBC programme had preceded it, many perceived it as Granada's response to the threat of *EastEnders*. Furthermore, because *Albion Market*'s scripts occupied the middle ground between The Street's alleged staidness and the BBC programme's achingly PC nature, it almost seemed as though Granada, while stubbornly refusing to radicalise The Street in the style of *EastEnders*, were acknowledging that *EastEnders* was doing something The Street wasn't but in a rather pusillanimous, hive-off of a way.

David Liddiment, who became *Albion Market*'s executive producer in February 1986, fiercely insists that none of this is the case. London Weekend Television, which as its name suggests held the weekend franchise for London, was rather jealous of the ratings/advertising asset Thames Television – which held the capital's weekday franchise – possessed in the shape of The Street episodes in the richest area of Britain on Mondays and Wednesdays. Liddiment: 'This was a Granada initiative to help the weekend schedule by giving them a weekend soap opera that was designed to do what *Coronation Street* did in the weekday. So this was all about the politics of ITV and the balance of power of ITV and it didn't have much to do with *EastEnders*.'

Though the show gained an impressive 60 to 70 per cent share of the audience in the North of England, as it transpired the one region in which *Albion Market* did badly was London. When LWT lost faith in it, the show was doomed, as the London part of the network was paying more than 40 per cent of its costs. Its last episode was broadcast in August 1986, almost exactly one year since its launch.

The year of *Coronation Street*'s Silver Jubilee ended on another *EastEnders*-related sour note. During 1985, *EastEnders* had incrementally built on the almost instant success it had achieved upon its launch and by October had officially reached number one in the weekly ratings for the first time. Possibly in response to the fact that *EastEnders* was planning a Christmas Day broadcast, the year saw the first Christmas Day *Coronation Street* since 1972. It got the traditionally poor Bank Holiday viewing figures that had made Granada discontinue the 25 December episodes more than a decade previously, on this occasion 12.45 million. The only trouble was, the *EastEnders* Christmas Day episode pulled in a cool 15.2 million – and that only on the day itself; it didn't even include the weekend *EastEnders* omnibus broadcast viewings that had become a bone of contention between the programmes. BBC1 controller Michael Grade publicly jeered that if the Christmas competition had been a boxing match, the referee would have stopped the fight. This could be dismissed by The Street's staff as the braggadocio to be expected of a man whose crassness had ruffled many feathers among people who still believed in the public service principles established by the Corporation's first director general John Reith (many of which people being BBC staff). Another relevant point is that the BBC – which tends to pour a disproportionate amount of money into the Yuletide season – traditionally comes out on top at Christmas whatever the show. Not so easy to shrug off was the fact that this blatant imitator seemed to be nosing in front even as it was rewriting the rules of continuing drama serials.

Though *Coronation Street* had never been complacent about the introduction of *EastEnders*, it must have been taken aback at just how popular the BBC show quickly became.

The BBC had just never seemed to get TV soaps – and by now, that is what continuing drama serials with more than one episode per week were generally, and without judgment, referred to – right. Its responses to *Coronation Street* had been laughable. Luxury flats-set *199 Park Lane* (1965) was apparently designed to prove how hopelessly bourgeois the Corporation was. Contemptuously dubbed 'Carnation Street', it expired after 18 episodes. Largely rural *The Newcomers* (also 1965) was more proletarian and was popular enough to last until 1969 but most reading this text will crinkle their brow at its name. Meanwhile women's magazine drama *Compact* (1962–1965) and football club-set *United!* (1965–1967) were reasonably successful but their workplace orientation seemed to suggest nervousness about taking the fight into The Street's domestic territory. The success of ATV's *Crossroads*, Yorkshire TV's rural soap *Emmerdale Farm* (later just *Emmerdale*) and Channel 4's edgy *Brookside* seemed to have made it obvious that the successful ongoing drama serial was exclusively a commercial television phenomenon.

Enter *EastEnders*. Set in the fictional East London district of Walford, its dramatic hub was Albert Square, a grouping of houses surrounding a small, enclosed green. It had a pub – the Queen Victoria – and (in the adjacent Bridge Street) a shop and a café. Those *Street* old-timers who were put in mind by this of that now largely forgotten onetime threat to The Street *Market In Honey Lane*, might well have had a spooky feeling when informed that the outside lot of *EastEnders* had been built on the ground once inhabited by the exterior set of that ATV programme: the BBC had bought ATV's Elstree facilities in Borehamwood in the interim. It was almost as if the ghost of *Market In Honey Lane* was returning to haunt The Street.

The exploits of Albert Square's residents and workers were broadcast twice a week in half-hour episodes. So far, so *Street*. But there were significant differences. The Street had always agonised over the dilemma of knowing that, in order to be true to life, the introduction of black and Asian characters would have to culminate in the depiction of racial discrimination. *EastEnders* got around this problem by simply ignoring it: ethnic characters abounded and, though racism might be touched upon, their main white characters were miraculously uninfected by the very substantial anti-immigration/ethnic attitudes revealed to exist in the real world by opinion polls. Yet far from being condemned for this make-believe, *EastEnders* garnered praise for its supposed realism. Meanwhile, the ridicule directed at The Street over its increasingly unrealistic depiction of an urban community living in each other's pockets was not aimed at *EastEnders*. Smitten pro-PC critics seemed to see nothing unlikely about the denizens not only all speaking to each other with familiarity but knowing each other's names – and this despite Albert Square being in terminally unfriendly London.

Granada's sense of injustice over these matters must only have been intensified by the fact of just how bad *EastEnders* was. The programme was in no way just *Coronation Street* with Lahndan accents. Its scripts were absurd, already caricatured behaviour by the protagonists only made worse by the painfully self-conscious shoehorning in of social issues. And though The Street was no less guilty than any programme, book or film with regards to poetic licence in dialogue, the sing-song, call-and-response, sharp-witted speech in *EastEnders* was so far removed from the invective- and profanity-flecked inarticulacy of most real-life cockneys as to be preposterous. Even the casting was stupid: Den Watts – landlord of the 'Queen Vic' – was supposed to be a hard man but looked like a 'Before' panel in a bodybuilding advertisement. The programme was also infected by doom and gloom: the bonhomie of the cockney was nowhere in evidence in scripts and storylines that were totally humourless. On every level, *EastEnders* seemed a cartoon version of *Coronation Street*.

In fact, one of the curious things about The Street-*EastEnders* rivalry is that, if one didn't know otherwise, one would assume that The Street was the BBC programme and *EastEnders* an ITV product: the former's high-quality makes it seem steeped in Reithian values while the latter show's crassness gives it the smack of something created with an eye for the lowest common denominator and the attendant bedfellows of high ratings and advertising revenue. So much so that it was astonishing – and continues to be so – that the shows aren't an either-or proposition for the public: there seems to be a crossover of demographic that calls into question whether it was ever the intelligent writing and convincing acting on *Coronation Street* that made it beloved of the public.

Another source of a feeling of injustice at The Street was the fact that it had become widely believed that the BBC programme had displaced *Coronation Street* from the top of the ratings. Way back in 1970, John Braine – author of Angry Young Man novel *Room At The Top* and a big *Street* fan – had lamented that he couldn't understand 'why so popular a show should be shown once only. I know that I myself am not always home every Monday and Wednesday at 7.30pm.' Noting that he couldn't be alone in his frustration, he offered a solution: 'What objection could there be to an omnibus edition of The Street on Sunday?' It's not known whether 16 years later an employee of the BBC had recalled this article from a *TV Times* souvenir extra on The Street, but while ITV did not take up Braine's suggestion, scheduling an hour-long omnibus edition of *EastEnders* on Sundays is precisely what the Corporation did. TV ratings company the Broadcasters' Audience Research Board (BARB) permitted the extra figures for this broadcast – which added as much as eight million to the normal stats – to be included in an aggregated rating for *EastEnders*, and with the cruellest irony, it is this that enabled the latter to leapfrog over The Street in the weekly tables. Though Bill Podmore did his best to emphasise to the press that if *EastEnders'* omnibus figures were deducted The Street was the more popular programme, the newspapers preferred the story of the triumph of the new kid on the block, possibly because they were located in London themselves – a perceived bias that was yet another source of grievance in Granadaland.

To some extent, Granada and ITV had no right to feel aggrieved. There was nothing to stop them compiling and broadcasting their own weekend omnibus and thereby wiping out *EastEnders'* artificial ratings superiority. However, the network was reluctant to do this because it was thought that some viewers might not tune in to the weekday episodes if they had the safety net of the knowledge of a weekend repeat, thus damaging the Monday and Wednesday ratings 'tentpoles'. This was, John Stevenson says, a source of no little frustration to the programme's writers, who pleaded for a *Street* omnibus.

This sense of competition or rivalry might seem strange to some. After all, the two shows were not scheduled against each other. The BBC had in 1955 infamously tried to sabotage the first day of transmission of the ITV network by killing off Grace Archer in that evening's edition of radio drama serial *The Archers* (although this was officially denied) but they were hardly going to launch their great white hope in The Street's Monday and Wednesday 7.30pm slots. *Steptoe and Son* and *Blake's 7* were one thing, but two soaps going head to head could only have one result at this stage in history. *EastEnders* was instead broadcast on Tuesdays and Thursdays (originally at 7pm, later 7.30), thus communicating that it was something that might complement rather than compete with The Street in the public's affections. However, attracting big audiences early in the evening was considered very important by the broadcasters: even in this day and age of video recorders, it was assumed that once people had turned on a channel at 7.00 or 7.30, that channel had them for the rest of the night. For a quarter of a century, the success of *Coronation*

Street had meant that, with rare exceptions, ITV 'owned' Mondays and Wednesdays. Now the BBC had a similar audience-grabbing weapon.

If only for the sake of image and wounded pride, ITV and The Street had to respond to the threat, however indirect and abstract it might be. Following on from Alf's shop modernisation the previous year, 1986 saw a similar refurbishment of the Rovers Return, this one the consequence of a fire. The 18 June episode in which the pub was ablaze and Kevin Webster rescued a distraught Bet Lynch was the kind of big event The Street needed at this point. However, by the worst possible stroke of fate, the episode had to be brought forward to 6.15pm to enable transmission of an England World Cup match. Consequently, a *Street* episode got a rare repeat, going out again the next day and thus becoming the most watched episode of the year (22.75 million viewers – staggering for the summer) via the aggregation of viewings of separate transmissions that had so angered The Street when *EastEnders* did it. When the Rovers reopened in August, the Snug and the Select were history: the Rovers now had one big bar instead of two bars and a function room.

Perhaps it would have happened anyway, but the wedding in the 8 October episode of Kevin Webster and Sally Seddon was another ratings grabber, even if this wasn't one of the major, church-set splicings. Sally (played by Sally Whittaker) had first appeared in January. A pretty, perky, blonde girl from a rough family, she seemed to change her hairstyle monthly and was usually resplendent in the day's fashions – laughably 'Sooo Eighties' from this distance in time but then, for a certain demographic, impressive. The newlyweds lodged at No.13 with Hilda Ogden, who was delighted at the way they seemed to exist on 'love and fresh air'. Another marriage this year was intertwined with an intriguing storyline: Mike Baldwin tied the knot with Susan Barlow after seeming to propose only in retaliation for Ken decking him in front of his workforce. With gritted teeth, Ken gave Susan away to his arch enemy in the 14 May ceremony.

After all this, though, there was another Christmas Day bashing for The Street. This was the year of the Yuletide *EastEnders* in which Den Watts confronted his wife Angie about her pretence that she was fatally ill. Discovery of her ruse made him determined to go ahead with the divorce her pretence had been designed to stop and his seethingly delivered line, 'This, my sweet, is a letter from my solicitor', was seen by over 30 million (including the omnibus), while, following last year's damp squib, The Street ducked out of the big day altogether. Additionally, the end-of-year tallies showed that, thanks to that hated *EastEnders* omnibus, in 1986 The Street's usual dominance of the ratings had – to use a phrase that might crop up in *EastEnders* – gone for a burton. Though *Coronation Street*'s most watched episode was seen by 1.35 million more people than the most watched episode of the previous year, only one of its editions made the number one slot in any week – a whopping drop compared to the 32 episodes that had managed that feat in 1985. Once again, tabloid journalists had an excuse to write The Street's obituaries.

Ken and Deirdre became a high-powered couple in 1987. Ken had had good and vital storylines since becoming editor and one-third owner of the *Weatherfield Recorder* in 1983. (He managed to buy the rest of the *Weatherfield Recorder* by remortgaging in 1988.) Deirdre resigned from her shop assistant's role at the Corner Shop and stood as an Independent councillor, though was none too pleased when she discovered Ken was only supporting her campaign because he thought she would split the vote and let the Labour man win. In fact Deirdre triumphed. The pressures her victory would put on the Barlows' marriage were indicated by a denunciation Ken wrote in the paper of a junket on which Deirdre embarked once installed in office.

In The Kabin, Alan Bradley – who had moved in with the proprietor – persuaded Rita to close down the record department in favour of the type of video library then springing up all over Britain. *Street* fans with long memories will recall that originally Rita had a book lending service in the shop.

Cabaret agent Alec Gilroy became the major shareholder in the Rovers Return when Newton & Ridley decided to sell it. Bet Lynch didn't have enough to buy it outright but Alec – who had been fluttering around her recently – stepped in to save the day. They became more than business partners, though, with the pair marrying in September. The stout, bald, bespectacled Gilroy – who had first appeared (with a full-ish head of hair) as a working man's club manager in 1972 – was a calculating but somehow endearing character played brilliantly by Roy Barraclough, familiar to TV viewers from playing a housewife named Cissy opposite Les Dawson in the latter's comedy show.

Don Brennan also made his first appearance. Don was a taxi driver who started romancing Ivy Tilsley. It was the third stint in The Street for, and the third different character played in it by, Geoff Hinsliff. It was also the third era in which Hinsliff had appeared in the soap, if we define eras as being marked by sets: the actor had straddled the original studio *Street* 'interior exterior' set, the Grape Street set and the outdoor lot opened by the Queen. Exactly 10 years previously, his second stint in the show had been playing Eric Bailey for two episodes, a small time crook intent on robbing the Corner Shop with a mate via a diversionary double date with Renee and Bet Lynch. Even apart from his contempt for the stars' airs and graces, Hinsliff had felt a certain anxiety about his first stint in the programme in 1963. 'In those days, actors of any seriousness did not do commercials [and went] nowhere near soaps because of being typecast,' he says. The 1977 gig was easy to do, because it was again too short to adversely affect his career. By 1987, when Bill Podmore – whom he knew from working with him on the Stevenson-Roach-written *Brass* – asked him to appear in The Street again, Hinsliff was not simply deigning to do a short run in the show as a jobbing actor but had other objectives in mind: 'By then I was fifty years old and I was thinking, "Get in out of the cold Geoffrey. You haven't got a pension." Things like that were beginning to occur to me. Of course, I was full of all these memories of how it had been and how these people were and I thought, "Can I live with that? Can I do this for a couple of years with these people?"' He would play Don Brennan for a decade.

Despite his humble origins, Hinsliff has a cultured speaking voice. 'I went to RADA and my speech changed,' he explains. 'I didn't play working class characters initially. Way back in 1960, actors spoke well. The working class genre was just beginning. Everyone insisted at the time, "Look, you can't speak like that and be an actor." That's one of the things that *Coronation Street* [changed].' Don was an odd-man out in The Street in that he didn't have a Mancunian accent. Hinsliff: 'I was born and bred in Leeds and I just used the accent I used to have as a kid.' Also a stark contrast was the difference between Hinsliff's real-life mellifluous tones and the emphatic, almost wrenching enunciation of Don. Hinsliff explains, 'I thought he was an angry guy.'

Don Brennan would be a highly compelling character, but he could never be a replacement for Hilda Ogden, who departed this year. Jean

Alexander decided to hang up her rollers partly because of workload – she had noticed an increase of her lines per episode since major veterans like Len and Elsie had left – and partly due to the fact that she still had acting ambitions left that she wanted to fulfil before it was too late. Fittingly, The Street utilised the farewell of this much-loved icon to give a long desired bloody nose to the competition. The culmination of a storyline that had Hilda moving to Derby to become the housekeeper of a doctor took place on Christmas Day. The regulars in the Rovers assembled to see her off via a surprise party. Hilda sang – in that high-pitched voice the nation had at first been irritated by then come to love for the package that went with it – 'Wish Me Luck As You Wave Me Goodbye.' Appropriately, this landmark episode was given to Leslie Duxbury, another veteran, to write. Upon his retirement in 1991, he had racked up 411 *Street* episodes following his 1966 debut.

Excepting a video compilation, Alexander did one more turn as Hilda, although not in The Street proper but a mini-edition made for ITV's charity Telethon in 1990. Stevenson reveals, 'They've asked her to come back many times but she won't, and it's too late now.'

The Christmas edition meant that for the first time ever three separate episodes of The Street were broadcast in the space of one week. This time, *Coronation Street* was taking no chances with the Yuletide broadcast: the show got massive ratings anyway, but the first ever *Street* omnibus was broadcast the following Sunday – containing this and the previous episode – and ratcheted up the final viewing tally to a massive 26.65 million. Although three million shy of the previous year's Christmas Day *EastEnders*, it beat this year's Xmas edition of the BBC programme by nearly nine million. From here on, a Christmas Day episode would become a permanent fixture of the *Coronation Street* calendar, with the programme only ducking out once (1993) to date.

With Hilda gone, and with her being very fond of her former lodgers, Kevin and Sally Webster were able to purchase No.13 cheaply in 1988. Don Brennan and Ivy Tilsley married in the episode broadcast on 13 June. The big wedding of the year though was that between Derek Wilton and Mavis Riley. Derek proposed to Mavis through the letterbox of The Kabin. Many viewers were amazed that Mavis should accept, considering the way Derek had messed her around for years, but Adele Rose says, 'We thought it was natural. They were both complete ditherers anyway and they were just made for each other. They were the opposite of Len and Elsie: Mavis and Derek together were even stronger than as separate units and we got a huge amount out of that marriage.'

There was a genuine affection between the Wiltons that patently didn't exist in the marriage of Don and Ivy, which was more business-like. An early indication of the fact that Don Brennan had a broiling emotional sea beneath his avuncular outward appearance was his disgusted reaction when Brian Tilsley refused to service his taxi on the cheap now that they were relatives.

Geoff Hinsliff reveals that the longer his latest *Street* stint went on, the less he was perturbed by the celebrity of *Street* stars that had so upset him in 1963. 'I had a lot of friends at *Coronation Street*,' he says. 'As time went by in *Coronation Street*, things became very different and I was into the ambience of what they were experiencing.' What took him a bit longer to get used to was the sparsity of his stage directions. Hinsliff: 'As a theatre actor and an actor of serious plays on television, I thought acting was about reading the script and within the script you'd find the person you were playing and you would at all times be true to the scripts. In soaps, it's a bit different. Because of this aspect of playing yourself, very often soaps don't dictate anything to you within the script. In soap, it's about what you bring and what the writers write will be what they see you doing, not what they think you should be doing. Don Brennan evolved, but evolved very slowly from me because I didn't know I was supposed to do it.'

Ethnic faces had always been dotted around *Coronation Street*: the black bus conductor discriminated against by Len in 1963, the Asian nurse who tended to a hospitalised Minnie Caldwell in 1969, the coloured boys fostered by Emily and Ernest in 1974, the Afro-haired soldier who told Bet her son was dead in 1975, Janice Stubbs, the black waitress via whom Ray Langton had been unfaithful to Deirdre in 1978.... But there had never been any regular character of black or Asian extraction. When in 1988 The Street rectified this running sore, they did so big-time. Shirley Armitage was a beautiful young black woman who had been seen as an employee in Mike Baldwin's factory since 1983 but her moving into the Corner Shop flat made her The Street's first ethnic minority resident. Confronting head-on the dilemma that had always previously prevented The Street incorporating a character of race, the writers instantly involved her in a storyline in which Alf Roberts was clearly opposed to her living in the flat because of her colour. Not only did The Street – as with the Len Fairclough/black conductor story thread – run the risk of spoiling a main character in viewers' eyes (or alternately, legitimising his racism to sections of the populace), they also dived head-first into miscegenation: Curly Watts moved into the shop flat with her (Alf backed down after Emily Bishop remonstrated with him in front of his customers) and Shirley took Curly's virginity. The couple would split up the following year when Curly's new business ambitions made Shirley feel they were mismatched (in reality, Lisa Lewis, who played Shirley, left to have a baby), but the ground had been broken.

The Granada Studios Tour opened in 1988, a theme-park style affair which enabled the general public to walk on mock and real sets of Granada productions. Many people who attended were completely uninterested in the likes of a facsimile of Baker Street as seen in *The Adventures of Sherlock Holmes* but instead came just to grab the opportunity to walk down the genuine exterior lot of *Coronation Street*. Fans would have always surreal-seeming pictures taken of them outside the Corner Shop and get a personal video made in the Rovers exchanging lines of dialogue with a *Street* character. Most of the visitors were unaware that the New York-themed entrance area of the tour stood on the ground once occupied by the Grape Street exterior set. The tour was closed on Mondays to enable The Street's exterior scenes to be shot. The enterprise was closed down in 1999, not so much because of the inevitable quotient of visitors to the cobbles who flipped their blouses up for snaps that ended up in the *Sunday Sport* but according to John Stevenson because, 'It cost a lot of money in personnel to have people on all the corners and show people around and all that. It didn't make much money.'

The same year saw the demise of *Crossroads*. Recently, its raised production values meant that it had ceased to be the programme that launched a thousand spoofs, but that seemed to be missing the point: what the public wanted were surely its twangy Tony Hatch theme tune and its iconic characters like the Thatcheresque Meg Richardson, the idiotic Benny and the simpering Diane Hunter, and all had latterly been dispensed with. There was a brief two-year revival in the Noughties, but The Street had essentially seen off another pretender to its crown.

CORONATION STREET

The departure of John Temple in 1987 and the retirement of Bill Podmore the following year paved the way for a new regime at *Coronation Street*. The programme gained a new executive producer in 1988 in the shape of David Liddiment, while Mervyn Watson returned as producer. The pair would make 1989 one of the most seismic in *Coronation Street*'s history.

Though David Liddiment was officially exec producer, he had a hands-on approach with The Street one more readily associates with the role of producer. Liddiment had been at Granada since leaving university in 1975. As well as taking over as producer of the *Street*-esque *Albion Market* halfway though its run, he had produced a documentary made to mark The Street's 25th anniversary. Says Liddiment, 'I was asked by the director of programmes to take over the show as exec producer because I'd always shown a great interest in it.'

Under Liddiment came possibly the most comedic *Street* character of all, the garishly spectacled, colossally vainglorious Reg Holdsworth, manager of the Bettabuys supermarket where the upwardly mobile Curly Watts became a trainee assistant manager. Only intended to be a temporary character before Curly took over his job, the production team were so knocked out by Ken Morley's gloriously over-the-top performance on his October 1989 debut that he became a permanent fixture. However, Reg was the exception. Under Liddiment, the humour pendulum swung back a little. While Podmore had injected a much needed levity into a latterly dour programme, Liddiment concluded that in recent years this had been too much at the expense of The Street's gritty *raison d'etre*. That pendulum swing, though, was a very small tweak compared to the other changes Liddiment set in motion.

Before taking up his post Liddiment had made it clear to his higher-ups that despite his love for The Street – which went back to the days when Minnie Caldwell had reminded him of his own gran – he felt it needed a massive updating that would be in a different league to its standard periodic rejuvenations. 'And they were very sympathetic to that.' He explains, 'Bill had done a fantastic job, but it was starting to look a little tired because *Brookside* had arrived a few years before and then *EastEnders* came along and both of them looked like they were made at the time and of the time, while *Coronation Street* frankly was still being made in the way it had been made in the very beginning.' The list of problems with The Street, for Liddiment, was a long one: 'It was made in Studio Six, which was quite a small studio, which meant there could only be five sets across two episodes – The Rovers plus four others. The sets had to be put up every week and therefore they got bashed around a lot and the lighting time was limited. The location work was shot on film and the studio was done on video tape. So the show looked very old-fashioned. Each episode had about fourteen scenes, so it was quite slow in its pace. And you compared that to *Brookside*, which was all shot on location, in real houses, with a range of characters and stories that were rooted in what was happening in the early Eighties. And then along came *EastEnders*. It looked real. It had a dedicated studio, so the interior lighting of the sets was so much better. Many more sets were available every week, which meant there was greater pace and variety to the episodes.'

Liddiment was appalled at a story conference when the discussion turned to a plot thread revolving around Alf Roberts' humiliation over his credit card being refused in a shop because of wife Audrey's profligacy. Liddiment: 'John Stevenson said, "And Alf will tell the story to…" whoever it was. And I said, "Well we should see that moment. That's a fantastic moment – we should see him in the store." What John was doing, of course, was editing according to the resourcing of the programme.' Liddiment decided to shoot everything on videotape and to open out the show as much as possible. The programme now began to feature extensive location shooting not as the stuff of special event like the day trips of previous years but as a matter of course. He explains, 'Lightweight video equipment was now becoming commonplace so it was easier and faster to do more on location than it had been before. It never looked right [in] *Coronation Street* to shoot the interiors on video tape and the exteriors on film, so making it all video was better.' That static quality to The Street that had so often made it resemble a stage play or a shortened version of *Play for Today* – the famous, worthy but studio-bound, BBC drama slot – was gone forever.

Liddiment secured The Street some more studio space within the main Granada studio complex. This itself was a preamble to acquiring The Street its exclusive permanent space in 1990, the recently constructed studio Stage One, which in those days was used as a multi-purpose film stage. Handily, it was located right next to The Street's outside lot. 'It gave us a kind of little village to produce the show from,' says Liddiment.

'We took over that stage completely, where we could have as many as twelve standing sets, which just gave the writers and the production team much more flexibility. It meant we could have more sophisticated lighting to make the interiors look more realistic; meant they weren't battered around every time they were taken in and out of the studio. It meant that The Street could have its own headquarters with its own green room, its own dressing room, its own space.' Rehearsals could now take place on the actual sets on which they would be filmed, rather than – as hitherto – in a rehearsal room that was featureless bar the occasional chair or table and sticky tape marking out where walls notionally stood. In 1992, Granada increased the studio space available to The Street even further, partly by making use of facilities left redundant by the closure of the Granada Studios Tour.

There was yet more. A property developer called Maurice Jones persuaded Mike Baldwin to sell the factory after buying the Community Centre and surrounding land. Cue another facelift of the non-terraced side of The Street, but, more importantly, the one that finally 'took'. Recalls Liddiment, 'I went for a walk around Salford and I noticed there were pockets of development. There were big signs up with new housing and some industrial units all backed by European money, which was all about industrial regeneration. I thought, "The Street needs to not just move on in terms of production and location and modernise, the fabric of The Street needs to evolve as well." And that's where the thoughts for the new houses and the new factory unit came from.' Was the terraced side of The Street untouchable? Liddiment: 'Absolutely. Absolutely. And indeed, there were streets in Salford where the terraced houses were absolutely intact, and right adjacent to them would be warehousing and modern housing. So that redevelopment of the other side of Coronation Street was absolutely intended to mark a step change in this modernisation process. It did two things. It gave us a different kind of house that could mark some of the social changes that had happened to Britain. It also made the street a more interesting space physically to shoot in so there were more angles, which meant that we could write more of The Street *on* the street rather than just in the houses and in the shop and the pub.'

This was a long-term project, with the non-terraced side reduced to a building site for several months from late summer onwards (the demolition of the outside lot's Community Centre and factory shells was filmed from several angles for use in the programme) and the redevelopment not completed until 1990. But whereas the maisonettes had been a veritable joke and the Community Centre and Baldwin's Casuals only moderately effective, Liddiment's face-lift would almost double the dramatic potential of The Street in the way it finally provided both houses and workplaces whose inhabitants smoothly and visibly interacted with the people on the other side of the street.

Though the move wasn't done with it in mind, obtaining The Street its own studio is what enabled Liddiment to authorise yet another revolutionary move this year. Liddiment: 'This modernisation made the third episode possible.' In his 1981 autobiography, Harry Kershaw said of The Street, '...it has resisted every attempt to increase its weekly output. Two twenty-five minute episodes are as much as body, soul and any acceptable standards can endure and by restricting output to this level, successive producers have been able to produce what they think is a quality article.' Additionally, for three decades, producers had been lamenting that the turnaround time of one week was insufficient to produce even two weekly episodes of Coronation Street free of blemishes. However, Liddiment concluded that technology and resources had moved on sufficiently to offer a third episode without sacrificing quality. In fact, there was an increase in quality, as the extra studio time enabled directors to banish negative hallmarks of the programme like fluffed lines and boom shadows. Some have posited a feeling of a need to steal a march over EastEnders for the third weekly, Friday episode of Coronation Street but Liddiment and his crew felt that the increased quality and expansion of The Street had already dealt with whatever threat emanated from Albert Square. 'At the time, the story that was spun was that our researcher told us that there was the appetite for more Coronation Street,' confesses Liddiment, 'It was much more about the internal politics of ITV.' As with Albion Market before it, the Friday edition of The Street came into being through the desire of ITV franchise London Weekend Television (which transmitted from early evening on Fridays to Sunday night) to have an anchor point like Thames.

The first Friday night episode of The Street since 3 March 1961 was screened on 20 October 1989. The lack of consistent scheduling across the network that had done for The Street's rival Market In Honey Lane – and which would plague The Street's own omnibus, introduced this January, for years to come – was not an option. 'We wouldn't have offered a third episode had we not secured 7.30 on a Friday night and unanimity around the network,' says Liddiment. 'And they bit our hands off, I can tell you.' Despite the subterfuge mentioned above, Liddiment does admit that the public's response in the market research on the third episode was genuinely positive and the Friday edition's introduction beneficial: 'There was a nice pattern about Monday-Wednesday-Friday, even recognising that people tend to do different things on Friday night than a normal week night. The third episode was a wonderful extra boost to us because it gave a further shot of adrenalin to the show.'

When Alf and Audrey moved out of No.11 in December, the new residents were the McDonalds, a classic two parents-two kids set-up, introduced because it was decided that The Street was currently weak on family units. This deficit, explains, Liddiment, will inevitably occur quite regularly: 'The thing about soap opera[s] is they eat up stories and eating up story means you're breaking people up and you're breaking family units up and you're making new connections.' The McDonalds were belligerent, Irish ex-army man Jim (Charles Lawson), his flame-haired, tough-as-nails wife Liz (Beverley Callard) and their twin 15-year-old sons Steve (good-looking but shallow, played by Simon Gregson) and Andy (less of a looker but brainy, played by Nicholas Cochrane). The latter pair helped address another identified deficiency. Liddiment: 'The average age across the occupants of The Street was too high.' There would be more youth to follow. The days when someone like Lucille Hewitt could be the sole voice of the young generation on the show (one furthermore played by a woman five/six years older than her screen age) were perceived as increasingly unfeasible. This was a far cry from the Seventies when future *Brookside* creator Phil Redmond was invited to three story conferences by Bill Podmore and declined to come aboard when his ideas for more unlined faces were rebuffed.

Despite this, Liddiment admits that veterans Ken Barlow and Emily Bishop were as untouchable as the terraced side of The Street. 'As far as I was concerned, for as long as they wanted to be in the show they were in the show, and it was up to the writers to be ingenious and inventive in creating interesting stories for them,' he says. 'It's not sentimentality. It's, "What an extraordinary thing that one actor plays the same part for [their] virtual adult lifetime and what an asset that is to give a sense of continuity to a show that's about everyday life." Don't wilfully abandon that.' Again, a far cry from before. Podmore once wrote, 'Ken has side-stepped more assassination attempts than JR Ewing, and I'm sure that clandestine plans for half those little coups never even reached his ears.'

In many ways, Liddiment's rebuilding of the non-terraced side and his absorption of trends in wider society was an echo of what had been attempted by his predecessor Richard Everitt just over two decades previously. The main difference was that Liddiment was able to secure the one thing whose absence ultimately undermined Everitt's plans: cash. For the first time in its history, Granada stopped being parsimonious with the programme that like it or not (and some didn't) was their flagship. 'More money thrown at it,' is Adele Rose's recollection of the period. Says Liddiment, 'The advent of *EastEnders* and *Brookside* was a wake-up call to Granada and the ITV network to get its act together on its most popular show, invest in it and make it feel like people were living in the same Britain as its viewers. The whole business of the big Stage One studio, the rebuilt *Coronation Street*, more location shooting – not just on The Street but elsewhere in the area – a bigger cast, more scenes per episode, all cost money. It represented a very significant investment in the show from Granada.'

The tornado of rejuvenation reached everywhere this year, including that irritant, the illusion of *EastEnders*' viewing figures superiority. The aforementioned weekend *Coronation Street* omnibus was introduced by new director of programmes Steve Morrison. Though it took many years for ITV regions to agree a full networking and consistent time for the omnibus, it allowed The Street to fight back sufficiently to get rid of a nagging feeling of ratings injustice that Liddiment describes as 'infuriating'.

The Street's writers were not merely given new toys in the form of being able to set scenes in relatively exotic locations and more sets per episode, but were asked to rethink the way they did things. 'Thinking more ambitiously about stories and making the most of the story opportunities that come along, so seeds that are planted are fed and watered and grow into stories that everyone's talking about,' explains Liddiment. 'A little bit more longer-term thinking about where stories are heading. This is quite a delicate process.' Unlike other producers, Liddiment made his changes without alienating the writers. The excitement of the changes seemed to infect them. The Street's scripts became ever more sophisticated, the occasional clunkiness and sometimes manufactured cliffhangers of the show seeming to disappear with the advent of the third episode. The programme was now sometimes so rich in detail and nuance that it was almost difficult to keep up. It was the start of a golden era on the show rivalling, for aficionados, that of the early Sixties.

Liddiment also had to get the actors on side. The quality of the scripts they received put their minds at rest on one score. 'I wasn't sceptical so much as worried it was going to be stretching it,' admits William Roache. 'The writers did a brilliant job. Suddenly they're going to produce another fifty per cent.' However, there were considerations other than the aesthetic ones. Even before the third episode, the extra location shoots had meant the introduction of weekend work, necessitating Liddiment having to get rid of some Spanish practices. Liddiment: 'People get into the habit – those who lived in London – "We come up on a train on the Monday morning and we then have a quiet word with our director and say, 'Could you schedule my scene so I can get the four o'clock back on a Friday afternoon?'" That sort of thing was going on. It was a very cosy little pattern of work. It stopped the show moving forward....' Though there were compensations to the weekend shoots – 'They all loved the increase in location work because it was more like making movies,' points out Liddiment – the third episode required even more delicate manoeuvring. The exec says, 'I think there was a degree of wariness from certainly the longstanding cast. We explained to them how it was going to work, how actually there would be a little bit more work but not as much as they would think because there were going to be more members of cast, it'd be spread around more.' Naturally, the fact that the more episodes the cast worked on, the more money they earned also helped to dispel disquiet. As with the writers, ultimately, no cast members were lost in the shuffle.

The final – essential – element was getting the press on The Street's side. Though Fleet Street was always happy to write about the programme, in recent years it had often been in unusually disparaging tones. Liddiment thinks this was less to do with the London solidarity alleged to have made the capital-based papers prefer *EastEnders* than with neglected public relations. 'There used to be quite a strong Manchester-based press corps,' Liddiment says. 'They'd pretty much all gone by the time I took over. Within Fleet Street, The Street was regarded as a bit of a pain because they jealously protected their people and they didn't much want to join in with leaking stories and so on. Any newcomer, whether it was Channel Four or the BBC, was anxious to get as much press and publicity as they could, so they had a very different attitude. It was all part of the living-in-the-modern-world adjustment that we made. We were just a little bit more pragmatic about the need to recognise that the press have an agenda and doing our best where we can to help.'

It was Liddiment and Watson who appointed Daran Little *Street* archivist. The role had been vacant for several years since Eric Rosser's retirement. Little is a Londoner born in 1966, 'The week that Ena Sharples put up for shoplifting'. That he measures time via events in the programme's history is not much of a surprise. Little: 'I was brought up on a diet of *Coronation Street* by my grandmother. I used to ask her questions, I was interested in characters. When I was thirteen there was a couple of questions she couldn't answer, so I wrote to Granada asking the questions and I got a letter back from Eric Rosser. It was the first I'd ever heard of that kind of job. I remember saying to a teacher "That's the job I'm going to have." And I got it when I was twenty-one, my first job.' Little had made contacts with The Street office after moving to Manchester to do his degree in film and television production. His dissertation was on Tony Warren, who introduced him to the show's top brass.

Little inherited a card index system of Rosser's that he found patchy. Meanwhile, *Street* scriptwriter Barry Hill would come into the office after every story conference to use the resident computer – the only one in Granada at the time – to type a brief summary of what had happened to the characters over the previous three weeks. Little: 'I spent the next three-and-a-half years watching very single episode that had ever been made and I wrote down what happened in every single episode, every reference to any backstory, any reference to any characters we'd never seen. The first few years were on film, then it was on two-inch big tapes, which were disintegrating, then one-inch tapes, and then ultimately they were on Beta tapes. I transferred every episode onto Beta tape, which was the most modern thing then, and also got VHS copies of everything that was done. I could locate specific scenes by time-code and so I would write down key quotes and stuff like that. I used to keep a register which I used to alert the producers to, "Well, Julie Goodyear's coming up to two thousand episodes, we should give her a party", that kind of thing.'

During his 11 years as archivist, Little's job changed and grew. Little: 'I started off as archivist and then I became archives and researcher and then I became archives, research and merchandising, and they gave me this title which was Manager of Drama Serials, which was very grand.' The Street/Granada, he says, were 'raking in' money from merchandise based on the archives, including books, videos, key rings and caricatures that were sold by The Street's shop on the Granada Studios Tour, their mail order company and shopping TV channel QVC. At around this juncture, the first official *Coronation Street* magazine was published. Entitled *The Street*, it ran for three years. The second – *The Official Magazine of Coronation Street* – started in 1994 and was edited by Little. Though that too folded, Granada tried the format again in 2003, this time with a DVD. As with the previous efforts, it sustained enough interest to last a few years.

When a writer suggested at story conference a plot wherein the Rovers was painted blue, Little felt compelled to intercede because The Street brand over which he presided would be affected as the pub and its merchandise was historically green. His attendance at those story conferences, incidentally, led to him having a direct influence on the show he had always loved. Little: 'I was putting forward stories of my own: the death of Susan Barlow and discovering that she hadn't had an abortion. Things like Alf Roberts getting the OBE.'

He also wrote 11 books about the show, some the glossy histories one would expect, others creatively lateral views on the programme such as *Weatherfield Life* – which was predicated on the idea that the titular district was real – and *Around The Houses*, which went into great detail about who lived in all the houses right from their notional building date of 1902 and which used a mixture of childhood photos of cast members, historical pictures bought from the likes of Manchester antique fairs and Little's own family albums. All the backstory he devised in these books became part of The Street's official history.

15 February saw the death of Brian Tilsley in a violent stabbing when he attempted to save a young woman under attack. This story was inherited from Podmore, who – despite assuring Chris Quentin his character would not be killed off – had decided that Quentin's opting to spend most of his time with his wife across the Atlantic meant that there was no way to retain Brian. Podmore worried his betrayal would lead to Quentin refusing to come back to play his death scene so it was kept secret and for the first time ever the storyline was not distributed around the various departments at Granada who ordinarily would expect to receive it.

There was also a very dramatic storyline involving the mental and moral decline of Alan Bradley, who started the year by fraudulently mortgaging Rita's house in order to set himself up in business. When Rita uncovered his fraud, she threatened to go to the police, but Alan tried to suffocate her. He was only prevented from doing so by his daughter Jenny walking in. Tried for assault, Bradley was sentenced to the six months he had spent in prison and, walking free, came back to torment Rita by taking a job on the building site now located where the Community Centre/Baldwin's factory had been. The denouement of the story saw him fatally run over by a tram when he followed Rita to Blackpool, to where she'd fled to escape his evil stare.

Though intermittently exciting, the storyline frankly never felt quite right: Bradley's propensity for evil had not been properly established previously and the whole affair had the smack of a storyline being grafted onto a character. 'If you're asking me which was the best drama story The Street has ever had, that's got to be a contender, 'cos it played for months without getting repetitive,' John Stevenson demurs. 'Barbara Knox was absolutely brilliant as Rita as he gradually tore down her life and her own self-esteem and her own self-confidence, and Mark Eden who played Alan Bradley was terrific too, I felt.' Liddiment: 'You've got to respect the characters but you can't be slave to them. I think Alan Bradley was kind of going nowhere. He was a good actor but there weren't great stories coming up for him. There's a dangerous place in *Coronation Street*, the middling place he was in, and if the writers aren't inspired to come up with good stories for you, you're a dead duck. Peter Whalley had this notion that he would pretend to be Len Fairclough, which was the original name on the deeds of Rita's house. I thought that was a very clever idea. Once he'd deceived his wife, you can start to build on that. It wasn't, "Let's turn Alan Bradley into an evil person." What the writing conference does, it takes a simple idea, it captures the imagination of a group of writers and then they improvise on that over a period of time and the story evolves into something that in that particular case caught the public's imagination in a big way, stretched that actor in a way that he wouldn't otherwise have been, which in turn meant that the actors who played with him were all stretched to do different things.'

Far more plausible, and far more effective, was the affair embarked upon by Ken Barlow with Wendy Crozier. Wendy was a council secretary who was feeding Ken's newspaper details of confidential council committee meetings, which leaks brought Deirdre under suspicion. When – thanks to Deirdre – Wendy was discovered to be the source of the leaks and sacked, Ken took her on as his secretary at *The Weatherfield Recorder* and they fell in love. Deirdre discovered their affair and threw Ken out on New Year's Eve.

On an apparently more trivial but actually just as important note, in 1989 Jack Duckworth acquired the plaster holding his glasses together that would become iconic. The Duckworths' house gained something that would be just as iconic: stone cladding, then all the rage in Britain. It could almost serve as a metaphor for the way The Street had acquired a completely new look this year.

Part Five

The Nineties

In the year of its 30th anniversary, *Coronation Street* really began to take on a different look as the rebuilding of its non-terraced side was completed.

By the end of the first quarter of 1990, that side would have three houses (Nos 4, 6 and 8), all of which had gardens, a lush contrast to the other side's 'coal holes'. It also boasted two shops. One was bought by Rita, who transferred The Kabin from Rosamund Street, the other by Audrey Roberts, who opened a hairdressing salon. The shops had flats above them and there was another flat (No.12) whose entrance was next to The Kabin. An additional commercial unit (entrance actually in Rosamund Street) was attached to Audrey's salon and would in time become the home of the Streetcars taxi service. In a sort of irregularly-shaped horseshoe between The Kabin and No.8 was located a factory that would be bought by Mike Baldwin and a commercial garage repair unit (ultimately the property of Kevin Webster).

Never again would people legitimately be able to claim that *Coronation Street* was marooned in the 1960s, clinging to a boast of portraying ordinary folk that was debased by the fact that the architecture surrounding those folk was little seen in real life. With perhaps one exception: the archaic living arrangements in the terraced houses, unchanged in most of them since 1960. Who now spends the majority, or any, of their time in a combined kitchen-living room? As John Stevenson says, 'It was always a bit of an embarrassment because all those houses are supposed to have a front room just as you go through the front door, but you very rarely see that front room.' Having said that, it's somehow sweet that this means that several of the houses in Coronation Street retain floorplans and living arrangements based on the interior of the home of Tony Warren's long-departed maternal grandmother.

The architectural changes were reflected in the new title sequence, which began on 15 October, the first to be recorded on videotape rather than film. Once again a cat was included in the opening titles was maintained, although the serendipity that had occasioned it in 1976 was superseded by a calculating eye for publicity that resulted in a competition taking place for recruitment of the new feline star.

Derek and Mavis Wilton moved their belongings, their budgie and the trivia with which they surrounded themselves into No.4 in March. The Platts moved into No.8 from nearby Hammond Road in 1991. Carolyn Reynolds – shortly to become *Street* producer – explains of incorporating the Wiltons and the Platts (regular cast members but hitherto non-residents) into the Street itself, 'There was a sense that we had lost a lot of characters to a place outside of the street that people didn't know or care about, so there was a drive to make it more insular in a way, more, "Let's just look at this pocket of humanity on the street".'

By default, a white collar worker (Derek) broadened the social caste, but the biggest statement of Liddiment's determination to mix up the nature of the type of people who lived in Coronation Street was the February installation in No.6 of Des and Stephanie Barnes. Geordie Des (Philip Middlemiss) was a bookie's clerk and brash but decent. Steph (Amelia Bullmore) was the daughter of developer Maurice Jones, who had built No.6 and everything else on that side of the street. She was a make-up counter assistant. Personality-wise, she too was brash with a tinge of not always benign mischievousness. Though the word Yuppie had lately exhausted its shelf-life, Des and Steph were of that young, upwardly mobile professional class the acronym had been prompted by and who unquestionably not only still existed but were a growing presence in society.

Regarding the redevelopment, Stevenson says, 'That caused quite a big debate as to whether it would alter the whole nature of the programme, but it was generally thought not a bad idea because you'd get the contrast between the sort of people who'd always been in the terraced houses and the sort of people who would have their sights raised a little and would go for semis even if they were across the road from a series of dirty old terraces.' Liddiment: 'We were trying to live in the real world and in the real world…the working class that Tony Warren wrote about in 1960 was not as homogenous, and owner-occupation rather than renting your house was becoming more and more of a norm. Britain was changing. The aspiration of many people was starting to get realised. More and more people were going into education. The social behaviour of people was changing and it's important if you are Britain's most popular programme and you are about the lives of ordinary people that you understand that and reflect that.' How appropriate then that shooting in the first week of the Barnes' appearances should be attended by Prime Minister Margaret Thatcher, whom many credited with the social revolution that had made people like the Barnes possible. It should be noted, however, that in Northern regions like Manchester/Salford, Mrs Thatcher was not at all popular, with many there feeling that massive unemployment and steeply rising interest rates were as much hallmarks of her policies as self-improvement.

When Rita moved into the new Kabin's shop flat (10a), the vacated No.7 became a hotbed of the youth that Liddiment had wanted more of in The Street, inhabited first by Jenny Bradley and her fellow student, Asian girl Flick Khan (Rita Wolf) and subsequently colourful fashion student and pint-lifter Angie Freeman (Deborah McAndrew). Flick's little sister Joanne Khan briefly ran away to the Lake District with Steve McDonald this year.

Despite the acknowledgment of the new breed of the upwardly mobile in the form of the Barnes, and Manchester's Asian community in the Khans, there was still no addressing of the lack of homosexuals that many considered a problem with the programme. Though Liddiment is gay, he says he felt no moral obligation to tackle the issue. 'You take things one step at a time and the idea that you turn *Coronation Street* into *Brookside* or *EastEnders* would have been a mistake,' he says. 'You have to evolve over time…. What makes *Coronation Street* special is its unique blend of everydayness and music hall/showbusiness, so it's more important that *Coronation Street* retains its own way of being than it's gay or black or blue or middle class or working class…. It's what grows out of the characters and feels right for the characters, so it never crossed my mind that we should have this kind of sexuality or that. It was not an issue.'

fter a brief period living with Wendy Crozier, Ken Barlow decided that he had made the biggest mistake of his life and begged Deirdre to take him back. Deirdre refused and in the nasty divorce process that followed Ken was forced to sell the *Weatherfield Recorder*. The latter was in retrospect a bad move by the storyliners. A character is only as good as the plots he is given and since losing that high-powered role from which compelling stories emanated naturally, Ken has never seemed a truly dynamic character. Nonetheless, he was involved in a superb storyline this year that saw step-daughter Tracy feeling increasing contempt for him as he became ever more desperate to woo Deirdre back. Mortified by Ken complaining to her that her mother was 'going to bed' with her new man, Tracy screamed at him that he was 'Pathetic!' and fled. Alone in No.1, Ken set about committing suicide – only to be stopped by Bet Gilroy before he could swallow his bottle of pills. Incidentally, the time Ken spent cohabiting with Wendy and his subsequent few months living in a flat in an unnamed street are the only times in his entire life that Ken has not had a permanent home in Coronation Street.

In 1991 Mervyn Watson was replaced as *Coronation Street* producer by Carolyn Reynolds. Reynolds had previously worked for The Street in the production department under Podmore. She had been producer of *Families*, a massively ambitious daytime Granada ITV soap of over a hundred episodes shot in both the UK and Australia. She, rather like Harry Kershaw and Bill Podmore, would mould The Street by switching between producer and executive producer roles over a protracted period. Also like Kershaw and Podmore, she became so steeped in The Street and so associated with its successful periods that she would be brought back in when it was felt the show was in trouble in her absence. John Stevenson says, 'She was a great perfectionist and a very good judge of stories. I would put her and Bill Podmore as about equal tops [as producers]. She was good at managing people.'

25 January 1991 saw the debut appearance of Raquel Wolstenhulme. A cashier at Bettabuys, she was intended to be merely a plot device in a storyline exploring Curly Watts' frustrating love life but such was the brilliance of the performance of actress Sarah Lancashire that she would become a longstanding character. 'She and John Stevenson really created

that character,' says Liddiment. 'It was a sort of riff of John's in a story conference. He came up with this extraordinary name, this wonderful contradiction of "Raquel" – which evoked Raquel Welch, a glamorous name – and "Wolstenhulme", which is very down to earth and convoluted, awkward. The character came out of the name and the actress picked up on what she got from the writers and the writers picked up what she was doing with the character. The writers and the actors rarely meet, but they feed off each other in the most exciting way.' Originally a rather hard-faced young woman, as with so many *Street* characters down the years, Raquel was necessarily softened up to inspire viewer empathy and ended up as a sort of modern day Irma Ogden/Barlow, an ingénue who made up in good nature what she lacked in intellectual depth.

Recently, Mike Baldwin had had a rival as the most ruthless man on Coronation Street in the shape of businessman smoothie – and boyfriend of Deirdre Barlow – Phil Jennings. Inevitably, the two were mates. Both men came unstuck in 1991. Mike was awash with money after the factory sale but lost it all in a bad Spanish land deal. He became a humble salesman for a while, before landing on his feet by marrying into money. When Mike refused to help out a financially embarrassed Phil, he paid the ultimate price for his lack of sympathy: Phil told Jackie Ingram – Mike's wife of one week – of the financial motivations behind his wooing her following the death by heart attack of her husband Peter. Though Mike was temporarily reduced to living above the Rovers, with a £100k-plus-Jag pay-off from Jackie, he wasn't as badly off as Phil, who had to flee to escape his debtors – but not before a woman present in his house when Deirdre went to see him dropped the bombshell that she was his wife. Peter Ingram, incidentally, was played by Tony Osoba, who had been Wesley McGregor in The Street prior to that part being recast for the spin-off *The Brothers McGregor*.

Amelia Bullmore had decided that one year in The Street was enough and she was written out via an infidelity story that culminated in Des setting fire to the Barnes' boat after a disastrous canal trip on which the Platts had been their horrified guests. The caring side of Alec Gilroy was seen when his teenaged granddaughter Vicky was orphaned and he adopted her. Vicky seemed 'toffee-nosed' to a contemptuous Tracy Barlow, but her posh Cheshire background furthered the Liddiment cause of broadening the caste range that people associated with the programme.

Three 1991 storylines highlighted The Street's imperishable ability to play funny without resorting to slapstick or undermining the drama. Curly Watts engaged in an apocalyptical tussle with building society worker Adrian Gosthorpe for the affections of Kimberley Taylor in a period in which Curly was the most compelling character in The Street, something assisted by some superb tragicomic performances from Kevin Kennedy. Mavis Wilton turned out to be a woman of hidden passions when Derek was failing to fulfil his matrimonial duties, and after seeking the advice of her female friends decided to feed her husband parsnips. It worked a little too well. Vera Duckworth's mother died this year and it was at her funeral that she first met Joss Shackleton, the man who claimed to be her father. That was never fully established – nor was Joss' claim that *his* father was King Edward VII. Vera, though, was tickled pink that she might have blue blood in her veins and invited Joss to share her home. Jack, though, thought he was a fraud and was infuriated by his royal pretensions like demanding a pinch of tarragon in his scrambled eggs.

Martin Platt and Gail Tilsley married in September, despite Gail's reservations about Martin being 10 years her junior, and the Platts moved into No.8 three months later. Reynolds attributes the new house lying empty for so long simply to the fact that the programme's writers had felt they already had enough storylines to be getting on with.

Demonstrating that The Street was now embracing the idea of Christmas Day episodes with a vengeance, there were not one but two episodes broadcast on 25 December in 1991, separated by 3½ hours. Not only that, but the first episode featured an audacious conceit whereby Alf Roberts sat down halfway through to watch the Christmas Day Queen's speech – which then proceeded to be shown for real, The Street resuming immediately afterwards.

The start of 1992 saw a tragedy that was the making of Jim McDonald as a character.

The previous year, his wife Liz had been surprised to find out she was pregnant. Jim talked her out of a termination. However, Liz's acquiescence on the grounds that this was her last realistic chance of having another child ended in tears and shattered dreams when baby Katie died on 2 January, one day after she was born. Jim was genuinely grief-stricken and actor Charles Lawson was finally given a chance to do something other than condescend to Liz, bawl out his sons and aim gratuitous insults like 'Fatso' at Alf Roberts. A public that had initially been sceptical of him and his sometimes incomprehensible Irish vernacular began to be won round.

1992 was the year when the Broadcasting Standards Council took it upon itself to deliver a broadside against The Street. This regulatory body – or Taste And Decency Watchdog to use the tabloid term – was headed by Lord Rees-Mogg, who back in 1967 when he was plain William Rees-Mogg, editor of *The Times*, was widely credited with springing Mick Jagger and Keith Richards of The Rolling Stones from prison by publishing an editorial that was scathing about their apparently discriminatory drug use-related sentences. Similar liberalism seemed to inform his organisation's October 1992 claim that The Street was '...out of touch with reality and living in the Harold Macmillan era' because its failure to feature anything like as many ethnic faces as *EastEnders* and *The Bill* (an ITV police drama that had taken on the look of a soap by changing its format from one weekly hour-long episode to two half-hour broadcasts per week) made it only 'an accurate portrayal of life 25 years ago.' The BSC had come to its conclusions via research drawn from 12 discussion groups and a telephone poll of 500 people, where the consensus was that the lack of non-whites on *Coronation Street* was unrealistic, with an interesting point being made that had not often been before: Manchester now had a large Chinese population.

John Stevenson: 'It would come up from time to time but in the Seventies and Eighties the black community – I mean black, as against Asian – was very much in one small pocket on Moss Side and in most of the working class streets you wouldn't see a black face, so it wasn't quite the turning the face away from reality that people sometimes said it was.... There were occasional black characters and occasional Asian ones but it was always felt you shouldn't be writing to anybody's social thesis.' The official response from David Liddiment, who this year became Director of Programmes at ITV, was, 'Lord Rees-Mogg might like to talk to any of the eighteen million viewers who watch *Coronation Street* and discover an entirely different view. The idea that serial drama is there to directly reflect real life is a false one. It is there to entertain, not provide a demographic reflection of Britain.' This seems a strangely anodyne response for a man who had done so much in recent years to ensure that The Street more accurately reflected British life. It may have been the result of a 'bullish' feeling Reynolds recalls in The Street's offices. 'Very little reaction,' is her recollection of her and her colleagues' feelings on the Rees-Mogg condemnation. 'There was an air of "We're changing things." We believed in what we were doing really. We thought if you mention our name, you'll get a headline.'

Some fans of The Street cited an 'A Different Kind Of Reality' defence, one summed up by Adele Rose, when she says, 'It doesn't matter that it is a Britain that doesn't exist anymore. I'm not sure that that's true either, but what does matters [is] that people like it. Maybe if it is a reminder of a Britain that doesn't exist anymore, that is why people want to watch it – because it gives them a kind of reassurance to know there is a community where people pop in and out of each other's houses and help each other out and slag each other off. People live much more isolated lives these days and I think it's comforting to know there's a community somewhere, even if it's only in fictional TV land.' Says Daran Little, 'If you don't have a sense of community, you don't have a soap opera. No one's saying soap opera's realism. You can't say that. It's ridiculous. Maybe it was a slice of life in the Sixties when *Coronation Street* started.'

Rees-Mogg may have been interested in the fact that two months after his organisation's broadside – 14 December – came the first appearance of *Street* regular Fiona Middleton (Angela Griffin), who was black. Reynolds and Liddiment say this was coincidence. She was a young woman who served as assistant to another new character, hairdresser Denise Osbourne (Denise Black), an Elsie Tanner-like woman (bright hair, colourful past) who in December opened up The Salon on the refurbished side of the Street.

1 9 June saw Mike Baldwin marry Alma Sedgwick, the woman he had discarded in his pursuit of Jackie Ingram but whom he had always really loved. However, an overhang of a previous relationship cropped up in the form of his son Mark. The boy's mother Maggie Redman had initially kept his existence from Mike. In order to aid the drama of the events they wanted to engineer – Ken Barlow fell for Maggie and was horrified to find out the identity of the father of her son – the writers made Mark two years older than he would logically have been. It was an appropriately absurd first instalment in a long, sorry saga involving Mike and children he didn't know he had.

The comedy highlight of the year came when Alec Gilroy put a mouse-eating exotic spider on display in the Rovers. It escaped at the most inopportune moment – when the environmental health services were inspecting the pub. Alec ended up dispensing with the beast behind his back as he spoke to one of the latter's staff, the expression on a torn Alec's face as he attempted to maintain a polite conversation while forcing himself to squash to death a hairy beastie with his bare hands was a masterclass in comic acting from Roy Barraclough. Meanwhile, Derek Wilton found himself made redundant by Pendlebury Paper Products and careened from one dead-end job to another, his face set in that perennially put-upon expression that Peter Baldwin had made his trademark.

6 July saw the BBC launch yet another continuing serial drama in a blaze of publicity. Hopes for it were high indeed: at a time when *EastEnders* was still only semi-weekly, newcomer *Eldorado* was to be broadcast three times a week.

The news of the programme was greeted with equanimity by Carolyn Reynolds. She says, 'There was a lot of discussion about, "Oh is it going to have an impact on everybody?" The *Emmerdale* producer rang me to say, "Are your writers being nicked to go and write on *Eldorado*?" and I said, "No they're not", and she said, "All my writers are being pinched." I remember putting the phone down and thinking, "No threat there, then".' ITV thought differently. As was customary, the BBC serial wasn't put up directly against The Street but the fact that the programme was to be broadcast at 7pm constituted an indirect and abstract threat to both The Street and the independent network: people might, the thinking went, watch the programme and then not bother to switch over to *Coronation Street*, or indeed ITV all evening. It was a thought process riddled with second-guessing, questionable assumptions and little consideration of the increasing use of VCR machines (partly for a reason – advertisers don't like thinking about them because people often fast forward through commercials when watching a recorded show). However, it was adjudged something had to be done and ITV decided to counter the new threat by broadcasting on the day of *Eldorado*'s launch the first ever hour-long *Coronation Street*, one whose starting time was 7pm. 'We had no choice in the matter,' says Reynolds. 'It was very, very much the days of ITV versus BBC1 and those two guns just sat permanently staring at each other. It was very much, "They've got something – we've got to kill it at birth." The BBC were always viewed by Granada and ITV as, "The ones that have got all the money, the ones that have all the scheduling power and we don't. We've got to do whatever we can".'

In point of fact, the hour-long episode was actually two regular *Street*s artificially stitched together, but happy coincidence provided a feeling of a special event justifying a double: it so happened that the storylines of these episodes encompassed an attempted suicide by Don Brennan. Don was upset that Julie Dewhurst, a woman with whom he'd been having an affair, didn't want him as a permanent part of her life and tried to kill himself via a car crash. He survived but had to have a foot amputated.

The use of The Street as, to use Reynolds' term, 'a battering ram' seemed to work – *Eldorado*'s first episode pulled in a disappointing 7.3 million – but it's difficult to imagine that without this piece of sabotage the new programme would have thrived. *Eldorado* seemed misconceived and inept on every level. The fact that it was set among a community of British expats in Spain suggested that its creators Julia Smith and Tony Holland had failed to understand that the fundamental point of soap opera is permanence of community, not a convergence of lives built on financial and cultural conditions subject to change at any time. This patently obvious cast-iron rule was simply ignored because – it seemed obvious – of a rush of enthusiasm for what is now called the European Union. The EU was then rapidly expanding its borders and powers and its quality of an international brotherhood of man was something that went down very well in a broadcasting organisation that was increasingly corporately if not leftist then certainly politically correct. The fact that the location gave it a chance to proffer its own variant of the sun-dappled Australian soaps may also have played a part in the Beeb's self-delusion.

Compounding this deep-seated flaw was a multinational cast that even when it spoke English as a native language was often inexperienced or simply incompetent; characters who were frequently unprepossessing but never sufficiently so to tip over into attractive anti-heroism; clumsy and banal scripts and – unforgivably – acoustics that had not been set up properly come the first broadcast. Ex-*EastEnders* producer Corinne Hollingworth was brought in to buck things up after a while but despite a visible (and, indeed, aural) improvement, the show was never destined to last and disappeared in July 1993, almost a year to the day since its first broadcast.

Some might suggest the law of probability wasn't in the Corporation's favour, whatever the quality of the product. The BBC had tried for a quarter of a century to create serious competition to The Street and, before *EastEnders,* had consistently failed. Pulling off miracles isn't done to order.

The Platts turned out to have a cuckoo in the nest in 1993 – or at least a young lady who was cuckoo – when their nanny Carmel Finnian revealed the plan that had been simmering since her debut the previous year to supplant Gail in Martin's bed and as the mother of their kids.

The letters The Street got from some viewers protesting that the casting of actress Catherine Cusack as Carmel demonised the Irish provides, from Daran Little's point of view, another reason why it is problematic bringing ethnic minorities into the show. 'You always like to think the best actor gets the role but sometimes you have to go, "Yeah but this character cannot be black or Asian or Chinese or anything because we're gonna get slammed in the press"', he says. 'When was the last time you saw a bad ethnic minority person on *Coronation Street*? It's very difficult. The majority of characters that you bring into *Coronation Street* have a detrimental effect on characters who are already there. You always bring in a villain or a bitch.' He also points out that to some extent the introduction of ethnic minorities is doomed to failure. Little: 'Every time you create a character whose skin colour is not white, you get a bad reaction from the public. Viewers are very hostile to new characters anyway because they're taking screen time from the people they want to see, but if you look at the non-Caucasian characters who have been in the show, lots of them come and go very, very quickly.'

The developing evil of Terry Duckworth in recent years reached a crescendo this year. Terry's estranged wife Lisa – staying with Jack and Vera – was tragically killed in a traffic accident, leaving Terry as their baby's legal guardian. Terry wasn't the fatherly type but instead of leaving young Tommy in the care of his parents, who doted on him, signed over the legal guardianship to Lisa's folks, who lived in distant Blackpool. Lisa's parents had agreed to pay him £2,000 per year in exchange for this arrangement. Vera begged her son not to go ahead with the plan. Jack exploded, telling Vera that Terry wasn't going to change his mind because 'There's nothing in it for 'im!' He then decked Terry. His son, lying on the floor, told him he would allow his dad to do that to him – once. It was a barnstorming, brilliantly scripted and superbly acted scene that resonates in the memory to this day. Terry has popped up occasionally since but has become almost a caricature, seemingly employed by The Street purely to provide an equivalent to Nick Cotton, the *EastEnders* bad boy who returns like a bad penny, commits a nefarious act and disappears again.

Though long-term *Coronation Street* viewers were used to the Corner Shop changing hands, 1993 saw the most bizarre interlude in that business's history when it was purchased by Brendan Scott upon Alf Roberts' retirement. Scott was an ex-Bettabuys senior manager who made the purchase from under the nose of his nemesis Reg Holdsworth. Actor Milton Johns sublimely portrayed the sickly-looking, painfully old-fashioned and slightly sinister Scott. Brendan transformed 'Alfred Roberts' as it had lately formally been called into 'Mr Scott's Provisions', a title that summed up his antediluvian business vision. Deirdre – working there again – was required to wear an old-fashioned pinny and part-time worker Nicky Platt (son of Brian and Gail) became a modern day equivalent of a butcher's boy, delivering orders on a museum piece of a bike. However, a dispute with Nicky over Scott's tartar-like behaviour saw Nicky sacked and left the proprietor rushing hither and thither on the bicycle himself. On 20 August, he keeled over from a heart attack and died.

Scott's unexpectedly young, blonde and fast-living widow put the shop on the market. Alf Roberts attended an auction in which his house was to be sold but after becoming over-excited when he realised that the Corner Shop was another of the lots, ended up accidentally buying it back. He then had to hastily withdraw his own house before it went under the hammer. Audrey was glad of the development, having realised that if she and Alf were left alone together in a life of retirement, they would have nothing to talk about. Another sign of the emptiness of their marriage came on the day of Alf's reopening party when he drunkenly told an embarrassed Rita that he loved her and not Audrey. Reg Holdsworth finally got his hands on the shop the next year when Alf had to devote himself to his mayoral duties.

The gradual mental decline of Don Brennan continued this year. A man considered a pillar of the community once again betrayed an interior life that was little less than seething. When Denise Osbourne found herself receiving odd phone calls and got a friendly telephone company employee to track down the culprit, they turned out to be coming from No.5. The culprit was not Ivy – with whom Denise was on less-than-friendly terms – but her husband. Don had lent Denise a sympathetic ear as well as some money recently when she got into financial difficulties and had been upset when she let him know she wasn't interested in him romantically.

No doubt avid viewer Lord Rees-Mogg was overjoyed to see another black face entering The Street when Andy McDonald – now working his way up the Bettabuys career ladder – fell for a cashier named Amy Nelson. This union was to have led to a major storyline: The Street's first mixed-race marriage. 'It would have been fantastic and that was going to run and run and run,' says Little. Unfortunately, Louise Duprey, the actress who played Andy's Trinidadian fiancée, had a nervous breakdown and had to be written out. In a scene that verged on farce, Andy listened to Amy's reasons for breaking it off sitting on a sofa talking to a carefully shadow-shrouded stand-in actress. Following her exit, Duprey said, 'I was simply worn out after working eight months solid. I was being written into the show more and more. I didn't feel frightened about it, but I didn't want to let anyone down.' She also said, 'I can now live my life normally, and know that in a couple of months I'll probably be old news,' a comment that came true in a way that she can't have envisaged. Her other credits included the Russ Abbot drama *September Song* and comedy series *One Foot In The Grave*, but her career following The Street stuttered to a halt and she became a recluse. She died in 2000 of a suspected overdose, aged just 42.

With Carolyn Reynolds moving up to executive producer at the end of 1993 and with Sue Pritchard replacing Tony Wood as producer following his short stint, by 1994, *Coronation Street* had an all-female production team.

Marriage bookended 1994. In the edition broadcast on 26 January, Reg Holdsworth tied the knot with Maureen Naylor (Sherrie Hewson), the woman whom he'd lost as a young man because of the censure of her mother. However, when they met by chance through Maureen working as a cashier at Bettabuys, Reg was determined that this time he would not lose this woman who remained flighty and delightful even in middle age, despite the fact that said mother, Maud Grimes (Elizabeth Bradley), continued to glower her disapproval from her wheelchair. On 25 November came Deirdre Barlow's marriage to Samir Rachid. Samir was a Moroccan man young enough to be Deirdre's son whom Deirdre had met on holiday. This whole storyline never rang true, stretching the plot of Willy Russell's play *Shirley Valentine* beyond the point of credulity by positing the relationship as a permanent one instead of a holiday romance. It comes as little surprise to find out that the whole story was written for non-organic reasons: Deirdre moved to Morocco because Anne Kirkbride needed to be written out for several months to recover from non-Hodgkin's lymphoma. Matters were worsened by actor Al Nedjari seeming perpetually unconfident in the role of Samir. An examination of the facts makes clear why: not only was he a Londoner rather than Moroccan, but he landed the role just three days after he left drama school.

A wedding that wasn't the subject of another artificially created hour-long *Street* on 18 April. The previous Monday, the BBC had introduced a third weekly episode of *EastEnders*. Though it pulled in 5.5 million viewers fewer than the edition of The Street that it immediately followed, the complicated audience-nurturing impetus that had caused ITV and the Beeb to view the *EastEnders-Coronation Street* situation as a rivalry led the following week to ITV extending an episode of The Street so as to overlap with that Monday's *EastEnders* – the first ever instance of the two programmes going head to head. The Street episode saw the culmination of Emily Bishop's romance with priest fiancé Bernard Morten. Bernard broke it off when he discovered to his horror that Emily had had mental health problems in 1992. It pulled in a rather low 14.9 million, but it was still a lot more than the 8.1 million the BBC programme garnered.

Two characters who would later become regulars made their first appearances in 1994. However, both were far more unpleasant on first appearances than in their somewhat more avuncular later incarnations. Fred Elliott (John Savident) was an astoundingly overweight, irredeemably sleazy butcher who took a leering shine to Audrey during a black pudding contest in France that Alf's new role as Mayor of Weatherfield had taken the Roberts to, while Norris Cole was a salesman acquaintance of Derek Wilton's who was only slightly less unprepossessing in his self-centredness and oiliness. Norris was played by Malcolm Hebden, who had been seen in The Street 20 years previously as a Spanish waiter who had a bedsitter in the same house as Bet Lynch and who proposed to Mavis Riley because he wanted a residency permit. He had also appeared in two other *Street*-related shows, *The Brothers McGregor* and *Albion Market*.

As with producers before her, Carolyn Reynolds frequently found herself having to address strange or inappropriate behaviour by cast members. She explains, 'We'd had a run of artists trying to put very expensive clothes on their costume rail and turning up with fantastic tans. Obviously the tanning issue became completely different when tanning salons were practically the only shops open in some of the streets in the North, but when I had the conversations with them you had to go abroad to get those kinds of tans. These artists earn good standards of living and they can forget the characters that they're playing on occasions. Mostly it was individual conversations. One of the trickiest is something that probably quite a lot of producers have where I had to ask an actress, "Could you possibly start using deodorant?" You couldn't write the script when it came to what happened in your day. It was certainly varied.'

In the second quarter of 1994, Reynolds found herself contemplating one of the most bizarre-ever examples of cast behaviour when the woman who played Ivy Brennan underwent cosmetic surgery. Collagen implants to create fuller lips was a highly fashionable procedure at the time, but it was bizarre that 63-year-old Lynne Perrie should avail herself of them. 'Lynne had this star thing that belongs to *Coronation Street*,' says Geoff Hinsliff, her screen husband. 'I warmed to her and liked her as a kind of knocking-on, middle of the road lady. Now Lynne thought of herself as a star singer and a fabulously attractive star to boot.'

Because she never appeared in The Street again following her surgery – Ivy was written out by her leaving for a religious retreat and would die off-screen of a stroke in 1995 – it has been widely assumed that Perrie was dismissed over the issue. Not so, according to Reynolds. 'There were other issues at the time to do with what Lynne was going through,' she says. 'Even without those collagen implants, we would have had a problem. My meeting with her to talk about her future was already in place.' Her recollection chimes with those of Adele Rose and Geoff

Hinsliff. The latter says, 'There's a whole saga with Lynne. Drink was the problem.' The drinking was almost certainly related to the considerable stress in Perrie's private life: her son Stephen was stricken with AIDS. Reynolds: 'I took the decision that it had to come to an end and Lynne was almost relieved.' This version of events about the meeting is virtually identical to Perrie's own.

Which leaves the question: if the other issues hasn't existed, would Perrie have been sacked for her cosmetic surgery? Nips and tucks were actually a longstanding tradition among female members of the *Coronation Street* cast. By the time Perrie joined in the summer of 1971, Betty Alberge, Angela Crow and Jennifer Moss had all had nose jobs. Other women in the cast have had face-lifts, including Pat Phoenix and in more recent years Beverley Callard. However, such relatively subtle work was not jarring, especially in the days when people watched in black and white, which situation, as previously mentioned, persisted for most households well beyond the introduction of colour TV. Reynolds says *vis à vis* Perrie, 'With collagen implants, if that was the only issue, you look at things differently and say, "Well how does this have an impact on the show?"' It's unclear whether Reynolds is implying that Perrie could conceivably have stayed had her drinking not presented an obstacle, but the answer to her posed question must surely be 'disastrously'. Rose says, 'She did look very peculiar and it did affect the reality of her character.'

When Perrie turned up for work with a fundamentally changed visage resulting from an operation that simply would not be within the frame of reference or the financial means of the financially hard-up and religiously austere person she portrayed, it surely created a problem that would have been insurmountable. The credibility that was essential to the programme would have begun to drain from it as week-in, week-out this actress bustled about looking anything but the archetypal Northern working class housewife she was supposed to be. This was something that probably didn't occur to Perrie, a far more frivolous person than her character and to some extent an innocent (she never quite got her head around the fact that Reynolds' forename was not Caroline). Hinsliff sums it up when he says, 'How would you explain this look? She didn't look like her – which is the one thing you owe the programme.'

Alec and Bet Gilroy went their separate ways in 1992. Come 1995, Newton & Ridley – to whom Alec had sold back the pub – were putting the Rovers up for sale and Bet was left desperately casting around for the money to buy it. Rita (surname now Sullivan) declined to invest, puzzled why Bet would need any money from her if the pub was the goldmine she was trying to persuade her it was. The brittleness this engendered between the two old friends was finely drawn by the scriptwriters but in any event it had to be the case that no one would invest in Bet because Julie Goodyear had decided to leave The Street. Bet departed the Rovers and Weatherfield on 16 October feeling very unwanted.

The scriptwriters dovetailed Bet's ill-fortune with the good luck of the Duckworths, if coming into a great deal of money after Jack's brother Clifford died could be called that. Not long before, Jack had bitterly reminded Vera of their hard lives, 'This is as good as it gets!' But with £30,000 life insurance money in their account they could now fulfil their dream. The pigeon loft came with them to the Rovers' yard from No.9. The pub they now owned ceased to sell only Newton & Ridley products as Jack – a veritable kid in a sweetshop – turned it into a freehouse.

Deirdre returned for a visit and extolled the virtues of life with her young husband. Considering Samir had only ever been a device to allow Anne Kirkbride to recover from illness, she was never going to be allowed to exult in her happiness with him for long. His death came at the close of a storyline in which Tracy Barlow suffered kidney damage when she – as many 18-year-olds were then doing – took the drug Ecstasy on a night out. Samir offered to donate a kidney after Ken and Deirdre proved to have incompatible tissue types. However, his donation became a posthumous one when he died in mysterious circumstances on a towpath. It was hinted that the incident that led to his death was a violent attack by a gang of youths, but we weren't shown it and the plot turn felt sketchy, even lazy – something that really summed up the entire wretched Deirdre-Samir story thread. Just about the only note that rang true in the whole saga came when a policeman arrived to tell the wife of young Samir the bad news and was amazed and almost appalled to find that Deirdre was a middle-aged woman.

No.9 was bought in October by Gary and Judy Mallet. Though rough and ready, they were essentially a nice young couple, although the unavoidably cartoonish quality of new arrivals to The Street before they (and the writers) settle down was demonstrated by Gary annoying the neighbours with his drum playing. Other new characters included young, blonde and fun-loving Maxine Heavey (Tracy Shaw), who became Fiona Middleton's flatmate, and Roy Cropper, a solitary resident of a block of flats owned by Mike Baldwin in Crimea Road in which Deirdre was caretaker. Roy kept harassing Mrs Rachid in a brilliantly creepy, shuffling, tic-stuffed performance by actor David Neilson – one ironically that required the scriptwriters to nicen Roy up when its power compelled the production team to decide he should be brought back. When Roy became a regular in 1997, his anorak obsessions with steam trains, bats and suchlike were retained but he was recast from sex pest into lovable innocent.

Speaking of lovable innocents, Derek Wilton's problems with his missing gnome Arthur were a wonderful light contrast to the more heavy stuff going on in the programme. Derek became ever more perplexed and angry when postcards kept arriving from around the globe signed 'Arthur'. Then there was the ransom note accompanying a severed gnome ear demanding 50 chocolate doubloons for his safe return. The storyline went on for several months and never got tedious before the mystery was finally solved when Norris Cole revealed himself to be the culprit. Derek exacted horrible revenge by making Norris late for his wedding to the terrifying Angela.

Gordon Clegg returned to The Street to give Betty Turpin away when she got married on 20 October to her old wartime sweetheart Billy Williams. It was Bill Kenwright's final appearance in *Coronation Street*. Gordon Clegg was played by Geoffrey Leesley in the character's appearances in 2002 and 2004 because the role was recast after Kenwright expressed his unhappiness at having rearranged his schedule at a time of his father's serious illness for *Street* appearances that he says he was told would be substantial but turned out to be negligible.

Though he had been in and out of The Street over the years since his 1968 debut, it was only this time around that it struck Kenwright how different it was. He recalls, 'There was its own *Coronation Street* entrance. There was constant refreshments, food, a huge green room. The green room was the kids on one end and the grown-ups on the other end. I remember thinking, "My God, there's loads and loads of Lucille Hewitts/Gordon Cleggs in it now." The biggest change is when I first became an actor, you had to have elocution, you had to be in London – you could not be a successful actor by staying in the North – and you couldn't go for the audition with an accent.'

No doubt many old-timers in The Street were thinking circumstances had changed for Kenwright even more than they had for *Coronation Street*. Kenwright had long ago ceased acting even on a part-time basis and had agreed to appear for sentimental reasons associated with his surrogate mother, Betty Driver. The Street had to provide him with a small office so he could attend to his producer's work between scenes. When in 1968 Kenwright and Reg Marsh had set up David Gordon Productions (the title derived from their *Street* characters' Christian names), their aim was to both advance their own thespian activities and to offer theatre employment to *Street* actors on breaks from the programme. By 1995, Kenwright was already well on his way to being – with the possible exception of Lord Lloyd Webber – the pre-eminent British theatre impresario of his day. This was underlined by the fact that some viewers of the relevant 1995 episodes didn't remember his face from The Street's history but were familiar with it from TV interviews about his various productions. By 1999, he was rich enough to effect the schoolboy fantasy scenario of taking over his beloved Everton Football Club, where he is now chairman. By 2001, such was Kenwright's success as a theatre producer that a former colleague was claiming that Kenwright employed more actors in the space of a year than the BBC. 'I think that's true,' Kenwright says without apparent conceit, pointing out also that several of the thespians with whom he found himself acting on his 1995 return to The Street were ones who had worked for him previously. By 2007 Kenwright became an instantly recognisable TV face again just under 40 years after his debut in The Street had first made him famous when he acted as a judge in the BBC television series *Any Dream Will Do*, a show designed to find a lead actor for a new version of the musical *Joseph and the Amazing Technicolor Dreamcoat* of which he was co-producer.

Though he was awarded the CBE in 2000 and says his 2008 Lifetime Achievement Award from the Theatrical Management Association was 'a fantastic accolade for me,' he also says, 'I don't feel I've reached any plateau. I think the headmaster's going to come in any second and make me do a real job.' Not too likely. Kenwright has transpired to be surely the most successful person ever to work on *Coronation Street* in any capacity.

The wedding of the year was the one that took place between Curly Watts and Raquel Wolstenhulme on 8 December. The resolution of their courtship was an appropriately big event for a *Coronation Street* 35th anniversary edition that was the first-ever episode of the programme actually written to be an hour long, as opposed to being two episodes artificially spliced. Artificially spliced is also what could be said of the marriage: it was clear that Raquel didn't love Curly but was impressed by his innate integrity following her cavalier treatment at the hands of men like Des Barnes. Says the episode's writer John Stevenson, 'That, technically, was the most difficult episode I've ever had to do 'cos I had to take her on such a long journey in under sixty minutes from being in love with Des and thinking he loved her and finding out it was absolutely cobblers, depths of low esteem and thinking, "I'll have Curly, at least I'll be safe with him" and going in for the wedding and regretting it and clearly being most upset about it.'

Curly and Raquel honeymooned on the *QEII*, on which cruise coincidentally Rita Sullivan and Mavis Wilton were also booked after Rita's life assurance matured. The adventures the two pairs encountered on this trip were released in November as *Coronation Street – The Feature Length Special*, the first non-compilation *Street* video. Alec Gilroy also made an appearance. Recalls Reynolds, 'There was a drive to see whether we could try a VHS, have a separate entity for a different market. At that time a lot of actors on *Coronation Street* were going on the *QEII* for free holidays. They could take their family with them and all they had to do was a few talks about life working on *Coronation Street*.' Offered a similar deal, Reynolds declined because of the attendant lack of privacy, but it sparked a thought: 'I said, "But I am looking for a location actually 'cos we're thinking of doing something on a cruise." That's the reason why it went on the *QEII* – because they said, "We'll provide all the facilities you need".'

John Stevenson: 'When they wanted ideas for something outside the show, I said, "I want to do this because I want to take them on from the wedding...." We weren't quite sure that we'd got the permission to do this filming on the *QEII* but Carolyn said, "We'll fix it with the Granada people later, I'm sending you to New York on the *QEII*." So David [Hanson, video producer] took his wife, I took mine. While we were on it, [we] spent a fair amount of time – not a great deal really – looking round the ship for good places to shoot and getting a feeling of what life was like on the ship and so on and flew back and wrote it. Later in the year, they went back on the *QEII* while it was going out to the Med and shot it all in about ten days.' Though the video already possessed a grand feel because none of it took place in Weatherfield, Stevenson gives great credit to Mary McMurray for her cinematic direction.

It is presumably the fact that the product was marketed as something exclusive to video that was responsible for it selling in such vast quantities. In March 1997, however, the ITV network broadcast it, overruling the protests of Granada. Though there was in fact another straight-to-video *Street* special adventure in 1997, Stevenson claims that the fall-out from the successful legal action brought by some fans over the breach of promise is the reason why there were no other such ventures for over a decade. Stevenson: 'They threw away millions by that.' Reynolds disputes the latter point, saying, 'There was a change in the DVD/VHS market during that time. Quite a lot of people started to do them and they had less value and because they had less value the advance that you got was too small to actually make it cost-effective.' However, she agrees with Stevenson on one point: 'Trust from the audience went enormously…. It was an appalling decision by ITV to transmit it…. It was a classic case where individual companies have no control over ITV the broadcaster.' Reynolds – to add insult to injury – had to appear on 'an excruciating' edition of the TV viewers' feedback show *Right To Reply* to defend something that she had neither wanted nor been responsible for.

The final insult was that when the cruise story was televised, Curly's risqué references at the end to *Moby Dick* and *Free Willy* were incomprehensible to those who hadn't seen the original video. Stevenson: 'They cut down about twelve, fifteen minutes of it and made a balls of it.'

From 1 October 1996, those *Street* fans with access to satellite and cable channel Granada Plus were delighted to be able to tune in to *Coronation Street* episodes from yesteryear. Over the following eight years, different episodes were shown daily, with a weekend omnibus. This was of course a welcome and long overdue exploitation of The Street's archives, even if it was somewhat maddening that the repeats began from the relatively recent juncture of the 5 April 1976 edition in which Elsie Tanner returned to Weatherfield, a starting point chosen by Daran Little after Granada Plus told him black and white episodes wouldn't interest their viewers.

urly and Raquel Watts' fragile marriage ended after just a year when an increasingly confident Raquel was tempted by an aromatherapy job in Kuala Lumpur. Curly, realising the relationship was over, effectively let her go. Reg and Maureen Holdsworth got a quickie divorce when Reg – unseen at the Corner Shop or anywhere else in the programme since the previous November because Ken Morley, chafing at the lack of freedom of speech he complained his *Street* contract imposed, had not signed up again – turned out to be an adulterer. Ken Barlow's endless inability to keep his children manifested itself again this year when Denise Osbourne took their son Daniel to live with her in Scotland, the location, it might be remembered, of Peter and Susan's exile – and Denise wasn't even really Scottish. (Fiona Middleton bought the lease of the salon.) Denise bequeathed an excellent and longstanding character in the shape of Ashley Peacock (Steven Arnold), nephew of Fred Elliott and boyfriend of Denise's babysitter Kelly. This asthmatic-voiced teenager was no leather-jacketed rebel but rather a young man of such preternatural decency that within a short space of time he would become The Street's unlikely conscience. Another new character was beautiful Rovers barmaid Samantha Failsworth (Tina Hobley). However, though her flaming tresses were loud, her impact was muted. Not given notable storylines, she often seemed to be serving no dramatic purpose and her tenure lasted just two years.

Steve McDonald and Don Brennan both went into a precipitous decline in 1996 in brilliantly written and completely convincing storylines. Steve's troubles started when he bought the witness dock silence of a crook from whom he had bought some stolen alcohol – in which messy business he had to involve his wholesome wife Vicky (Alec Gilroy's granddaughter) because she was the one with the necessary money – and reached a crescendo when the estranged wife of the crook decided to rat on them both. Steve begged Vicky to take the rap, but she had had enough of the seedy world her marriage had taken her into. The year ended with Steve in Strangeways Prison and Vicky fleeing to Switzerland. Don Brennan's financial problems started when he and his new partner Josie were tricked by Mike Baldwin into paying over the odds for his garage business. Don's recurring nastiness made Josie leave him, the business was taken into receivership, the Platts failed to invite

Don over for Christmas and the final straw was a positive breath test which would mean the loss of Don's driving licence. On Christmas Day, Don tried to kill himself via carbon monoxide poisoning. The Christmas Day episode, though dark, was excellent, yet humiliatingly for Granada it attained viewing figures of just 10.3 million, including the omnibus, giving it only just enough of an audience to scrape into the ratings top 30. As recently as February, an episode had hit nearly 20 million. It was an embarrassing way to end a year in which more *Coronation Street* had been put on offer than ever before – the end of November had seen the introduction of a fourth weekly, Sunday episode.

'The network decided,' says Adele Rose of the episode increase. Explains Reynolds of the decision, 'ITV were following suit from what they'd learned in America where certain large channels who had enjoyed very large shares of the audience were now losing their share, so there was a view that you spread your big winners across the schedule.' Controller of Programmes Andrea Wonfor came in to announce the increase in episodes. Says Tom Elliott, 'Julian Roach said something which I've never forgot. He said, "Why compete with the worst?"' He adds, 'There's an old adage in the theatre: leave 'em wanting. And we weren't.'

Though the switch to three episodes in 1989 unquestionably went hand in hand with an improvement in the show's quality, this was due to a combination of the simultaneously raised production values, a concentration on improving the plotting of stories and a general adrenalin rush. The fourth episode felt like an unhealthy tipping point. Production-wise, with only so many hours in the day and with weekend shoots having already become common with the switch to three episodes, a way to magic up an extra episode had somehow to be found. The result was a jettisoning of the producer/technical run that had been a fixture of The Street since day one. That Bill Kenwright recollects rehearse-record being used when he was in The Street in 1995 indicates it was already happening; the move to four episodes seems to have accelerated the complete switchover to the process whereby cast would film a scene immediately after rehearsing it. 'They were doing it on the location scenes, so it was only the studio scenes that were different,' says Reynolds of rehearse-record. 'The arguments about keeping the rehearsal didn't really wash when we were having to shoot more stuff on location. The impetus [was] we had to. We had to speed it up.... It kept the rehearsals as long as it possibly could but ultimately it started really to tie in with how the rest of the industry was working.'

The actors were won round to the changes because the rejigging of the production process meant that even despite the higher number of episodes they had more time off, but John Stevenson was dismayed by the consequences. Though he perceived 'no harm at all' in the three episodes per week schedule, he says, 'When it went to four, something irrevocably changed there.' He explains, 'When it was two a week and three a week, on the Wednesday or Thursday they would have a technical run in which the players would know their lines although they'd still be carrying their scripts. You could go along as writer and watch them go though their motions and you could see where you could do a better line, you could see where they'd taken something the wrong way and they thought you were being satirical or vice versa. You also lost a lot of continuity because they used to do these tech runs in scene order, but once they got to rehearse-record obviously all your scenes in one particular set you do in a bunch and in no particular order, which is more convenient for the technicians. So from that time on you lost the ability to make these last minute improvements and the actors lost their knowledge of where the hell the scenes were going, especially if they were the sort who because it's so busy are only reading their own parts and don't know how they fit with everybody else's.' Additionally, of course, the reduced rehearsal time meant that actors would not always be word-perfect. Some – but not all – were so concerned by this that they voluntarily worked on their lines out of hours. Stevenson: 'It's fair to say that not all actors are as conscientious as others and some will arrange private rehearsals. Bill Roache and David Neilson and others really do take their work seriously and it shows.'

Rose: 'Three was tolerable, four was difficult. You were then in a factory almost of having to come up with so many more storylines and so many more characters and the whole thing became a bit unwieldy. Huge increase in the number of people sitting round the table, and the bigger a committee the harder it is to get things achieved.' That enlarged committee would see the story associates expand to half a dozen, drawing to a close the days of long-running storylining pairs like Harry Driver & Vince Powell, Esther Rose & Peter Tonkinson and Tom Elliott & Paul Abbott.

Harry Kershaw observed back in the days of two weekly *Street* episodes that for purposes of dramatic licence it more accurately resembled the goings-on in a hundred streets, not one. Now that the number of episodes had doubled, the number of streets whose goings on were represented increased exponentially, with obvious consequences for the willingness of viewers to grant dramatic licence. Stevenson: 'When it was two a week, it was very difficult to get things that wrong. When you get to four and five a week and you're desperate for material, people fall back on, "We'll get them into bed" or whatever. Or, "We'll catch him with his hands in the till" or "We'll bring a murderer in." And gradually you lose touch with the thing that made The Street so important to people – that they could relate their own lives to it.... Once you go in for a great deal of murder and crime and everyday serial sexual infidelity, you can't turn the clock back. You're stuck with it, and who knows where it's going to end.' Rose: 'One of our prime objectives was to keep it rooted in street reality and not to do things that were completely the opposite of what really might happen or those characters might do. They're forced now of necessity to do things like that. To stretch reality beyond breaking point.'

Finally, the fourth episode never sat well or felt right for another reason. Though an attempt was made by The Street not to just throw in an extra episode arbitrarily (Reynolds: 'We would always say, "Remember this is a Sunday and make sure we reflect that in our stories"'), whatever care was taken was sometimes lost: the unfamiliar weekend scheduling meant some regular viewers found they frequently forgot to watch it.

Few were worried that the year marked the first example of sponsorship of the programme: it was understood that Cadburys were not going to try to pressurise The Street into incorporating into the drama the chocolate family whose animated forms were now to be seen cavorting before the opening titles of each episode. But with the addition of that Sunday *Coronation Street* transmission from 24 November, for all the reasons stated above, 1996 was for some the year that marked the point at which the goose that laid the golden egg began to be drained of life.

'The Street is currently being terrorized by a smiling axeman.'

These were the words of *Daily Mirror* columnist Victor Lewis-Smith in 1997 as the Brian Park era got into swing at *Coronation Street*. He was by no means alone in his criticisms. Jean Alexander had kept her counsel about the show since hanging up Hilda Ogden's curlers, but Park's new-look *Street* moved her to state, 'I always thought

Coronation Street would go on forever – a great British Institution – but now I have my doubts.'

Park had been a Granada man for nearly 20 years, working across the board from drama to comedy to documentaries and had been head of entertainment, taking over from David Liddiment. Though Granada-bred, unlike previous *Coronation Street* producers like Liddiment, Park was no particular fan of the programme. His detractors – outraged by a cast cull, crass casting decisions and sensationalist storylines – would say that it showed. However, from Park's point of view desperate measures called for desperate remedies and he had been brought in to try to turn around the fortunes of a show he describes at this point as 'seen as a bit of a basket case.'

Park: 'It wasn't rating in the London area at all. Two major problems with it were spelt out to me. One was that it had an ageing viewing population, so it was the kind of show that had turned from the show that your mother had watched to the one that your grandmother would watch. There was also a big PR bias against The Street at that time, perceived as being old-fashioned, fuddy-duddy, while *EastEnders* was making all the running. The *Sun* and the *Mirror* were very pro-*EastEnders* compared to *Coronation Street*. I started in January 1997 and it had got thrashed at Christmas and that was always a great springboard for tabloid hysteria against [an] "ailing soap".'

Park felt a pressing need to introduce bigger, bolder and longer stories. Sitting down to view a programme he had last watched regularly with his grandmother as a child, he was dismayed by 'very creaky storylines. Some scripts individually themselves might have been okay but... I remember one great storyline: [a] little girl got her bike stolen and they managed to make this a central plank of an episode or two or maybe for the week. They were very small-scale. They were either that or they were overblown, like Liz McDonald took up with a gangster, so it was all sort of sub-*Sweeney*. The storytelling had become rather tired and we needed to shake it up.... Too often because of the whims of the story conferences, [they'd say], "Oh we're bored now, we don't see where we can go with that story." What I did do is impose an order on it to go, "No, that's got to happen, this story can go longer".'

All of this creates an incredible sense of *déjà vu* – squared. Isn't the anecdote about the triviality of the missing bike story rather similar to Derek Granger's recollection of being underwhelmed by the saga of Lucille Hewitt's missing purse? Hadn't it been less than a decade since

David Liddiment was addressing the allegation that *EastEnders* was making The Street look pedestrian and antiquated? And as for falling ratings, this was a recurring complaint since the mid-Sixties, one repeatedly seemingly solved by 'new broom' producers or exec producers. Added to all of this familiar territory is Park's conclusion about The Street using up stories too quickly. Haven't we already heard from Granger *and* Barstow *and* Liddiment that they insisted on the elongation of story threads? No doubt Park's detractors might point out the fact that this year marked the launch on a new terrestrial channel called Channel Five of the programme *Family Affairs*, yet another continuing drama serial about ordinary people that broadcast more than once a week – i.e., another show that would never have existed without *Coronation Street*'s boilerplate. It even featured Ken Farrington (the erstwhile Billy Walker) in its cast. However, Park's analysis merely goes to prove that restoring *Coronation Street* to the former glories it has allegedly fallen from is an unceasing task with which the people who paint the Forth Bridge will be able to empathise.

Executive producer Carolyn Reynolds is the person who recruited Park. She says, 'There's no doubt that it needed yet another assessment of where it was and what it needed to achieve and a bit of new energy round the table. I knew Brian already and he's a very energetic guy and he also knows how a good story works.' On the here-we-go-again issue, she says, 'It's a constant revaluation of what it is as a show. They're almost living and breathing organisms, these soaps. I can't think of any other TV show that's like it, I think partly because it has to reflect what's going on in society. So I don't think you can ever say, "Oh we've cracked it now, it'll be okay." It probably buys you about four or five years, max.' Is this treadmill of rejuvenation disheartening? Reynolds: 'If you're feeling a little weary with life or if you're feeling rather tired because you have a busy period then you will find it quite depressing, but if you just look at it rationally you just say to yourself, "This is part and parcel of that job".'

The problems facing the show were serious. Carlton – to whom Thames Television had lost the London weekday franchise in 1991 – were not happy about the way people within its transmission area were turning away from The Street. Even more serious was the disgruntlement of London Weekend Television, which with its Friday and Sunday broadcasts now had as many *Street* episodes as the weekday London franchise. With only Friday evenings and weekends in which to make their advertising money, LWT couldn't afford to carry programmes they perceived to be flagging. Park reveals, 'There were worries from LWT that on a Sunday night particularly – because it was a vulnerable night – it was dipping below fifty per cent viewing figures. This wasn't seen as being a disaster but it was seen as being a bit of a drift. It was seen to be going into decline, and a steady decline, while *EastEnders* was staying solid. And particularly with it having gone from three episodes to four episodes there was also debate as to, "Oh, did we get that wrong?" and "Have we killed the goose that lays the golden eggs?"' Though the two London franchises were, of course, not threatening to drop The Street, there was talk filtering through to Granada of them pulling out of the agreement that saw the original transmission of each programme at a uniform time of 7.30pm. Park admits that some of this was 'posturing' by Carlton and LWT, but he also says that had such a move taken place it would have been catastrophic for *Coronation Street*: 'Because then advertising would go away from it and it wouldn't be the tentpole on the ITV schedule. Mass still matters to advertisers, whatever they say.'

Park's methods to avert this catastrophe did not win him many friends at Granada or (initially) the press. On his first day in his job in January 1997, the programme's new producer effectively sacked Peter Baldwin by announcing that Derek Wilton was no longer to be part of the programme. A traffic incident saw Derek succumb to a heart attack on 7 April. Geoff Hinsliff recalls that Baldwin was devastated by the news that he was to be killed off: 'He loved The Street. There was the story of him being called up to the office and being told and Peter just being absolutely staggered and just saying "Why? Why are you getting rid of me? Why? Why?"' News leaked out of the other characters who would be following Derek through the exit door: Don Brennan, Percy Sugden, Andy McDonald, Andy's girlfriend Anne Malone, Bill Webster, Billy Williams and Maureen Holdsworth.

Moreover, some of the characters with whom Park replaced the alleged dead wood caused no little dismay. The introduction of the Battersby family – who moved into No.5 in July – offended on more than one level. The Battersbys were not lovable deadbeats in The Street tradition of the Tanners, the Ogdens and the Duckworths, but something below that level. They were the kind of people who had become increasingly common in Britain since the 1980s: loud, inconsiderate, ultra-prickly and of the opinion that the world revolved around them. Many claimed that such types were Thatcher's Children, the inevitable consequence of political philosophies of the 1980s that told people that self-interest was a good thing. While such an opinion is debatable – the rather proper Margaret Thatcher would have been horrified by the attitudes of the Battersbys herself – there was little doubt of their increasing preponderance in the culture or that this preponderance appalled most people. Many Britons understandably didn't particularly want to see this social phenomenon reflected on their TV screens in an entertainment programme. Compounding that issue though was just how badly the Battersbys were initially drawn. Moronic unskilled worker with a criminal record Les Battersby (Bruce Jones), his fearsome seamstress wife Janice (Vicky Entwistle) and their teenage daughters by respective previous marriages Leanne (Jane Danson) and Toyah (Georgia Taylor) were shown causing merry hell as soon as they arrived, both minor (loud music) and major (Les nutting Curly). Even allowing for that awkward introductory period where the writers are compelled to use broad brushstrokes to quickly acquaint the viewers with new characters' personalities, there was absolutely no subtlety in portrayal. Additionally, the manner of their introduction seemed insultingly lazy: they were housed in No.5 after the council acquired it with no explanation when Don Brennan was in prison.

As with many things about his reign, Park accepts responsibility but says the idea preceded him. 'I had just come at that point when they were talking about bringing a new family in and they were going to be trouble,' he says. 'They had to be a sink estate family that got up everybody's noses.' However, he also sounds proprietorial about them, and the radical approach that fleshed them out: 'In terms of working them out, they were introduced and established during my time. The brief for me was to change the show and give it a bit more pepper.'

Zoe Tattersall (Joanne Froggatt), introduced in May, also smacked of Park scraping the bottom of society's barrel for characters with sensationalist objectives. An 'underclass' teenager, her council estate tights-and-trainers combination was soon complemented by the inevitable fatherless baby.

'ITV wanted more younger people to watch the programme,' Park says. These days, The Street had more to worry about in the continuing drama serial stakes than pieces of social realism like *EastEnders* and *Brookside*. The Australian soap opera *Neighbours* had been shown on BBC1 since 1986 and had grown rapidly in popularity, not least because of the spin-off pop chart success of its stars Kylie Minogue and Jason Donovan. Its viewing figures of 12 million at best were not in the same league as The Street's even despite its twice-daily transmission (lunchtime and early evening), which made Park's predecessor David Liddiment dismiss both it and edgier variant *Home And Away* (which began broadcasting in the UK in February 1989) as 'like *Crossroads*.' Park, though, wanted this demographic. Park: 'There were no teenagers in [The Street] or even people in their early twenties.' Zoe was one part of the answer to that problem. Another was the final insult for many: Park decided to bring back Nick Tilsley with a different, more photogenic face. This was a rather devastating blow for Warren Jackson, who had literally grown up with the show, playing Nicky (as he was originally called) since the crib. Jackson had recently been absent to complete his GCSEs but had expected to return. Recasting an adult character had only been done before in The Street when actors were unwilling or unable to return but Park remains completely unbashful about having chosen Adam Rickitt to portray Gail's son because he looked like a male model. Park says in his defence, 'It put on viewers, it brought in kids to the show that would watch *Neighbours* or certainly would watch *Home And Away*, it's only a small part of the currency in exchange of actors that you have on that show. I feel vindicated in that it worked.' A defence he doesn't mention but could is that while he opted for heartthrob appeal over realism in his employment of Rickitt, he in the same year sanctioned the ultra-realistic casting of Georgia Taylor – a girl struggling with a considerable degree of facial puppy fat – as Toyah Battersby. Additionally, it was actually the start of a trend. The next few years would see several *Street* teenagers recast, even if less for reasons of attractiveness and more as a recognition that the hesitant, untrained child actors of yore were not quite up to the unremitting scrutiny of modern TV audiences.

Park says that, contrary to what has been claimed, he wasn't particularly interested in injecting social issues into the programme but admits this was his motivation with Geoffrey 'Spider' Nugent. Emily Bishop's 24-year-old nephew, played by Martin Hancock, was an eco-warrior. The latter were another recent societal trend, but the touchy-feely antimatter of Battersby-style self-centred yobbos. 'I thought that was a really good example where *Coronation Street* does things that other soaps don't,' says Park. 'You've got a *Coronation Street* twist on what was a fairly topical thing at the time because they had the Newbury bypass [demonstrations] and stuff like that and I thought [it] was very interesting that you had all those Guernsey-wearing, tweed-necked Home Counties dowagers making common ground with anarchic hippies. That's why we wanted to team up [Spider with] Emily rather than one of the younger members.' Park admits making Spider a Londoner was 'probably' an overture to that drifting South-Eastern demographic. That Spider was a man with a conscience at least made a merciful change from the identikit *Coronation Street* London bully – and was mild compensation for the fact that he had never been mentioned by Emily before.

'It wasn't my decision really,' Park says of Peter Baldwin's dismissal. Daran Little, who was privy to the decision in story conference, backs him up. Little: 'It was under Sue Pritchard that it was decided to get rid of Derek Wilton but the executive producers wanted to keep that for when Brian took over so that it was his first act, so straightaway you get the impression of him being this hard axeman. That often happens. From a publicity point of view, if you have a new producer coming in wielding an axe, then straightaway you're grabbing people's attention, but if it goes with an outgoing producer then it doesn't really mean so much.' Park: 'The decision had been mooted, though it would be fair to say that I [had] the opportunity to say, "No, let's keep him." None of this was to do with Peter Baldwin's acting abilities, but we had to get rid of some of these older characters…. None of them were my personal decisions as such. They all came out of story conferences, and, believe you me, most of the writers were much more vicious, but I ultimately took the decision that we could do without them, that we needed to create space. A lot of their characters had either got silly or peripheral. Often it's not the fault of the actors, it is a fault of the writers who'd give them nothing to do and then you'd go, "Let's get rid of, say, Maureen Holdsworth" and they go "Oh no, no, she's a great character, she can do this and she can do that." "No, they're just little things and you've let her do that for a year now and basically the character's dead." It's often the case when they're in that light comedic genre as well. You have to create space every so often to bring in new characters, and bring a new audience in with them.'

The observant will have noticed that in the above paragraph Park moves seamlessly from claiming writers were agitating for the demise of characters to admitting that he insisted on characters being written out against the writers' vociferous objections. Wherever the truth lies on who was responsible for the designation of dead wood, Park rejects the idea that he was insensitive in the way he embarked on his/the writers' 'cull'. 'We had decided at one of our conferences to get rid of six characters and it was presented to me the day afterwards that the *Sun* was about to doorstep everyone,' he recalls. 'So I had to have a rather unpleasant day where I just had to see six or seven people one after th'other and tell them they were going. And I think that sort of lives on in infamy.' As illustrated by his pantomime villain image and Smiling Axeman sobriquet in the tabloids at the time. 'It comes with the territory,' Park says. 'The shows all those years ago were perhaps more on page one than they are now – reality shows and the Cheryl Coles of this world have taken over slightly – so I don't think you'd have that interest now in a producer of a soap, but at that time that's the way it worked.' Of the fact that decisions easily made in script conferences and meetings affect people's livelihoods, he offers, 'I think you're lost if you say, "Oh I've got to keep that actor in sweeties." That doesn't mean that you're not aware of the human factor that's involved in it. I think after three years, something does change with them and they do tend to start to see it as a job for life. So the reaction against it can be – understandable – bitter, sad, catastrophic, depressive. You are aware of that, but there's another call, which is the longevity of the show and how you see the show going.'

'He was up to the job, believe me,' dryly says Geoff Hinsliff of Park regarding the necessity of imparting bad news to departing actors. It so happened that Hinsliff himself was not unduly concerned about his own dismissal. The actor reflects, 'The problem was with Don, he was going downhill. Each crisis brought him lower. There was only so far he could go lower – unless he came back up again.' This might be true, but many has been The Street actor before and after Hinsliff who became so comfortable that he ignored gnawing feelings of his character being past his sell-by date. Hinsliff was pleased to have the decision taken out of his hands. Hinsliff: 'By the time they did that, for two or three years beforehand, I was saying to myself, "Is that enough? For goodness sake should I get out now?" They actually said, "We're terminating you as of now and we want you to come back in six months time." My contract was still running until that time so I couldn't actually say no. I thought, "Well good – the decision's made then".'

As for Park's determination to 'shake it up' regarding the stories, seeing the results of this led some to assume that he was taking his cue from *Emmerdale*. Under the direction of *Brookside* creator Phil Redmond, that Yorkshire TV drama serial had recently acquired a sort of *EastEnders*-in-the-country glossiness and raciness that made its rural setting all but irrelevant. Park, however, says, 'Our focus had always really been on the rivalry with *EastEnders* and it was a way to compete with *EastEnders* without trying to carbon copy them.' However, another programme he cites as an influence on his *Street modus operandi* will only bolster the convictions of nay-sayers like Lewis-Smith. Park: 'I'd always been a great fan of *Dallas*, so I wanted big characters coming in. One of the first things I did was to go, "Right, who's the happiest, longest married couple in the show?" The only one that hadn't seemed to have an affair had been Kevin and [Sally] and therefore we introduced Natalie Horrocks, played by the redoubtable Denise Welch. Started to break up that marriage. That was some of my first big storylines.'

The affair embarked on by Kevin Webster fell flat from the get-go. Natalie Horrocks was the mother of Tony Horrocks, a mechanic in the garage Kevin now co-owned. After Natalie took over Tony's share, she and Kevin ended up as more than just business partners. The rationale for this – that Kevin couldn't resist the temptation when Sally had to visit her ill mother for a prolonged period – was patently a fig leaf for a provocative storyline. Though Denise Welch was attractive, it was being demanded of the viewers that they banish from their minds the Websters' deep-seated affection for each other. When family friend Rita later disparagingly asked Kevin why he had thrown away his happiness for a second-hand piece of goods, the viewers concurred. Yet, this would be a hallmark of Park's *Street*, a place where characters frequently seemed to be led by their genitals. Park defends himself by stating that the way the Ken-Deirdre-Mike storyline captured the public imagination was the kind of thing to which the show needed to aspire. 'You can't be complacent,' he says. 'Drama at the end can't be an exposition of the obvious and the predictable and, if it is, it stultifies. People go to watch it each week because they want to see twists and turns.'

The Websters-Horrocks story also enabled Park to give vent to his belief in extended plot threads. Park: 'Kevin and Sally and Natalie went on for months more than you normally would and you did the twist and turns, and then we finished that one big story, then we brought in another huge story: Deirdre being done by a conman. Controlling the storylines much more and making storylining as important as the scriptwriting was probably the thing that I affected most, 'cos I got rid of probably half the cast but I also got rid of half the writing team that had been there for ages.'

Tom Elliott, by now a scriptwriter, worked under Park for three or four months before leaving the show, although not primarily because of the producer. He says, 'That writing team was very strong. It was dictatorial. The writers drove that show. The writers were very, very powerful and that power had to be broken and I think it was broken. I heard constantly just prior to that, "Things have got to change." He wanted to take that arrogance, if you like, from the writing team. Maybe we were too big for our boots. We'd made The Street work for so long, it was very successful and we felt we had property rights.'

Among those thrown overboard were three of the show's longest-serving writers – Barry Hill, Julian Roach and Adele Rose. Roach was suspended for three months after a vituperative performance at a story conference that caused complaints. Though Roach had excelled even his own traditional causticness, some felt Park (who claims he wasn't responsible for the original suspension but admits he vetoed a suggestion that Roach be allowed to attend long-term conferences at this point) wouldn't have been displeased if – as happened – Roach's pride got the better of him and he refused to return after his exile. Roach had written 267 episodes. Though Hill wasn't quite as esteemed as a *Street* writer, the fact that he had been there since 1971 and contributed 263 episodes hardly suggests someone who didn't know what he was doing. Adele Rose, meanwhile, was the longest-serving *Street* scriptwriter of all time. Her 454 screened episodes are a record. She had seen no fewer than 24 producers (let alone executive producers) come and go since her 1961 *Street* entrée. As Rose says, 'When a show runs as long as that, you go through an awful lot of producers…. Most of us had been there a lot longer than any producer ever was.' However, she denies that the writers saw new producers as interlopers: 'We worked as a team, including the producer.' Asked about three other producers, Rose volunteers that they were 'lovely'. No such encomium is offered by her for Brian Park, to whom she refers by his surname. She puts her departure down to a 'dispute' with Park: 'General stuff. My attitude to one particular storyline, something I'd done that he didn't like. I wasn't the only one. There were a couple of other writers who got the same treatment. Quite a few left. [They] came back when he'd gone.' (Rose was actually invited to return to the team by Granada executives while Park was still there, but she declined. Her move away from London to a location from which it was not so easy to fly up for *Street* conferences explains why she did not countenance returning when Park's tenure was over.)

Carolyn Reynolds refuses to criticise Park over the issue of Rose's departure. 'You're into the thorny issue of whether someone as a writer is continuing to write for a period they're in now and also Brian's take on what would work for the show,' she reasons. 'I accept totally that Adele was a very special case because of pure longevity, but we can't ignore the fact that this is quite a brutal business. You have to back certain producers when they come in…. I can talk to you about endless writers who were taken off that show and felt aggrieved that they shouldn't be.'

Park readily admits that he was not a writer's producer. He says, 'It was four episodes a week. It was a very voracious beast in terms of story and script. My feeling was that it had to be guided by myself. The viewing population changes and you can't bring in a new viewing experience and expect it to adhere to the brand loyalty. I had to make decisions, the pace of storytelling had to change. We had to make sure that Monday's episode linked to Wednesday's episode, Wednesday's episode linked…. You wanted people to see the last scene of Monday's show and go, "I can hardly wait till Wednesday to see how this picks up and where they go with this." Within that, there were certain people who couldn't keep up with the pace, certain people didn't want to keep up with the pace – it wasn't the kind of show they wanted to work on.'

Under Park's regime, storyliners were, probably for the first time in The Street's history, no longer the poor relations of the scriptwriters. He had a team of three storyliners plus script executive Ann McManus. Park: 'I shifted a centre of power to the storylining department and we made sure that we were telling stories properly, because there's always a potential conflict in that writers – certainly in *Coronation Street* – had been allowed to take up the storytelling cudgels and write it often within their own parameters and that didn't necessarily mean enduring storytelling.'

Though Park retained the time-honoured *Street* story conferences, he felt no obligation to sit through the extended heated debates they had always generated simply because by this point decisions had frequently been made outside of the room. 'It used to be about two days and I think I cut it down to one day,' he says of the story conferences. 'So that we could say, "No, this is the storylines, we've agreed 'em, go forth and multiply and write them".' Did he say it as bluntly as that? 'I was fairly direct – but I think they appreciated it. Those story conferences weren't for the faint-hearted and you had remarkable, redoubtable characters that had been there for ages – people like John Stevenson and Peter Whalley – and brilliant practitioners in their art, therefore you had to argue your case with them. But I was very conscious that there's a tendency to settle on a storyline and someone starts to argue it out, so you come back to point zero again if you don't watch it. Myself and Ann McManus worked very well and we knew what we wanted to do with a story and to block it through and we'd go, "Right, we've got enough for that story, let's move on", and maybe that wasn't something they were quite used to.'

Some may be cringing at Park's apparently preternatural belief in himself but to some extent one gets the feeling that he is trying to live up to his own image of crassness. John Stevenson doesn't recall power particularly being shifted away from the scriptwriters to the storyliners, while Carolyn Reynolds says of the apparently flippant impetus of the Kevin-Natalie affair, 'It's very easy to say those things after the event but it certainly wouldn't have been sold that way when looking round the writing table.' Stevenson also comments, 'I'll say this for Brian: You could say, "Brian, just hang on a minute, just think about that, because if you do that, bang, bang bang…. That follows and it doesn't work." He would listen to this and if whoever was saying this was right, he would get the point and say, "You're right, we won't do that." I always found he was very straightforward and reasonable. I liked Brian.'

Those members of the general public who became aware of the loss of star scriptwriters were probably mostly unmoved, but the departure of Mavis Wilton was of far greater concern. The widowed Mavis left the show on 10 October, moving to run a guest house in Cartmel. Hinsliff says of Baldwin's dismissal, 'Thelma was so upset that she said, "Well that's it…."' This commonly held idea that Mavis' alter ego Thelma Barlow resigned in protest over Peter Baldwin's treatment is one that Park denies: 'No. The fact was that Thelma Barlow was leaving before Peter Baldwin. She'd announced she was leaving and that was one of our prime [reasons] to kill off Derek. A little-known fact and I'm never quite sure where that story came from that she resigned.' Reynolds backs up Park: 'Thelma wanted to leave. We talked to the writers and everybody felt that they didn't want Derek on his own and if Mavis was going, Derek should go too.'

After all the furore and claim and counter-claim, it can't be denied that *Coronation Street* was immensely watchable under Park's regime. There were certainly wrong notes in the stories in 1997. For instance, the Duckworths having to cede 50 per cent of the Rovers' ownership to Alec Gilroy over their unpaid VAT seemed a premature vote of no-confidence in the dramatic potential of Jack and Vera's helming of the pub. However, there were also story threads that were nothing less than excellent, a prime example being Don Brennan's descent yet further into his personal hell with the smirking face of Mike Baldwin hovering over him. Don tried to murder Alma but that went wrong and he ended up in prison, where he began to lose his mind. Admitted to hospital with cancer, Don – as Martin Platt, his nurse, delicately put it of the amputee – 'hopped it.' Aiming to murder Mike, Don died in a ball of flame as his car screamed into the viaduct. It was all superbly and believably done. 'I thought it was a good way to go,' says Hinsliff. 'The one thing you want to be when you leave The Street, however you leave The Street, is quite definitely dead. You don't want there to be any chance of you coming back because if there's that, looking for work: "You're not going back, are you?"' The actual filming, however, was bitter-sweet: 'I'd been away for about four or five months and just came back for three or four weeks to shoot the final scenes of Don Brennan in the car and attacking Johnny Briggs and so on. I was a bit out of the game so [it] was a bit, "Oh well, he's been away, don't even know him much and in any case he's leaving in three weeks' time", so among the cast I was a bit passé.'

Hinsliff is glad that he had a career before going into The Street. 'In soaps most people are cast on who they are now, the personality they present,' he says. 'Young kids think, "That's it, I'm an actor, that's me, and what's more I'm world famous already." Well, they're world famous as that particular person and it doesn't particularly make them an actor for other mediums. No one's knocking that talent. Some are extremely talented people in soaps, but they won't necessarily be able to take that outside the soap.... I didn't fear being outside The Street. I had thirty years experience before coming into it seriously. It wasn't death. I knew I was an actor and I knew I was employable. It's the young kids you should worry about. The ones who are eighteen and suddenly think they're the bee's knees 'cos everybody thinks they're wonderful. I would have done. I would have thought I was King Shit if at eighteen I'd got that kind of fame. Very often they've done nothing apart from this.'

Other compelling stories were the broody Mallets' purchasing of Zoe's unwanted baby and the arrival into Deirdre's life of a handsome airline pilot called Jon Lindsay who was not what he seemed. There were also Ken Barlow's hilarious, death-strewn escapades as a male escort. Park: 'If they were to remain, what would be the most bizarre situation to put them in to justify that they're still there? It proved there was always life in the old bugger yet in terms of storylines. What you couldn't just do was go Ken-and-Deirdre, Ken-and-Deirdre.' William Roache had no problem with this plotline. 'I think it's always fun to explore a character and to do things against character, providing when I play Ken that he would do what has been written for him to do,' he says. 'So long as I can do that, I'm happy to try anything.'

Meanwhile, three men vied for the affections of Fiona Middleton: Jim and Steve McDonald and her corrupt police officer fiancé Alan McKenna. The media had gleefully reported Rees-Mogg's criticisms of the lack of ethnic minorities in The Street but with this story it now revealed a different side. Recalls Reynolds, 'I do remember being quite shocked when Angela Griffin was getting married and Tracy Shaw was bridesmaid and several magazine covers said they wouldn't put Angela on the cover. Which was unheard of. When you had a big name on *Coronation Street* getting married it was an automatic [thing] that you'd get certain covers of women's magazines because there is a wedding dress. Basically what they said to our press officer was, "We'll put her on if we've got Tracy Shaw with her".'

Following on from the (tainted) success of *The Feature Length Special* video, another such release appeared in 1997. *Viva Las Vegas!* was shot almost entirely on location and saw Jack and Vera Duckworth, Fiona Middleton and Maxine Heavey involved in an adventure across the Atlantic. Jack and Vera got married properly for the first time when Jack confessed he had taken two years off his age when they first met, making their wedding unlawful. Someone in the *Coronation Street* production team had the superb idea of hunting down Neville Buswell, who was known to be working as a croupier in the desert gambling city since mysteriously quitting acting back in 1978. Fans of Ray Langton were delighted to see Buswell reprising his role – if a little shocked at the ravages time had wrought on the face and (especially) hair of the former *Street* glamour boy. (Buswell returned to The Street proper in 2005 to make amends to daughter Tracy before his impending death from stomach cancer.) No less a star of stage and screen than Joan Collins made a guest appearance, and the opening titles and ponced-up version of The Street's theme tune were deliberately redolent of *Dynasty*. The show – written by future *Doctor Who* producer Russell T. Davies – got a television broadcast in July 2000.

It was a rollercoaster of a year but it became clear that by no means had Park done with inducing earthquakes – it was announced that 1998 would see The Street introduce a transsexual.

'**G**et in, do the job and get out,' says Brian Park, who left *Coronation Street* in late 1998, replaced as producer by David Hanson.

The faster-paced, edgier and sexually rampant show Park turned The Street into was not to everyone's taste, but under him The Street's ratings picked up. Yet his post-*Street* career will probably confirm the feelings of those of the view that his *Street* tenure was a huge misstep by Granada. He revamped Channel Five's already ailing *Family Affairs* by killing the central family in a bloodbath. He also founded Shed Productions, a company specialising in glossy but vacuous fare like *Bad Girls* and *Footballers' Wives*.

'I didn't agree with everything he did, but on balance he did more good than bad,' says David Liddiment. 'He was another shot of adrenalin and you just need it, particularly now there's so many episodes, so much story. My God, it's a tough show to run – much tougher than when I was involved.' John Stevenson: 'He made one or more mistakes but he was good for the show.' Of course, several writers who departed under Park would no doubt beg to differ.

1998 saw the Battersbys transformed from cartoons into humans. Toyah tried to overcome her ghastly home environment and ridiculous name (clearly gormlessly bestowed in honour of the Eighties alternative chanteuse) and attempted to be a better person like her idol Spider Nugent. Leanne and Janice also revealed hidden charms. While charm is one thing Les could never be mistaken for possessing, Bruce Jones' perennial belief in his permanently bristling character made him grimly compelling at all times. At the time of writing both Janice and Leanne are still *Street* regulars, while Toyah is not only because Georgia Taylor tired of the role, and Les would still be had Jones not allegedly broken his contract by speaking to the press about plotlines.

When Nick Tilsley was stunned to realise in his college class that the visiting lecturer Iag was the man who killed his father Brian, he embarked on a cack-handed plot with new wife Leanne to get his parole rescinded by whatever means necessary. Des Barnes was murdered less than a month into his marriage to Natalie Horrocks after rescuing her drug dealer son Tony from some of his own sleazy associates. Natalie also became landlady of the Rovers this year after Alec bought out the Duckworths but then tired of difficult customers and moved to Brighton. Spider persuaded his 'Auntie Em' to join him in the ranks of the eco-warriors when the council decided to build on the Red Rec, i.e., the Red Recreation Ground, Weatherfield's oft referred-to but infrequently seen green area. Memorably, Emily Bishop – starting a sit-in with her nephew in a tree – intimated she might very well urinate on a council workman. Jim McDonald ended up wheelchair-bound and suicidal for a period after a confrontation with son Steve on a scaffolding over the fact that Jim had slept with Steve's current girlfriend Fiona Middleton. Les Battersby's long-lost son Greg Kelly turned up on The Street. Though his good looks and high grooming made him dissimilar to his father on the surface, he transpired to be a ruthless operator whose self-centredness was an unmistakable Battersby hallmark. Zoe Tattersall – who had snatched back the baby, Shannon, she had sold to the Mallets – began to resent the restrictions her child imposed on her life, but was shattered when she died and ended up kidnapping Fiona's baby by her fiancé Alan. In her vulnerable state, Zoe ended up in the hands of a religious cult. Sally and Kevin Webster split acrimoniously and Sally fetched up with Greg Kelly, who couldn't get her children's names right, spent her inheritance on a business venture and beat her.

The storyline about Deirdre's lover Jon Lindsay was one of the two most notable plots this year. Lindsay was no airline pilot but a Walter Mitty fantasist. Once Deirdre had dumped him, she ended up being charged with obtaining money and property by deception: they had shared a house and he'd given her a credit card, both acquired fraudulently. Jon glanced smugly at Deirdre's dumbstruck face as he walked out of the dock, leaving her to face 18 months' imprisonment. Over the following few weeks, there were several harrowing scenes depicting Deirdre in a women's prison.

Recalls Liddiment, who had continued to be involved with The Street, if indirectly, as Director of Programmes at ITV. 'You can just smell the potential of a story like that. That was a "Don't do it Deirdre!" moment. When the audience knows something that the characters don't, it's wonderful stuff.' The suspense created by the story was for Park a vindication of his determination not to allow plots to be dispensed with too quickly. 'I'd gone on holiday and that originally was going to run for about four weeks,' he recalls. 'Well it ran for about five months at the end and it built up a momentum and we absolutely twisted and turned that plot and put on the viewing figures and got it talked about and got it onto the front page of the tabloids.' Which itself could be said to vindicate Park's insistence on courting the media even when they continued to print leaked plot spoilers. The storyline captured the public imagination more than any previous *Street* story – even Ken-Deirdre-Mike. Not only did newspapers jump into the spirit of things with campaigns to get Deirdre out of clink, but so did the Prime Minister Tony Blair, who in Parliament called for the Home Secretary to intervene. The Downing Street press office had phoned Granada before the relevant day's Prime Minister's Question Time and the call had been put through to Park, who recollects, 'They said, "The Prime Minister does think he may be asked a question about when's Deirdre going to be released." They wanted to know some background. I thought it was a hoax.' John Stevenson is scathing about Blair's stunt: 'Fancy a Prime Minister getting up in Parliament to debate the rights and wrongs of an imaginary character being sent to an imaginary prison for something she didn't do. We should have known then.' William Roache, though, enjoyed the intervention, adjudging it 'fun'. Perhaps more disturbing than Blair's commentary was the fact that even as the millennium approached, some TV viewers were still so unsophisticated that Granada's duty officer had to field calls from people in tears over the injustice. One viewer even sent a £5,000 contribution to the Free Deirdre campaign. Deirdre, in fact, was released after three weeks when a campaign by The Street's residents to clear her name attracted the attention of a previous victim of Lindsay's scams. In prison, Deirdre was looked after by a hard-as-nails scouser called Jackie Dobbs (Margi Clarke), whose teenage – and temperamentally opposite – son Tyrone (Alan Halshall) would become a *Street* mainstay.

The other big story was the transsexual one that had caused outrage and/or derision when it had first been trailed. Park: 'At the time we'd been asked – slight pressure – did we want to bring homosexual characters into The Street, which they'd never had. We thought that that's really slightly done to death by *EastEnders* and *Hollyoaks* to an extent and didn't want to be seen to be chasing their tails so much. So when we had our transsexual character brought in, we thought that neatly transcended it, but in a slightly *Coronation Street* way: we went one step further but didn't shake it to its foundations as well.... I can't remember whose idea that was. I think maybe Ann McManus came up with it. And I said, "Brilliant!"' The way Park talks about his objectives on this score now ('Let's shake up The Street, let's get it talked about') seems only to confirm the salacious motivations he was accused of at the time by the media. However, though that may have been the conception, it was not the execution.

Hayley Patterson was introduced as an assistant at Firman's Freezers, where Curly and Alma now worked. Hayley was slightly gauche but possessed of an incredible sweetness of nature. The similarly nice (nowadays, anyway) Roy Cropper was attracted by her independence of spirit – and then horrified when 'she' turned out to be a 'he': a pre-operative transsexual, real name Harold. Several months later, Roy travelled to fetch Hayley back from Holland – a trip we actually saw in the programme – where Hayley had had her operation, and the two returned together to the street. Hayley took a job at Mike Baldwin's latest business, lingerie manufacturer Underworld. When Mike found out about Hayley's past through her name coming up as 'Harold' on her tax details, he too was uneasy. Hayley decided to tell the rest of the staff that she was a transsexual, much to the disdain of Baldwin, who pointed out that her colleagues weren't *Guardian* readers. After initial difficulty, though, Hayley was accepted by the workplace and the wider community, the fact of her complete lack of malice making it impossible to dislike her for any reason.

Actress Julie Hesmondhalgh was brilliantly cast as Hayley. Park says, 'We had hoped for her to be a sympathetic character and we didn't want to make her big and blowsy and looking like Pete Burns. There was a debate: did you have a man play [her] or did you have a woman play her? It's a testament to Julie's acting skills and what she brought to that character that it's lasted as long as it has.'

If Brian Park's reign – and the introduction of Hayley Patterson – proved anything, it was that The Street can survive just about any outlandish story idea or apparently crass tilt at viewing figures as long as it retains its time-tested storyline, script and casting processes. Because Park's vision – like that of all producers before him – was filtered through the exhaustive and meticulous story conference system (however truncated under him) and then through the sensibilities of the best team of scriptwriters in the business – not to mention a none-too-shabby casting procedure – the Hayley storyline ended up as anything but cheap, gimmicky or distasteful. Hayley Patterson was no cardboard cut-out but a fully realised, rounded character with her own fascinating quirks and mannerisms that themselves had little to do with the fact of her transgender nature. That rounded – and loveable – character ensured that an idea that might sound on paper like a ratings-related freakshow with an inherently short shelf-life has become a fixture of The Street who in no way feels out of place.

On New Year's Day 1999, Alf Roberts died sitting in a chair at the Platts' house. No sooner were viewers getting used to the concept that Alf was dead, they were hearing that – in the ultimate example of the way Alf's ailing health had been mirrored by that of the man who portrayed him – Bryan Mosley had passed away on 9 February.

The new woman in Kevin's life in 1999 was Alison Wakefield, a machinist at Underworld. The latter was played by Naomi Radcliffe, an actress who epitomised a braveness in the *Street*'s casting that has been there from the beginning. While by no means ugly, Radcliffe possessed a startlingly bulbous pair of eyes. Such features are, of course, commonplace in everyday life but stand out a mile among the inordinately symmetrical faces usually to be seen on TV. Realism rather than feminist principles seems to be behind such casting as Radcliffe's and Georgia Taylor's: the squat and vaguely comical looking Alan Halsall (Tyrone Dobbs) and later cast member Gray O'Brien (Tony Gordon), who had a left eye noticeably bigger than its counterpart, are examples of television-unfriendly male faces from the programme. Such actors' appearances are at first almost alarming and certainly comment-provoking, but as they become more familiar soon seem unremarkable.

Les Battersby ended up in hospital and in the ultimate example of 'I'll have what she's having', demanded from Martin Platt, his ward nurse, the medication prescribed a woman in the neighbouring bed. When Martin refused, Len took advantage of an unlocked medicine cabinet. He went into a coma. Martin was subsequently put through hell as Les launched a legal action against the hospital, a story thread that accurately reflected the 'compo culture' that had lately turned medical negligence in Britain into less a misfortune and more a pools win.

Ashley Peacock got the surprising news that Fred Elliott was not his uncle as he had always been led to believe but his father. This storyline was on the face of it just as implausible as the revelation that Gordon Clegg was Betty Turpin's illegitimate son, but it was done sensitively and convincingly. Ashley married Maxine Heavey this year.

Following a period of ownership by Maureen Holdsworth, 1999 was the year that the Corner Shop finally got what many corner shops all over Britain had acquired in the last few decades: an Asian owner. New proprietor Ravi Desai was played by distinguished British Asian screen actor Saeed Jaffrey, whose face was familiar from the likes of *Jewel in the Crown* and *A Passage to India*. Jaffrey had spoken to journalists of retiring into his new role, but seven months after his introduction was axed.

Granada insisted that the decision to end his contract was made two days *before* an altercation with two women on a train that led to Jaffrey spending a night in the cells before being cautioned. However, Jaffrey's wife and agent accused Jane Macnaught – who had taken over from David Hanson as producer in the second half of the year – of being out to make a name for herself. Whatever the truth, the scripts were rewritten to have Ravi going back to India to deal with his recently deceased brother's estate. He sold the shop to his 30-something cousin Dev Alahan.

Roy Cropper and Hayley Patterson got spliced. A sympathetic female vicar performed the ceremony, which took place five years before transsexuals were legally allowed to marry. In a turn of events that few predicted, the Croppers took over the mantle of devoted and eccentric *Street* couple from Derek and Mavis Wilton. Also this year came the coupling – or re-coupling – that so many *Street* fans had so long wanted to happen. When Tracy Preston (Barlow as was) turned up in Weatherfield after leaving her husband, Ken and Deirdre found them-selves working together to reconcile them. As they did so, their own old spark was reignited. They would remarry in 2005. William Roache says, 'I remember when we were split – I think Deirdre was even married to someone else – and one of the writers was going through the couples, the Duckworths and various characters, and [he said] "Ken and Deirdre." I said, "What do you mean 'Ken and Deirdre?" "Oh no," he said. "We always regard you as together." There was a sort of feeling that inevitably we'd always get back together.'

Terry Duckworth turned up again and, as usual, misery came in his wake. He sold an unroadworthy car to Vera. It was involved in a crash when Judy Mallett was a passenger. Judy consequently died of a leg embolism. New character Jez Quigley (Lee Boardman) shared Terry's look of dark-eyed malice but was even worse than Terry, if it can be believed. A drug dealer, he turned Leanne into a woman so desperate for cocaine that she was soon resorting to crime, including a scheme to rob the Rovers. Jez, though, had only just begun.

Monday 8 November through to Saturday 13 November saw *Coronation Street* being shown nightly, or rather a version of it, for these programmes were in addition to the regular episodes and were billed in listings magazines (though not in the opening titles) as *Coronation Street – After Hours*. They have lately come to be colloquially referred to as the Brighton Bubble ('bubble' being a phrase used to describe an offshoot of a soap opera that was coined for a pioneering *Brookside* effort in this area

– *Damon And Debbie* – in 1987). The six-parter consisted of a self-contained story revolving around a trip to Calais by way of Brighton by Steve McDonald and his new friend Vikram Desai, cousin of Dev Alahan. It saw the temporary return of three old favourites: Reg Holdsworth, Bet Gilroy and Vicky Arden/McDonald. Reg's oily attempts to get Bet into bed were vaguely amusing, but the programme pulled no punches about what incredibly nasty characters Steve and Vikram were and how much better Vicky was with her ex-husband out of her life.

The final year of the 20th century saw the enriching of *Coronation Street*'s exterior lot. Buildings in neighbouring streets would no longer be merely referred to in dialogue or feature via interior sets but now had concrete outsides. A medical centre was placed in Rosamund Street and a builder's yard behind the adjacent betting shop. Victoria Street – home of Roy and Hayley Cropper's Roy's Rolls business and Elliott's the butchers – was constructed. There was also a new viaduct, not the one at the Corner Shop end but a hitherto unmentioned one to be found when turning right into Rosamund Street at the Rovers end. It made no sense. A moment's thought (and the title sequence, then and subsequently) made it obvious that it led nowhere. The prosaic truth behind it was that it conveniently blocked from view a Granada office block.

Part Six
The New Millennium

As *Coronation Street* entered the 21st century, it was clear that Jane Macnaught was transpiring to be, like Brian Park before her, the opposite of a 'writer's producer' – and this despite her moving the scriptwriter's credit (along with the director's credit) from the closing roll to the opening titles.

Her regime saw the end of John Stevenson's quarter-century tenure as *Street* scriptwriter, despite the fact that he had ridden out even the body-strewn Park regime. Says Stevenson, 'Jane came in with the attitude that the writers were against her. I just got fed up of the atmosphere in the story conferences and that was because of the way she treated the whole writers' body.' Ken Blakeson, a very well thought of *Street* scriptwriter since 1989 (off and on) also left, as did talented newcomer Jan McVerry.

Some had felt unease at Macnaught's appointment. Carolyn Reynolds offers, 'I had no part in *Coronation Street* during that period. I knew Jane. We worked together in production many years ago. She was a very good entertainment producer. She was a huge fan of *Coronation Street*. But she had no drama experience. It was quite a hard show to just come in cold on, especially with a team of writers who might not know that she'd not read many scripts before now. I think she had a rough ride. I don't think she got much support from Granada.'

Macnaught's predilection was for blockbuster stories and there was no storyline more headline-grabbing in a year of sex, greed, crime and violence in The Street than the one began on 21 February 2000 when it was revealed that Gail Platt's 13-year-old daughter Sarah Louise (Tina

O'Brien) was five months pregnant. The idea came from Stevenson, one of whose near-neighbours had gone through just such a trauma. The father of the baby was her schoolmate. Sarah (as she was nowadays referred to) decided to keep the child. That she seemed alarmingly young for such an adult responsibility was suggested not just by her doe-eyes but the fact that she had to be talked out of naming it Britney in tribute to Ms Spears. When she gave birth on 4 June, she compromised on Bethany.

Almost as sensational as that storyline was the one involving Jez Quigley. Steve McDonald had borrowed money from Quigley to set up his business Streetcars with Vikram Desai. When Steve refused to ferry drugs for Quigley, the latter threatened him by telling him what had happened to Tony Horrocks – whose recent death was a mystery – when he tried to stand up to him. Steve blew the whistle, but Quigley was acquitted at his trial. A terrified Steve now lived in fear of Jez exacting revenge. He was almost relieved when he was hospitalised after a savage beating arranged by Quigley because it meant there was no longer a threat hanging over him. Jim McDonald was not so philosophical, and hospitalised Quigley for his troubles. Quigley then went looking for Steve in Weatherfield General, but as he was trying to sabotage the medical equipment around his bed, collapsed and died of a ruptured spleen – the culmination of a fabulous, blood-spattered, rollercoaster of a storyline.

Mike Baldwin's son Mark had begun working for him at Underworld in 1999. He had also started seeing Leanne Battersby. Mike's disapproval of that was – naturally – as nothing compared to his feelings when Mark had a relationship this year with Linda Sykes, the fiancée of Mike, who was now divorced from Alma. Mike found out at his wedding reception when a self-loathing Mark confessed all. Intriguingly, Jacqueline Pirie, the actress who played Linda, was Scottish and adopted a Manc accent for her role – a far cry from the days when a North-West accent was best covered up if one wanted to make progress in thespian circles.

Despite its pacy and vigorous nature, The Street tried to show that it was not sacrificing its artistic ambition and sophistication with a New Millennium special edition (even though it was not the first *Street* broadcast of the year, being transmitted on 2 January). It featured the first-ever two-hander in The Street's history to last an entire episode. Furthermore, this episode ran to 45 minutes. *EastEnders* had taken to using two-handers recently and it might be assumed by some that The

Street was stumbling in that programme's shadow on this score, but John Stevenson, the writer of the episode, denies he had ever seen an *EastEnders* two-hander at the time. As the creator of Raquel Wolstenhulme and the author of some crucial Raquel stories, Stevenson – asked if he had any ideas for a special – suggested the return of Curly's former wife because he felt it was 'unfinished business'. The episode saw Raquel tell Curly that he had a three-year-old daughter. 'That was a special programme and it was done in virtual secret to keep it a surprise,' Stevenson recalls. 'I must say I was very pleased with that. It was very good. It got a huge audience and it was very well received. I've got a feeling it was the last time The Street got twenty million or more.'

Though it did indeed get a high viewing figure of 18.17 million (albeit including the omnibus) and though its intentions were admirable, frankly it is one of those ideas that sound better on paper. The Len and Elsie half-episode two-hander in 1968 might have been a milestone but it was rather self-consciously epic and strayed into both absurdity and tedium. As for the Raquel-Curly edition, surely the opening out of The Street in the late Eighties had been done to banish that static, play-like feel of which this episode was the quintessence? Meanwhile, the revelation during it that dizzy Raquel was engaged to a French count was laughable, not least for anyone who remembered Ken Barlow's vain attempts to teach her the French language a few years back. Stevenson is willing to admit to one flaw though, namely that Kevin Kennedy didn't shine in the way Sarah Lancashire did: 'I thought she was excellent in the two-hander and Curly wasn't. He'd been much better at the dress rehearsal. He wasn't quite at the top of his form.'

The Street's enduring bedrock values are demonstrated by the way it ticks over with storylines of a relatively mundane but still absorbing nature. Examples this year were: the feckless, self-absorbed piling up of debt by Gwen Loveday, new lover of a by now mobile Jim McDonald; the steady, irritable disintegration of the Platts' marriage; Tyrone Dobbs' first love affair with kennelmaid Maria Sutherland; and Rita's relationship with bookshop owner Anthony Stephens, a man made lonely by his wife's Alzheimer's.

Though the New Millennium was undoubtedly the bigger milestone, 2000 also saw a huge landmark for The Street itself: its 40th anniversary. This time, the programme didn't mark the passing of another decade with simply a *TV Times* souvenir edition or a television special. Instead, it was decided to broadcast an hour-long edition of The Street on 8 December featuring the culmination of a recent campaign by residents to save the street's cobbles, which the council was trying to replace with ordinary tarmac. Even that was relatively standard. The real headline-grabbing aspect was the fact that it was decided this episode would be the first live *Coronation Street* since 3 February 1961.

It seemed an idea bordering on the insane. Only William Roache and Eileen Derbyshire of the present cast had ever known what it was like not to get a chance to do a *Street* scene again if the lines were badly fluffed or the equipment went wrong. Roache says he was, 'Terrified. Just terrified.' He adds, 'You can't help but be when you know twenty million people are watching and eighteen million are sadists waiting for a mistake.' Not only that, but times had moved on since 1961 – illustrated by the fact that it was reported that an extra was thrown off the set on the night, with the implication that said person had been planning to sabotage the programme on a bet, possibly with bad language. There were also significant practical problems: the episode took place on a single day, so almost all outdoor scenes had to be crowded into the start because the sky would get progressively darker during its course. Meanwhile, because the final scene took place outside the Rovers directly after it emptied, the events in the pub near the close had to be shot not on the proper Rovers set in Stage One but inside the Rovers on the outside lot, which of course was usually an empty shell.

However, though she had her critics, on this score Jane Macnaught knew what she was doing. As Daran Little points out, 'No one else could have done a live show, 'cos that was her background.' For good measure, on the night, fortune seemed to be smiling on the show. Roache says he can't recall any fluffed lines. He points out, 'I think the *Sun* rang up and said, "It's going too smoothly. I don't believe it's live".' Quite rightly, the last man standing from episode one got the final line, although it went with an action that posed potential problems. Roache: 'I had scenes right through but I had a final speech which involved opening a bottle of champagne as well. I said, "Oh please let this go alright." And it did. It went well.'

An hour before the anniversary programme began at 8pm, the very first episode of The Street was repeated, with an introduction by Roache from the outdoor set. There was then a cheesy montage of *Street* actors posing for the cameras to the accompaniment of the song 'You're Nobody Till Somebody Loves You', climaxing in a caption reading 'Coronation Street – Forty Years – Thank You.' The latter rather ruined the segue feeling intended by the start of the new episode, which did not have a title sequence but instead a first scene (Sarah telling David his breakfast is ready) rendered in the type of scratchy, blemished black-and-white in which viewers had originally seen episode one. After an event-packed edition involving a scrape with death for Vera, the revelation that Terry might not be Jack's son, Hayley determining to leave Roy, Natalie deciding to relinquish the Rovers and (pre-recorded) cameo appearances by newsreader Trevor McDonald and Prince Charles, the cobbles were spared at the last moment. Though a preservation order was obtained, it was late, and the usually moralistic Ken Barlow had no qualms about cooking up an interim fake one with recent businessman character Duggie Henderson and one Stan Potter (Noddy Holder of rock group Slade).

Cobbles are a type of road surface far more suitable to horsedrawn transport than cars and therefore little seen in modern day life. Almost a cliché of early 20th century poverty tableaux, their retention in the programme was a fitting plot development for a show that had so long been accused of wallowing in the past yet had triumphed with the public regardless.

Though the trivialities of life continued to appear in The Street, Jane Macnaught's policy was to augment them with huge, issue-related stories at a deliberately steady/relentless rate of one per month.

In April 2001, Toyah Battersby was raped and left for dead in the ginnel, her assailant unseen. Phil Simmonds, a friend of Toyah's, proved to be the culprit. Other storylines included Roy and Hayley Cropper disappearing with their foster child Wayne because they were concerned for his well-being and a storyline involving Sarah Platt that reflected a disturbing new trend in society: teenagers being groomed by predators on the internet.

Though, as ever, these storylines were never anything less than tastefully done and well-written, some viewers found them too near the knuckle or inappropriate. Others just felt that The Street was turning into a Northern version of *EastEnders*. Leaving aside the implicit humiliation in having to ape the new(ish) kid on the block, the thought of Weatherfield descending into the relentless misery of Albert Square was too much for many in its fanbase to bear. Jean Alexander opined at the time, 'What The Street is desperate for is more humour. It's not a place you'd want to live in any more.'

Then there was the decision to kill off Alma Sedgwick – who had grown in recent years from a shallow divorcee into a kind and compassionate Everywoman – by making her the victim of cervical cancer. 'Sometimes you have to get rid of characters,' shrugs Little. 'When you sit round the writing table every three weeks coming up with new stories, the easiest thing in the world is to create a new character because they've got no baggage. So the easiest way to create a new story for Steve McDonald is to give him a new girlfriend, if he wasn't married. She brings an ex-boyfriend, and there's a kid. And if the ex-husband works out and he's a great actor, you go, "Oh, let's have something for him." So suddenly you've increased your cast just by having one story.'

While the spokeswoman for the charity Macmillan Cancer Relief approved of Alma's exit story because reminding women of the need for regular smears might save lives, she was coming from a health angle, not one of dramatic plausibility. Amanda Barrie condemned her alter ego's demise as a 'cheap ratings ploy'. She said, 'Cervical cancer takes years and years to develop. No consultant would make a pronouncement as quickly and as bluntly as that. I felt straight away that it gave completely the wrong message.'

Additionally, it seemed a good character was being replaced by boring ones. Matt Ramsden (Stephen Beckett) and his wife Charlie Ramsden (Clare McGlinn) were a professional pair who had moved into No.6 the previous November. Matt was a GP who worked at the medical centre on Rosamund Street, Charlie an English teacher at Weatherfield Comp. Ostensibly a zesty young couple, they were totally unprepossessing and unconvincing. Matt seemed too young to be a doctor – though admittedly Beckett looked younger than his 33 years – and his fashionable haircut and ties worn with denim shirts didn't help in the plausibility stakes. Charlie was permanently brittle, including in the classroom, where her approach to teaching seemed as counter-productive as her husband's unsubtle bedside manner.

The affair between Janice Battersby and Dennis Stringer (live-in lover of new No.11 tenant Eileen Grimshaw) was simply groan-inducing. Dennis was a character with decency written through him like a stick of seaside rock and the entire story was therefore nonsensical and a transparent grab for headlines and ratings. The presumption of the programme that there would be any pathos surrounding a guilt-stricken Dennis' death in a car crash was therefore infuriating.

Peter Barlow was now played by Chris Gascoyne, whose debut as the character went almost unnoticed amid the hullabaloo of the live 40th anniversary episode. With this baptism by fire, Gascoyne became no less than the sixth actor to have played the role after John Heannaue, Christopher Dormer, Linus Roache, Joseph McKenna and David Lonsdale, a *Street* record. Asked if the ever-changing face of his fictional son got disorienting, William Roache says, 'No, not at all. There's usually a big gap and then Peter comes back as someone else, but the character is written in a particular way. The interesting one was Tracy of course. How Tracy would go upstairs and two years later she'd come down as somebody different.' Meanwhile a different actress played Peter's sister Susan this year, Joanna Foster showing her face only to be killed off and leave an orphaned boy – raised in Scotland – behind. It was a pretty desperate storyline, involving another new, hitherto unknown son for Mike Baldwin, and another one that led him into conflict with longstanding nemesis Ken Barlow, who as grandfather, wanted custody. At least the boy concerned, Adam, had a Scottish accent, which Peter and Susan had mysteriously never acquired.

Sally Webster got married to her partner Danny Hargreaves, first seen in 1999. There was another wedding, but it was hardly the depiction of love's young dream. Karen Phillips (Suranne Jones) was a clothes-obsessed, prickly Underworld machinist first seen in the programme in 2000. She and Steve McDonald agreed to marry to win a bet, both thinking the other would chicken out. Luckily, the newlyweds soon found they did have genuine feelings for each other. Lovable barmaid Shelly Unwin (Sally Lindsay) was a new face. By coincidence, Lindsay received the news that she had landed the part when working on post-modern sitcom *The Royle Family* with Doreen Keogh aka Concepta Riley/Hewitt. Keogh celebrated the announcement by gifting Lindsay a photograph of the original cast with the inscription, 'From the first barmaid to the newest.'

When Streetcars switch operator Eileen Grimshaw rented the house of the now fractured McDonald family, she brought with her two teenaged sons, academic Todd (Bruno Langley) and his athletic half-brother Jason (Ryan Thomas), aged 16 and 17 respectively. The boys were heartthrob material, but anybody imagining their introduction was going to herald shallow storylines would be wrong. Explains their creator Daran Little, 'I'd been at drama school with Sue Cleaver, who played Eileen, and when they were bringing in two kids for her, I did this breakdown and I wanted to give Jason the story of finding his father whom he'd never known – which is something that had happened to me – and Todd the whole gay thing, which again has happened to me.'

The year saw the first head-to-head of half-hour episodes of The Street and *EastEnders* when the BBC launched its fourth weekly episode of the latter on Friday 10 August. The ending of the truce was down to the BBC: with it already long known that *Coronation Street* was being pushed back to 8pm by a special hour-long *Emmerdale*, the Corporation scheduled its serial directly against it, only making the announcement at 3.30pm that day. The result was too close to call, although the fact that both shows recorded fewer than six million viewers demonstrated how increasing competition from digital channels and timeshifting – the word now used in the industry to describe viewings of programmes that take place after their original transmission – was reducing the audience for individual programmes.

However, as far as it was now possible to determine (or even define) victory in the ratings war, *EastEnders* had seemed to be nudging ahead all year round, even if this meant more stealing The Street's limelight than its viewers with flashy, imagination-grabbing storylines like the mysterious shooting of Phil Mitchell. It's not known whether that, the alienation of long-serving staff or the controversy over some of the subject matter is what did for Jane Macnaught at The Street, but her sudden removal from her post in October was certainly a surprise. Some have posited her switch to New Dramas producer at Granada as a demotion in all but name. That her replacement was safe-pair-of-hands Carolyn Reynolds could also be viewed as a form of a rebuke. Reynolds recalls the panic at The Street of this period being tied up with the disintegration of the franchise system: 'What they said to me was they were in desperate need of somebody who knew the show to get it back on track. There were all sorts of mergers going on. The North in effect for ITV became less about Granada and Yorkshire and more about ITV as a whole and that's when I was asked if I would go back and help them because they had a problem with their figures. Because I liked Jane enormously and felt that she'd have enough of a run to make it or not, I suggested that she worked with me on some other drama and that I would change producers on *Coronation Street*.'

Daran Little defends Macnaught. 'She put a lot of effort into *Coronation Street*,' he says. 'She put a lot of herself into the show. It was her life. She was very good at giving the network what they wanted – and David Liddiment was network at the time.' Little's contrasting opinion on Macnaught to that of John Stevenson may be something to do with the fact that she was the first of the eight producers he'd worked with to give him the opportunity to write a trial *Coronation Street* script. Having passed the test, he made the ultimate *Street* fanboy's fantasy graduation to scriptwriter on 14 May 2001, when his first episode was broadcast. He would write for The Street – with gaps – until 2010, when he departed to pursue other ambitions. His replacement as *Street* archivist was a person with the superb and appropriate name Helen Nugent.

The same month as Macnaught's departure effectively saw the introduction of a fifth episode of The Street. Broadcast on Thursdays, it was started without fanfare and explained by Granada to journalists who enquired as a 'run of specials' and not necessarily a permanent thing, even though it lasted through to mid-December. ITV advertising revenues had slumped by 12 per cent this year and the network was facing the possibility of acquiring a lower annual share of the TV audience than the BBC for the first time. If a fight back was going to be mounted, The Street was unquestionably the biggest weapon in ITV's armoury. Many were predicting that a regular fifth weekly episode of *Coronation Street* was only a matter of time, especially when it was announced that Keiran Roberts – who had overseen *Emmerdale*'s switch from three to five episodes a week in recent years – was to become the programme's producer in December.

5 January 2002 saw The Street's opening titles change for the sixth time in its history. The change was made necessary by the new-fangled technology of wide-screen broadcasts but The Street took advantage of another example of new science – computer-generated graphics – to make the titles the most comprehensive and sophisticated yet.

CGI enabled aerial shots of the titular street for the first time. Generic terraces had always been shown in aerial views in the title credits before because Granada's buildings and driveways would have been visible around the programme's outside set. Now the aerial view showed terraced rows stretching back behind the ginnel, a street beyond the Rosamund Street viaduct featuring kids playing football and even a tram going by on the Corner Shop-end viaduct, all of it the result of digitally melding Salford street scenes with film of The Street's lot. Miraculously, there was absolutely no way to see the 'join' – a far cry from the pitiful painted backdrops of the Sixties. The tradition of a cat in The Street's title sequence was maintained.

Keiran Roberts had come out with the usual 'Nobody on this show is bigger than *Coronation Street*' comments expected of a new *Street* producer. (Reynolds remained as executive producer.) Roberts also said, 'The mood of viewers has changed since the tragic events of September 11. Perhaps there's an appetite for more comedy now.' It was presumably to this end that *Royle Family* co-writer and star Craig Cash came aboard The Street in 2002 as a creative advisor. Some found the move risible, although that may have been mostly due to the fact that they associated him with Dave, the gormless character he played in said post-modern comedy. A producer who believed that the show should be driven by the scriptwriters, Roberts also brought on board Jane Macnaught-era writing exiles John Stevenson, Jan McVerry and Ken Blakeson, as well as a pair of acclaimed outside writers in John Fay and Carmel Morgan.

One of Roberts' casualties turned out to be Duggie Ferguson. Though he had never been a compelling character himself, his death on 6 February sparked off one of the iconic *Street* storylines. Richard Hillman – the ex-Gail Platt's husband as of July – took advantage of Duggie's death to try to dig himself out of a terrible hole: he preferred to raid his pockets and his safe rather than alert the authorities when he suffered a fall at a building they were redeveloping. Between now and March 2003, the financial difficulties of Hillman (played by Brian Capron) would see him con the Duckworths out of their life savings, attempt to murder Emily Bishop and Audrey Roberts – both for insurance-related reasons – and succeed in murdering both his grasping ex-wife Patricia and Maxine Peacock (the latter had seen too much). Eventually, with the net closing in, he would attempt to wipe out the entire Platt family and himself. The story illustrated an essential dilemma of the new action-packed *Street*: Duggie's death was the 18th on the street in five years, giving it a mortality rate 50 times the national average. But this only strained plausibility if one reflected on past episodes for a great length of time, and the sheer zest, great writing and superb acting of the whole Hillman saga made one disinclined to do anything but concentrate on the exciting present. The finest of its many heart-in-mouth moments was a subtle one: Hillman was trapped in Audrey's house, which he had broken into, when Audrey unexpectedly returned with Gail. He hid himself in the pantry and the suspense when he nearly gave himself away by dropping a can was almost agonising.

A new arrival was Archie Shuttleworth, an undertaker who was stepping out with Blanche Hunt and who asked Audrey to use her hairdresser's expertise on his corpses. He could guess somebody's height – or, rather, their coffin size – with one glance. Ostensibly a good, quirky character, he never really clicked, and one suspects the casting of Roy Hudd was to blame. Though the celebrated veteran actor and comic was a working thesp on one level, he also had such a cultural presence beyond The Street – which tends to make stars rather than hire them – that it smacked of novelty, while Hudd himself didn't have the dedicated character actor's magic. Ironically, the suspicions of novelty surrounding the casting of Ciaran McCarthy – a charismatic navy friend of Peter Barlow – proved unjustified: the Boyzone singer Keith Duffy played the part surprisingly well.

The big news of the year was the return of Bet Gilroy to the programme proper following the *After Hours* appearances. It all went horribly wrong though when after her return in a blaze of publicity, Julie Goodyear disappeared from the show after filming just 17 episodes, pleading exhaustion over the four episodes per week schedule. On 24 May she informed Roberts she couldn't go on. It was suggested that she would make regular one-off appearances in the future but she would have only one further and brief *Street* stint the following year. Some sources said she was infuriated at not been allowed to smoke in her own dressing room. Adele Rose caustically observes, 'Nobody is bigger than The Street itself. That's the mistake a lot of them made. They thought if they went, that they could come back and name their own price. But they find The Street goes on without them.' Her departure was a shame: the screen crackled with energy with Bet's scenes, especially a reunion with Rita that started out friendly but soon descended into Bet accusing the redhead of still feeling like she was 'a cut above.'

A new family, the Nelsons, appeared in November. Mechanic Tommy (Thomas Craig), his wife Angela (Kathryn Hunt) and their two children,

17-year-old Katy (Lucy-Jo Hudson) and 12-year-old Craig (Richard Fleeshman) moved into No.6, mercifully vacated by the Ramsdens. Nelson, though, wasn't their real name, but rather Harris: they were in a witness protection programme since having had their previous house burnt to the ground after giving information to the police.

Les Battersby, abandoned by Janice, got a housemate in the shape of Maria's uncouth but sweet brother Kirk. They pretended they were a gay couple so that the council wouldn't evict Les, who wasn't allowed lodgers. Gay rights campaigners were furious at their ostentatiously limp-wristed escapades, but then they didn't know what Daran Little had up his sleeve for Todd Grimshaw.

There was controversy in 2002 about a new system for working out television ratings that was said to have 'lost' The Street more than three million viewers. That The Street's Wednesday episode was often knocked back to Thursday this year by live football didn't help. Nor did the broadcast on Monday 3 June of what must surely be the worst episode in the programme's history. As acknowledged in the press this year, The Street had come under pressure in recent times from the ITV network to provide hour-long specials and it is presumably this that was the impetus for the 60-minute edition on this one-off Bank Holiday called to celebrate the Queen's Golden Jubilee. Mark Wadlow was the writer, but he alone can't be blamed for this farrago of stupid story and unbelievable motivation. Nor for its artificial sense of occasion. Some people ridiculed the campaign to save the cobbles in the 40th anniversary live episode as typical of how boring The Street supposedly is, but the backbone of this edition – a historical re-enactment of a Weatherfield battle – was ridiculously uninvolving. Its absurd denouement – Roy Cropper, of all wallflowers, almost killing his re-enactment opponent Fred Elliott with a pikestaff held to his throat until coming to his senses – seemed to recognise this fact in its smack of over-compensation. No doubt the network was disappointed with the pitiful 8.19 million viewers and shocking 17th place in the weekly ratings, but it should have been relieved that this lowest-rated episode of the year was witnessed by so few. The pikestaff scene, by the way, seemed in poor taste considering that Fred's alter ego John Savident had notoriously been stabbed in the throat in an incident two years previously that had seen him hastily written out of the live 40th anniversary episode.

From 9 September, The Street was to be seen twice on Mondays, at 7.30pm and 8.30pm. The division of episodes was ungainly but inevitable because of the necessity both to avoid going head-to-head with *EastEnders* and not to finish before it. As in 2001, the fifth episode was initially said to be temporary. However, though some Mondays towards the end of the year only saw one episode screened, this time the fifth weekly episode ultimately became permanent. 'Again, it was total broadcaster-driven,' says Reynolds. As if to acknowledge the fact that the two Monday episodes should logically be shown continuously, there were no closing credits after the first, something that was replicated when the Sunday episode became the second Friday episode in 2008. Asked about the goose/golden egg ramifications of the regular fifth episode, William Roache says, 'I think we're okay, but I think any more will be pushing it a bit.' Admiration for what seems honesty is tempered a little when contemplating the fact that he probably came out with such a formula of words when the fourth episode was instituted. Daran Little is representative of what seems to be the majority of those onetime *Street* insiders who no longer have a vested interest in toeing a *Street* party line when he opines, 'I think *Coronation Street* is diluted. It's not special anymore. Nowadays you have to hunt round the schedules to find it and there's so many episodes you feel like you can't possibly watch them all, so it doesn't become event TV.'

It should be pointed out that the increase to five episodes did not mark as huge a jump in *Street*-related screen action as might be imagined, for over the years there had been a gradual and surreptitious shaving away of the content between the start and finish of each episode. 'It was because there weren't so many commercials,' Adele Rose says of the greater non-advert time in The Street back in 1961. 'Our running time was cut from 27 point something at one time to about 21, 22.' John Stevenson: 'The running time of the show has dropped formidably over the years. It was just a stealthy creeping thing: a half a minute here and then a few years later another half-minute, and then you'd realise that every time you'd written a script you'd get the producer or the director on when they got into production week saying, "We're going to have to take five minutes out." "Five minutes? Bloody hell, it's not that much over." Then you'd realise it was because the running time was being cut down.' The dual desire of advertisers to have a platform in the most popular show on television and the ITV network to cram as many 'advertisements in the commercial break as possible is something that was presumably also responsible for the fact that for a while in the Nineties The Street actually began at something like 28 minutes past seven rather than the 7.30 the TV listings claimed.

Nor, as touched on before, has the ever increasing episode count necessarily meant the jump in workload for the actors as might be automatically imagined. 'There's a bigger cast and the load is spread,' Roache says. 'When you do have your intensive period of work, they are intensive. You're in the studio eleven hours a day, and then you've got your learning at night. So you can have a few weeks which is to the exclusion of everything. But then that passes and others take the load.'

Though not related, the gradual decrease in the show's overall running time has been mirrored by a reduction of the length of each scene. *Coronation Street* was never, of course, in real time. However, in the Sixties so leisurely was its pace that it somehow seemed that way – and this was not something that was at all perceived to be to its detriment. Though scene length always fluctuated depending on the relevant producers and writers, the fast cutting to be found in contemporary *Street* episodes is a world away from that long, stately opening scene in the Corner Shop in the very first edition of the programme. Stevenson: 'If you looked at a show from 30 years ago or 50 years ago and looked at them now, whereas before there might have been 12 scenes in an episode lasting 27 minutes, you'd probably see now 24 scenes, some very short, in an episode lasting about 21 minutes.' Both Stevenson and Rose attribute this to the conviction that the modern public have short attention spans, an attitude that Rose says is 'very patronising to the viewer.' Tom Elliott thinks it a 'myth' that producers assume a short attention span. He dates the scene shortening to the Liddiment era and attributes it to the changes of that period that allowed more exterior scenes and more sets per episode, as well as an increased cast. Daran Little offers an additional reason: 'In the old days in the Sixties you used to have one or two stories per episode running through. Now you can have five strands running through an episode and you've got to try and put in about 30 characters to get through that. So each scene has to go quite quickly.' Another possible reason is emulation of the quick pace/brisk scenes that *EastEnders* deliberately made one of its hallmarks.

A 70-minute 2002 Christmas Day episode marked the return of Tracy Barlow. She was no longer played by Dawn Acton – who'd debuted in 1988 – but by Kate Ford, who was the winner of an audition involving five other actresses, including Acton. The decision to throw actress continuity to the winds was no doubt partly due to the successful recasting of *Street* teenagers lately but the disastrous tenure of Wendy Jane Walker as Susan Barlow in the mid-1980s probably had an influence too. Brought back for consistency reasons after she had portrayed Susan in 1970/71 – though it's unclear why Suzie Patterson, who played Susan from 1979 to 1981, was overlooked – her sweetness and lack of sensuality immediately made Mike Baldwin's interest in her unfathomable, while Walker herself didn't have sufficient thespian grounding to handle some dramatic scenes. Little: 'There were things you couldn't do because her portrayal was very one-note.' Bill Podmore came to the quick realisation that he had 'dropped an almighty clanger.' Unfortunately, the stories involving her took two years to unravel.

Tracy had not just had a head transplant but also a character conversion: this was not the nice girl we had known, but a grim-faced, short-tempered type who would ultimately stoop to murder. It was Little's idea to bring Tracy back as an anti-hero. 'I always found her unpleasant,' he says. 'You only have to look at a character whose parents got divorced when she was very young and then pulled her either way to find out this woman is very flawed and has a chip on her shoulder. So you take that and bring her back a few years later as a very selfish person. I never brought her back to have her being a murderer, but if you have characters who are just nice then they are dull.' It seems incredible that a man who knows more about The Street than perhaps anyone else alive should be of such an opinion – many will recall Tracy as a broadly happy young girl before and after her parents' traumatic divorce – and one can only assume that a trade-off has occurred in Little's mind between needing to maintain script plausibility and the understandably pleasing power and high remuneration that comes from making a graduation from fan to successful scriptwriter.

After all the fear about the new ratings calculations unfairly affecting The Street, the programme's end-of-year statistics were not at all bad. Though its highest-viewed episode had only mustered 15.01 million, none of its episodes – now up to a staggering annual tally of 223 – had failed to make the week's top 20, as opposed to seven that had the previous year. Additionally, 34 had hit number one – as opposed to just three in 2001. As ever, The Street's perennial popularity almost redefined the meaning of crisis.

On 13 January 2003, Ashley Peacock came home to find his wife Maxine dead in a pool of blood. The killing off of Tracy Shaw's character had gone ahead despite an attempt by ITV to stop it. A holidaying Carolyn Reynolds received a phone call from the Director Of Programmes who she says was responding to an objection raised by Charles Allen, executive chairman of Granada. 'Charles had made it clear that he knew Tracy quite well and she didn't want to leave the show and could I change the story,' recalls Reynolds. 'I was very annoyed by this. The share price of [Granada] was not doing well at the time so I very rudely suggested that I go and run [Granada] to the City and he can do the storylines on *Coronation Street* 'cos it can only improve our share price.'

This was a year when The Street led a revitalisation of the fortunes of ITV, or rather ITV1 as it was now called, following the creation of digital channel ITV2 in 1998. The 16 million that watched the Maxine murder episode was The Street's highest audience since exactly two years before when 15.6 million tuned in to watch Deirdre tell Mike Baldwin about his unknown son. Not only that, but in the week of the murder, The Street secured a historical ratings grand slam by claiming the top five places of that seven-day period. Furthermore, just under 20 million watched the 24 February episode wherein Hillman admitted to Gail that he was a murderer.

It wasn't just the ratings that justified the Hillman storyline, however: it was in The Street's best traditions of believability. The balance struck in that narrative, though, was nowhere to be seen in the plot thread that ensured that before the year was out Peter Barlow was a bigamist. Peter virtually prostrated himself at the feet of Shelley Unwin after she wanted to finish with him when he had let her down. The sympathy the viewers had invested in a genuinely contrite man was made a mockery of by the writers' haste in having him fall for florist Lucy Richards (Katy Carmichael) just weeks later and dithering his way into two concurrent marriages.

A far better storyline was the one that made Les Battersby an unlikely recipient of viewer sympathy. After antagonising Mick Hopwood, the policeman boyfriend of ex-wife Janice, he found himself charged with assaulting a police officer – even though it was Mick who had beaten him up. Worse, the normally virtuous Emma Watts – Curly's policewoman wife – perjured herself to back up her colleague. Les ended up in prison. The Watts departed to Newcastle by the end of the year after Les had proven his innocence to Janice, if not to the courts.

Of Curly, Little recalls, 'His character was just drained to nothing and people were saying, "Right, let's get rid of him." He was a comedy character. Jane Macnaught tried to turn him into a family man by marrying him to the policewoman and stuff. Just didn't work for the character.' Getting rid of Emma (and their baby) would have been difficult, as Raquel – another of Curly's exes – had also been written out. Little: 'There were three conferences and Kieran Roberts wanted to keep Curly because he was very fond of the character, John Stevenson and I wanted to keep Curly and everybody else wanted rid. Kieran [said], "If you can come up with a story, we'll keep him." John and I met on our own, we tried to come up with different stories and ultimately we didn't come up with anything good enough.' This was a double shame for Little because Kevin Kennedy and he are good mates. Little: 'You have to leave that at the door sometimes. Some of my closest friends are members of the cast. It's a professional thing. You must never tell an actor what's going on to their character.' Little reveals that when Kieran Roberts departed as producer, his last words around the table were, 'Remember Curly Watts. Bring him back.'

Ashley Peacock hired a nanny called Claire Casey (Julia Haworth) to look after his son Joshua. As sweet-natured as Mavis Wilton but without the latter's mouse-like qualities, Claire was instantly recognisable as a solid character and she settled in for a long run. Cilla Brown (Wendi Peters) – snarling new paramour of Les and remarkably possessed of a bigger gob than even Les's ex Janice – was also clearly going to last. In contrast, cleaner Harry Flagg (Iain Rogerson) – featuring in his first full year in The Street after his debut in September 2002 – was instantly recognisable as too lacking in that combination of good casting, good storylines and a backstory that provides dramatic potential to make him destined to be anything other than another of the countless semi-forgotten passing-through characters in The Street's history.

The stories given to Kate Ford to act out demonstrated that it might have been better to have made her character a completely new one rather than give Tracy Barlow a personality transplant, for she was truly mesmerising in her malevolence. Nowhere more so than in the plot thread wherein she drugged Roy Cropper in order to entice him into her bed and then gave him cause to believe that her unborn child was his. After she charmingly told Roy that she wouldn't allow one of his 'freaks' into the world, Cropper – feeling he had been 'touched by evil' – attempted suicide.

Making her last *Street* appearance was Bet Lynch/Gilroy, in a storyline in which she planned to marry brewery boss Cecil Newton (of '& Ridley'), which story dovetailed with Jim McDonald going on the run from prison where he had been serving a sentence for the manslaughter of Jez Quigley. Bet's bleak, resigned, 'He's not coming, is he?' when her intended was late was truly moving – so much so that one didn't know whether it was better or worse that her intended hadn't jilted her but had dropped dead.

The Grimshaw brothers began in earnest the sagas that Daran Little had planned for them since their inception. Jason met his father for the first time. This half of the saga didn't quite work, partly because of casting. Alan Igbon, who played dad Tony Stewart, is black. This was not physically impossible – famously, the father of white footballer Ryan Giggs is a black man – but it was statistically unlikely enough for it to distract from the storyline when – as absurdly happened here – at no point did anybody remark on the colour disparity. (Igbon, incidentally, had played the young Afro-sporting soldier who'd told Bet Lynch of the death of her son in 1975.) Meanwhile, on 5 October The Street finally broke its gay duck when Todd Grimshaw instinctively leaned over and kissed Sarah Platt's brother Nick when they were alone in the flat that the in-denial Todd was sharing with Sarah. That there would be a further seven months of furious denial and self-deception on the part of Todd just shows how intricately planned was one of the most significant *Street* storylines of all, for Todd had been intended to be homosexual from day one. So much so that Bruno Langley had been bewildered when his character had embarked on the love affair with Sarah. Infuriatingly for Little, because the kiss coincided with the return to *EastEnders* of its most famous character Den Watts after a 14 year absence, some newspapers posited it as a cheap way of stealing the rival show's thunder. 'I'd spent two years building the story of Todd being gay very, very carefully,' Little protests. 'I was the first openly gay writer on the show because Tony Warren was never out, so I was treading very carefully because it was something that we'd never done.' Some might dispute that Warren had never been out, but one can sympathise with Little's irritation when he reveals, 'I'd had to go to London to see a theatre production which Adam

Rickitt was in to talk him into coming back to play the story nine months before we actually did the kiss.'

The year saw the publication of *Coronation Street: The Epic Novel* by Katherine Hardy, a doorstopper that traced the events of four decades of *Street* life but did so with some licence, shuffling events for dramatic and practical purposes. Unlike Harry Kershaw's novelisations, it was released into a world that had access to many old episodes of the programme. It also wasn't a prequel/backstory affair, like Christine Green's *The Way To Victory* (2000) or Daran Little's *Keeping The Home Fires Burning* (2001), which were set in the second and first World Wars respectively. Yet in an age where novelisations have begun to disappear – DVDs seem to scratch that itch – it did well enough for revised editions to appear in 2004, 2008 and 2010.

January 2004 saw Tony Wood returning to The Street's producer's seat. One can forgive him for the way he amused himself during his two years there by naming bit-part characters after players from present and past teams of his beloved Tottenham Hotspur, but not for a major lapse in continuity.

While, as Daran Little says, *Coronation Street* in the 1960s was scattered with continuity errors, this was down to the fact that the programme didn't yet have an archivist, let alone the benefit of computer databases. There were no such defences available in 2004 when Mike Baldwin was portrayed as having a brother, Harry, rather than being an only child as had always previously been stated. In May 2004, Harry's son Danny moved to Weatherfield along with high-maintenance wife Frankie (itself an encroachment on what we knew to be the name of Mike's father!) and their teenage sons Jamie (Frankie's stepson, played by Rupert Hill) and Warren (Danny Young). Danny (Bradley Walsh) had brought an equal partnership in Underworld and before long was wide-boying it on the factory floor along with uncle, while Frankie (Debra Stephenson) busied herself by shocking the staff at Audrey's salon by enquiring whether they offered Brazilians.

Nonetheless, there were some good storylines on Wood's watch. Case in point: Karen McDonald demanded a divorce so that she and Steve could have a ceremony more dignified than their previous one. Unfortunately, Tracy Barlow had decided she also wanted Steve, whose baby she was carrying – conceived when the McDonalds were on a break – and kept pleading with him to abandon the wedding. The wedding took place across two episodes on 16 February. 'You slag!' Karen screamed at Tracy when the latter gatecrashed the event and relayed the news that Steve was the father of her baby daughter, now currently in the care of wedding guest Roy Cropper, who was under the blissful impression he was daddy. Ratings-grabbing wedding episodes had certainly changed since the slushy Elsie Tanner one of 1967 kicked them off.

Dev became engaged to shop assistant Sunita Parekh (Shobna Gulati), something that did not go down well with Dev's disturbed ex, Maya Sharma (Sasha Behar). A vengeful Maya persuaded Leanne Battersby – briefly a Corner Shop employee – to file a dishonest claim for sexual harassment. The case – which, ridiculously, was heard within two weeks – ended disastrously for Maya and Leanne, but Maya's campaign continued. In the week beginning 21 November, no fewer than eight *Coronation Street* episodes were aired. The Street had of course successfully assimilated various aspects of other programmes like *EastEnders, Brookside* and even *Neighbours*, but in this week it mimicked the properties of American TV thriller series *24* as it followed Dev Alahan in real time as he tracked the trail of destruction Maya had wreaked on his retail empire. On 24 November, Maya almost succeeded in murdering Dev and Sunita but in the end only the Corner Shop and Maya were casualties – the first spectacularly immolated, the latter accidentally run over after rising vampire-like from an apparently fatal injury. When the Corner Shop was rebuilt and reopened in 2005, the door was located on the Viaduct Street side for the first time since 1965, when Florrie had moved it because of draughts. This new relocation was something still not reflected in the opening credits five years later.

Charlie Stubbs, a builder who had made his debut the previous year, became more prominent in the show. Despite his soot-and-chimneys surname, he was a handsome, entrepreneurial type – if a complete bastard. He wooed Shelley Unwin's mother Bev, then Shelley herself, then Liz McDonald, with certain overlaps. After such shenanigans, the blossoming love between Ashley Peacock and Claire Casey was as refreshing as a drink of cool mountain water. They wed on Christmas Day.

It was a year of celebrity cameos in The Street. Comedian Peter Kay made an appearance as drayman Eric Gartside, who went on a date with Shelley Unwin. Norman Wisdom, a comedian of a different vintage and method, jogged (rather hammily) down The Street in July. September saw ex-Avenger/Pussy Galore Honor Blackman make an appearance less comical but equally over the top as an old showbiz friend of Rita's named Rula Romanoff.

Jack Duckworth had to don drag to take the place of Hayley Cropper in the Rovers' ladies bowls team when it was discovered by a member of the Slaughterman's Arms opposition that transsexuals were ineligible to play. This story thread marked one of the few occasions that Hayley's transgender status was ever an issue in The Street these days: because she basically lived the life of a woman and was assimilated and accepted, many newcomers to the programme must have been unaware that the character hadn't been female from birth.

As the arrival of his first – and Sarah Platt's second – child grew closer, Todd Grimshaw's world started unravelling when he realised he was attracted to Karl, a nurse with whom he worked at the hospital as a cleaner (a career he'd improbably embraced in preference to going to Oxford). Todd embarked on an affair with him, but couldn't bring himself to leave Sarah, even when mutual friend Katy threatened to expose him – a state of affairs Karl accurately summed up as 'his head's all over the place.' The truth came out on 23 May and its aftermath played across three separate episodes on the 24th (the final one of which was at 10pm) – the first time The Street had been the recipient of three separate episode broadcasts in one day. Sarah was naturally devastated, Todd's brother Jason uncomfortable and Gail Platt disgusted (although the latter's comment when she saw builder Jason in a safety hat – 'Here he is – the other one of the Village People!' – was genuinely funny). The liberal Martin was more upset by the fact that Karl's duplicity was probably the cause of Sarah giving birth prematurely – baby boy Billy died – and gave Karl a kicking in the hospital. Though Todd's endless prevaricating had at one point verged on boring, even infuriating, it was ultimately the storyline of the year and did full justice to what a landmark it was in the programme.

Such a landmark that by the late summer The Street had a second gay resident, the camp Sean Tully (Antony Cotton), an acquaintance of Todd's who became Eileen's lodger and an Underworld stitcher. Like Todd, Sean was a creation of Little, but the latter hates the character – or rather the role he has assumed in the programme with Bruno Langley's/Todd's departure that September – even though he is closer to Daran's own personality than the could-pass-for-straight Todd. 'It's not what I want to see as a gay reference on television,' Little says. 'It becomes very much sort of the granny's favourite. It's a safe bet. It's a Larry Grayson. I wanted to create initially, which I did with Todd, a real person who was going through social confusion and came out the other end. Unfortunately, just as we got him out the other end, Bruno said, "Oh, I want to leave".'

The Street entered controversy in 2005 by allowing itself to be used as a willing tool by the Year of the Volunteer campaign.

Charles Allen, now CEO of ITV, ordered a storyline in which Claire Peacock became involved in a crusade to save the Red Rec as part of the network's Britain on the Move campaign, which the viewers were invited to find out more about at the end of each episode. The same impetus was behind Streetcars driver Patrick being seen on screen extolling the virtues of pedometers. Ex-*Street* producer David Liddiment was scathing about this breach of the longstanding *Street* tradition of not – the 50 pence piece scene in 1971 excepted – acquiescing to politicians' or campaigners' requests to use it as a platform. Writing in the *Guardian*, he said, 'Soap, corporate agendas and politicians make a heady mix best avoided.' Not least, he could have added, because of the necessarily fatuous dramatic justifications for the intrusions: Patrick's interest in pedometers was explained as a determination to find out how many miles his lazy sons walked when he was at work.

The Street, in any case, had enough problems without adding to them. Its increasing disregard for continuity went from bad to worse this year when viewers were now asked to accept that Danny Baldwin was not Mike's nephew but in fact his son, the result of a long-ago fling between Mike and his sister-in-law. For those who had lost count, Danny was the third boy Mike had sired whose existence he had been initially unaware of.

All of this might suggest that The Street was a laughing stock, but those black marks were the exceptions in what remained the most compelling and well-written show on television.

Just when Tommy Harris had become resigned to the relationship between his teenaged daughter and the much older Martin Platt, Katy became pregnant. So outraged was Tommy that he convinced himself Martin was cheating on Katy with Sally Webster. Katy believed her father over the affair. By the time they both realised they were wrong, it was too late – Katy had gone ahead with an abortion. On 4 March, a devastated Katy confronted her dad in the garage where he worked for Kevin only to find him virtually taunting her. When he turned his back on her, she hit him over the head with a wrench, killing him. Angela initially took the rap for her daughter and was remanded in custody. Diabetic Katy eventually committed suicide with an insulin and sugar overdose, leaving Craig as the only character from the original family who was anything approaching longstanding.

Martin himself departed permanently in November. His exit story – moving to Liverpool with a rather charmless new girlfriend called Robyn – was rather less dramatic than the one originally planned for him. Little reveals of the abortive storyline, 'He met a girl, he had a relationship with her and then discovered she was underage because she looked older. We didn't do it because Sean Wilson refused to do it. He said, "I have children and it's [bad] enough that I've been going out with Katie who's sixteen. If I now start having relations with someone who's younger, then they're gonna get called names at school." It was the one and only time I've ever known an actor to refuse to do a story and for that actor's wishes to be honoured.' John Stevenson, a scriptwriter for far longer than Little, can think of only one other similar occurrence, and that itself preceded his 25-year (off and on) stretch on the show. Referring to Violet Carson/Ena Sharples, he says, 'In the Sixties, whoever was in charge of the show then wanted her to marry again. She'd talked about her dead husband a lot and she said, "No I won't marry anybody else ever because it's not true to the character. I've said he was the only man in my life and I won't do it and if you insist I shall have to leave".'

Diggory Compton debuted in 2005. He was played by Eric Potts, in his first regular *Street* role after four different bit parts. With a body as doughy as the goods he sold in his bakery in Victoria Street and a comedic face that masked a feeling of self-loathing, Diggory initially seemed the kind of a character who would last in the programme. Ultimately, though, it was his daughter Molly (Vicky Binns) – who also debuted this year – who would be the enduring character.

Streetcars driver Lloyd Mullaney was another first seen in 2005. Played by ex-*Red Dwarf* star Craig Charles, he became co-owner of Streetcars with Steve McDonald. The Street got another new black character this year in the shape of London-born mechanic Nathan Harding (Ray Fearon). This meant there were suddenly four regular black faces in the programme: longstanding Underworld machinist Kelly Crabtree (Tupele Dorgu) had graduated to a speaking part the previous year while Streetcars driver Patrick was also black. Daran Little liked the fact that The Street adopted *EastEnders*' don't-mention-his-colour approach for Nathan. 'It was never once mentioned that he was black, which is perfect,' he says. But is that realistic in a programme whose bedrock is supposed to be realism? Little: 'I live in Manchester and I live in a multi-cultural society. The people who say, "Ah, but this is Salford and there's all this clash" – well, have they ever lived in Salford? Do they know Salford?'

Mike Baldwin's exit story began. Sitting in the Rovers one day, Baldwin suddenly couldn't remember the name of the vessel in which drinks are contained. It was understated, but at the same time an unmistakable, deliberate clue, because lines are written for a reason. This first sign of Alzheimer's – that mind-wasting disease that was called senility when The Street first came on the air – was therefore chilling. The story thread was the idea of writer John Fay. Recalls Daran Little, 'We were at a long-term conference. The producer said, "Anyone else got anything?" He goes, "Yeah, yeah, I've got a story for the death of Mike Baldwin." And the producer said, "Well that's not going to happen." He read the story and we were like – "Oh my God, yes. That's a two-year story. Let's do it." That story was played out in a very sympathetic, caring, well-planned way. That's something that The Street does amazingly well.' Perhaps not so caring of Johnny Briggs, who of course was going to lose his job as a consequence of it. Briggs' good friend John Stevenson says, 'He wasn't happy about it but he could see it was a good story for him and I think that reconciled him to it largely. I think he feels some grievance that he should still be there, but nothing that's disfiguring his life.'

The celebrity cameo to end all celebrity cameos occurred when the rock band Status Quo showed up in Weatherfield. The Quo had frequently been mentioned by Les Battersby as his idols – an astute choice by the writers. Les rushed to meet them when it emerged they were drinking in The Rovers, only to be decked in turn by Francis Rossi and Rick Parfitt for respectively causing Francis neck problems via his over-excitedness at an Eighties gig and requiring Rick to have to listen to endless complaints from Francis about such ever since. Les agreed not to sue the band if they did him the honour of playing at his not-quite-legal wedding to Cilla Brown. The story was a gimmicky, over-the-top idea done reasonably well.

In the summer, *Celebrity Love Island* was screened by ITV. It was a new reality show that was a sort of tropical variant of Channel 4's *Big Brother*. The programme was so much the network's new Great White Hope that it had no qualms about scheduling it in such a way as to push back the first Monday *Street* episode to 8.30pm. Little says, 'Their viewpoint was, "Moving it around, we might get some new viewers off the back of *Celebrity Love Island*, young people with money to spend." *Celebrity Love Island* got a raised viewing figure but actually *Coronation Street*'s figures dropped considerably because our audience was different. A woman who ran a nursing home rang up the duty officer at Granada and said, "I want to know why *Coronation Street* isn't on at 7.30 when all my old people in the nursing home are expecting it and now it's on at nine o' clock when they've all gone to bed".' It was a salutary reminder to ITV that the overtures to younger viewers of recent years were all very well, but they neglected the older demographic at their peril.

Steve Frost took *Coronation Street* into 2006. For good or ill, the producer was another graduate from the modern, pacy, racy *Emmerdale*, where he had become producer in 2001.

Sally Webster was furious when she found out that daughter Rosie was having sex with Craig Harris. After she told Kevin, with whom she had been reunited, the couple were jointly furious when the police were uninterested because though both were a year below the age of consent, they were the same age. The storyline was irritating because it required the viewer to forget the events of 2005 when Sally had embarked on an affair with her boss. Rosie put an end to it by threatening to tell Kevin. This latter fact was conveniently forgotten when Sally found out to her horror that Craig and Rosie were not merely – to use their Goth parlance – 'companions in darkness': the young lovers could have threatened to expose Sally if she told Kevin.

A churchgoer named Ed Jackson befriended Emily Bishop. He turned out to be the robber who had inadvertently killed Ernest Bishop in 1978. Confusingly, back then he had been referred to as Tommo. Even more confusing was the choice of actor. Dave Parke, who played Tommo, would seem to have drifted away from acting (his credits peter out in 1979), but did The Street really have to muddy the waters further by giving the role to Chris Walker, a man who had as recently as 1997 played a completely different character in The Street? The storyline saw Emily behaving unusually hard-heartedly when Ed horrified her by revealing exactly who he was. When her disinterest in his determination to make amends brought Ed to the brink of suicide, her essential decency flooded back in and she gifted him one of Ernest's old cameras as a token of forgiveness.

David Platt continued his transformation into a demon child, one that had just about been made plausible by his distress over the break-up of Martin and Gail and his dad going out with a girl of around his age. He slammed the car door on the hand of his mother's new boyfriend and began tormenting his mother by sending her cards signed 'Richard Hillman'. However, when he informed a fleetingly returning Maureen Webster and the rest of the assembled at Christmas dinner that her husband Bill Webster was having an affair behind her back with Audrey Roberts, he was for once on the moral high ground – if a little too gleeful in being the bearer of the news.

Becky Granger made her first appearance. A skinny, abrasive, peroxided blonde – Sarah Platt thought she was 'minging' – she was intended as a short-term character. Katherine Kelly's portrayal was so powerful that she was shortly brought back to be a regular, undergoing The Street's traditional de-nastification regime prior to the return. In her first stint, she framed up Kelly Crabtree for theft and tried to pinch her boyfriend Lloyd Mullaney.

Steve McDonald decided to buy the Rovers from current owner Fred Elliott. (Fred passed away shortly after the sale.) Charlie Stubbs, who had been jilted by Shelley Unwin at the altar over his cheating, took up with Tracy Barlow, but that didn't stop his wandering ways. Tracy reacted in a different way to Shelley. She set out on a campaign to convince neighbours – especially Claire Peacock – that she was a victim of domestic violence, so as to set up an 'abuse excuse' when she eventually wreaked her terrible vengeance on Charlie.

Mike Baldwin died on 7 April, succumbing to a heart attack after a year in which he had careened between confusion and lucidity, much to the distress of the people around him and the terror of himself. Though the rivalry between him and Ken Barlow had lessened in recent years, it seemed right that the ruthless capitalist and the idealistic socialist were together at the end. Says Daran Little, 'I was stunned when I was given the death episode to write because I thought John Stevenson as the guy who'd created Mike Baldwin and as Johnny's personal friend would have been given it to write. I think it was because I'd banged on and on at conference about how he had to die in the rain on the cobbles in Ken Barlow's arms.'

Danny Baldwin had persuaded Mike to give him power of attorney as he deteriorated, but he discovered to his horror that Mike had signed a revised will leaving everything to one of his other sons, Adam. However, he and new partner Leanne Battersby conspired to hide the will. One of the reasons Danny had fallen for Leanne was that she had her 'eye on the main chance' so it wasn't too shocking that Leanne blackmailed him when their relationship soured, demanding £100,000 to keep her copy of the new will to herself. Danny agreed, in two instalments. However, Adam (Sam Robertson) found out about the will anyway and Danny had to cede 40 per cent of the factory to him rather than go through the courts. Adam showed a teenager's impetuousness when he shortly sold his share to a pair of businessmen, Paul and Liam Connor (Sean Gallagher and Rob-James Collier). Soon they would be sole owners of Underworld: Danny sold up too. They were on one level bizarre: Irish Mancunians, brothers and a combination of older and talented (Paul) and younger and more charismatic but a bit of a hothead (Liam), they seemed blatantly modelled on Noel and Liam Gallagher of rock band Oasis. Nonetheless, they were good characters and brought with them two females equally strong: budding businesswoman Carla (Alison King), Paul's stunning but deadly wife, and barmaid and part-time singer Michelle, their younger sister. The latter was played by pop singer Kym Marsh. Though Marsh is incandescently beautiful, her casting originally seemed stupid: she was a former member of Hear'Say, who were then a laughing stock because of the precipitous waning of their fortunes after shooting to fame in TV talent contest *Popstars*. However, she proved an estimable actress. Michelle had a teenage son, Ryan (Ben Thompson).

In 2006, the highest-rated episode of *Coronation Street* mustered 12.6 million viewers. This was a shockingly paltry audience: it was the type of viewing figure that the lowest-rated *Street* episode of the year traditionally attracted (invariably a summer broadcast when people are on holiday/out enjoying the sunshine). This was not an indication of any crisis for the programme but of a disturbing trend for television. Forty-four of the year's 258 episodes made number one in the weekly ratings, a healthy proportion for The Street. Not a single *Street* failed to make the top 20. However, even as it retained its position as the most popular show on television, *Coronation Street* no longer had anything like the pulling power it had possessed as recently as 1999 when nearly 20 million watched the year's top-rated episode, a figure adjacent to the type of peak figure the programme had garnered back in the two-channel, no-spending-power Sixties.

John Stevenson opines, 'I think the days of the twenty million audience are probably gone forever, whatever you do.' Whether people are watching less television or about the same amount but spread across the almost infinite number of channels accessible through cable, satellite and set-top boxes, one could make the argument that the transformed ratings are a barometer of a healthy amount of television choice and/or raised living standards. It does seem a shame, though, that *Coronation Street* is now almost just another television programme and will never again be a collective national experience. Observes Tom Elliott, 'I'd go out into a supermarket or travel on a train or a bus and I'd hear people discussing last night's episode. That doesn't happen now.'

In terms of introducing new characters, 2007 was a dire year for *Coronation Street*.

Harry and Dan Mason, a father and son team who took over the Rosamund Street bookies toward the end of the year, were thoroughly nasty pieces of work, not criminal as such but possessed of hearts of granite and impossible to consider a welcome screen presence. They were both gone by November the following year. March 2007 saw the intro-duction of the Mortons, who would inhabit No.6 and who would run a fast food outlet on the former site of Diggory's bakery on Victoria Street. Father Jerry (Michael Starke) had a belly as big as a living room. His clan comprised his father Wilf (Rodney Litchfield, who lasted mere weeks), older daughter Jodie (Samantha Seager, who was gone by November), teenage twins Darryl (Jonathan Dixon) and Mel (Emma Edmondson), 13-year-old Kayleigh (Jessica Barden) and youngest child Finlay (Ramone Quinn, who differed from the others in that he was black).

Things got off to a grisly start when the viewers were effectively asked to find it admirable that Jerry tricked a signmaker out of his proper fee and they never really recovered from there. From the nuisance Jerry caused the neighbours by playing The Jam at full blast to the saga involving a shed-cum-house they installed in the back garden for Daryl to occupy; to Mel's uninvolving dilemma about whether to join the police service in defiance of the criminal life once led by her granddad; to Daryl's unconvincing relationship with Dev Alahan's daughter Amber; to Kayleigh's precocious clubbing escapades; to Ramone Quinn's complete lack of acting talent; to Jodie's complete lack of a personality, the Mortons were simply uninteresting when they weren't completely unlovable. A disaster from start to finish, they would all be gone from the programme by October 2009. Ironically, Jerry Morton's vile ex-wife Teresa – played by Karen Henthorn – had more of a screen presence than the rest of the family put together.

A friend of Claire Peacock's named Casey Carswell – a mother who had recently lost her son – abducted Freddie, Ashley and Claire's first child together. Baby-snatching stories were now a *Street* tradition, proven to be ratings' grabbers back when Christopher Hewitt went missing in 1962. This time round, though, real-life events made The Street abruptly halt their intended plot, which was to have lasted several months: it was feared it would distress the parents of British child Madeleine McCann, who had disappeared from a holiday resort in Portugal.

Leanne Battersby returned to The Street after a few months away and started going out with Liam Connor. She seemed a well-to-do young businesswoman and, in a way, she was. However, she kept secret her profession of prostitute – until she turned up for an appointment only to find her client was Liam's brother Paul. The latter's world came tumbling down when Carla found out about his passion for hookers and told him they were finished. A distraught Paul bundled Leanne into the boot of his car and sped off, but he died when the car crashed. Leanne was unharmed physically but had to face the disgust of Liam – who dumped her – and the contempt of Carla. (The latter was left Paul's controlling share of Underworld.) Meanwhile, the outstanding £50,000 owed to Leanne by Danny Baldwin – something that would have removed the rationale for Leanne being on the game at all – was simply not addressed.

Another Battersby (or Battersby-Brown as Les now styled himself, like his 'wife') was abruptly written out. Bruce Jones had been accused of giving away plotlines to the press. Though he denied it, he left the show by mutual consent and Les's absence was explained away by him becoming tour manager of a ZZ Top tribute band. Cilla Battersby-Brown left not long after, having been bequeathed some valuable jewellery. It was an altogether messy scenario – particularly as Cilla's son Chesney implausibly remained on the scene – and one wonders whether The Street would have done better simply to give Jones a warning.

Liz McDonald married her on-again, off-again drumming boyfriend Vernon Tomlin (Ian Reddington) on the last day of the year. The marriage, though, was not destined to last: Liz had decided to call it off but married Vernon out of pity when he was beaten up by her ex-husband Jim. Said beating was a writing *faux pas*. When Jim had beaten up Jez Quigley, he had screamed at him, 'You're a bully!', something that displayed (his prior beating up of Liz notwithstanding) that Jim was no brute himself.

Sarah Platt had fallen in love in recent times with Todd's brother Jason Grimshaw, and the two planned to wed following a previous attempt that Jason had ducked out of by escaping through a toilet window. Sarah's brother David had been spinning out of control. The suspicion of attempted murder of Jason hanging over him saw him banned from the wedding. Infuriated, David left a suicide note and on the day of the wedding drove his car into the very canal that Richard Hillman had tried to slaughter him and his family in. He survived, and it was left ambiguous as to whether he had intended to do away with himself. Sarah got revenge on her brother for taking the gloss off her nuptials by planting Ecstasy on him and thus kyboshing an invitation from Audrey's Canadian son Stephen to work for him in Italy, nabbing the job for herself. However, it wrecked her marriage, as Jason – appalled at her treachery – refused to go with her.

Tracy Barlow went through with her plan to get revenge on Charlie Stubbs – one given impetus when he told her to leave No.6, which he owned these days. While pretending to give him an amorous evening, she hit him over the head with a heavy lamp. Arrested, she cited the abuse that her parents and Claire Peacock had been tricked into believing she was suffering. The police, however, were sceptical of her self-defence claim when they realised the effort the average female would have to employ to heft the lamp. She was charged with murder, though was at least given bail. Tracy's trial occurred the few short months after the crime that for practical reasons is traditional in soapland. It was preceded on 25 March by The Street's second ever two-hander episode. In it, Tracy admitted to an appalled Deirdre that she was guilty. Deirdre was horrified but decided to stick by her, but it was Deirdre's confused evidence on the witness stand that was partly responsible for Tracy going down for a minimum of 15 years.

Kim Crowther took over as producer from Steve Frost in 2008.
Increasing health problems had prompted Liz Dawn to ask to be written out of the programme. The first month of the year saw the end of her tenure of over a third of a century as Vera Duckworth when her character died peacefully while sleeping in a chair. The husband with whom Vera had so frequently and deafeningly been at odds was distraught.

Michelle Connor discovered that her son Ryan was not really hers: another baby had been accidentally switched at birth. At first she fought the idea that this changed anything, but couldn't resist arranging a meeting with her biological son Alex (Dario Coates) and developed an attachment to him that was understandable considering he looked unnervingly like her dead husband. It was a reasonable enough storyline, but it petered limply out. Alex hasn't been seen since April 2008. Meanwhile, Gail met her father, Ted Page (Michael Byrne) for the first time. He continues to be a regular character in The Street. Since Ted turned out to have caught 'the other bus' in the half-century since he had got Audrey Roberts pregnant, it meant that the days when people complained about the lack of Weatherfield homosexuals were now an increasingly dim memory. As was, apparently, Gail's own opinion stated when her daughter's fiancé turned out to be gay that homosexuality was 'disgusting'.

David Platt seemed halfway to redemption this year when the early months saw him find love in the shape of Tina McIntyre (Michelle Keegan). However, it didn't take David long to find a reason to be unhappy. When he discovered that Tina had, with Gail's encouragement, had an abortion behind his back, he pushed his mother down the stairs of No.8 in an argument. In July, Ken Barlow went to a university reunion and was embarrassed to contemplate the fact that he alone of his classmates was still living in the same street in which he had been born.

The consequence was that he dug out the novel he had been seen writing in 1962. He found that the gap of 46 years hadn't made it any better and abandoned his plans to be the new Alan Sillitoe.

Daran Little says, 'If you do a bad thing on *Coronation Street*, you have to be found out, you have to go to prison, you have to suffer. There's some sort of moral code. That's a voluntary thing.' Leanne Battersby, however, seemed curiously immune to The Street's crime-doesn't-pay subtext. Finding her new life as a restaurateur a grind, she decided to burn down the business for the insurance money. She has yet to be caught for it, her accomplice Paul Clayton (a son of Terry Duckworth) having copped the blame and fled before his trial. A little later, Janice Battersby decided to nab the Underworld lottery syndicate's modest winnings for herself. When her theft was discovered, she took the rap despite the fact that it had been her step-daughter's idea. The matter did cause Leanne, however, to get dumped by boyfriend Dan Mason, who had been able to tolerate her being an ex-hooker but objected to her being an 'ex-human being'.

The major figure in The Street in 2008 was Tony Gordon, partner – in a romantic and, soon, business sense – of Carla Connor. In the first of the episodes of 8 August, Tony visited the last holdout in a site he wanted to redevelop. His freakishly large left eye seemed to balloon with rage at the obstinacy of the pensioner in question. Said tenant was Jed Stone, whose last appearance in The Street had been on 28 September 1966, a 42-year gap for an actor – Kenneth Cope – reprising a TV role that must surely be a record.

The ravages of age are always shocking and the contrast between the white-haired, puffy-faced and somewhat asthmatic sounding Cope of 2008 compared to the vigorous young man he was when last seen in the programme was jarring. Even more jarring – in character terms – was how the mighty had fallen. While Jed Stone had a roguish charm – certainly enough to thrill his landlady Minnie Caldwell – he was the type of person who nobody really wants as a neighbour. An ex-jailbird, he was constantly ducking and diving. His being reduced by time and circumstance to a fragile and solitary figure virtually helpless in the face of the aggression of Tony, the type of alpha male he used to be, was a sad sight.

The original plan had been for Tony Gordon to be hassling an arbitrary old man, one Mr Gamble. It was casting director June West's idea to resurrect Jed, whose last significant mention had been in 1974, when he had been supposed to visit Minnie but had sent in his place a man of exactly his kind of twinkle-eyed quasi-villainy, Eddie Yeats. In stark contrast to the programme's expedient continuity lapses of recent years, hard work went into ensuring the thread was picked up adroitly from 1966. As he'd always done in the Sixties, Jed permanently wore a cap. The name of his beloved cat Sunny Jim also displayed great depth of knowledge about *Street* history: this was the nickname Minnie Caldwell had given her beloved lodger, as well as her own new cat when Jed departed The Street for good.

Another of Gordon's developments, incidentally, was a block of luxury flats on Victoria Street called Victoria Court, theoretically enabling the opening up of The Street to more characters from the professional class. Later that year, Tony turned from bully to murderer. Insanely jealous at the best of times, the affair between Carla and Liam Connor that the pair didn't know he was aware of drove him to hire one Jimmy Dockerson to kill Liam in an ostensible hit-and-run.

With most of the Battersbys gone, there was a chav-sized hole in The Street, but it wasn't long before the producers rectified that offence against the programme's traditions. The Windasses moved into No.6 in December. Eddie Windass (Steve Huison) had a scraggly hairstyle whose length was unseemly for his age and was work shy in a way the benefit system hadn't allowed in Stan Ogden's day, being permanently 'on the sick'. Incongruously, he was a dab hand at cake-baking. His wife Anna (Debbie Rush) was not much brighter but had more of a conscience about the nuisance her family caused neighbours. Teenage son Gary (Mikey North) was as nasty as David Platt, and unlike David had the fighting prowess to back up his mean talk, as David found out to his cost. Eddie's brother Len (Conor Ryan) – a peripheral family/cast member – was a ducking, diving wideboy who Gary looked up to. The blatant 'fart-arse' variation that their name constituted was an over-the-top touch but the Windasses were a worthy contribution to the Tanner/Ogden/Duckworth/Battersby tradition.

October gave The Street's fans a chance to find out what Hayley had been up to in her year away doing voluntary work via the DVD *Out of Africa*. This sun-baked production also featured Cilla Battersby-Brown, her daughter Fiz Brown, Chesney Battersby-Brown and Kirk Sutherland. It was the first *Street* spin-off since 1997, back when VCR was still the medium on which such things were issued.

Two longstanding *Street* marriages that had already seen infidelity on both sides were in 2009 put under strain once more. This time it was the men in the Ken & Deirdre Barlow and Kevin & Sally Webster axes who were the straying partners.

Kevin found himself increasingly smitten by the youth and vivaciousness of Molly Dobbs, Tyrone's wife since January. Kevin sat Sally down on Christmas Day to tell her he was leaving her – only to be told by Sally before he could break the news that she had breast cancer. This plot turn mirrored the real life breast cancer of Sally Whittaker. Stricken with remorse, Kevin finished with Molly. Ken, meanwhile, had fallen for Martha Fraser, played in another example of a *Street* celebrity guest appearance by Stephanie Beacham. Paradoxically, although most *Street* actors are far more famous to most UK residents than Beacham, her tenure in the glitzy *Dynasty* conferred a certain allure that those playing ordinary people in an ordinary street somehow don't posses. Houseboat-residing Martha was an actress who as an aesthete and an intellectual offered Ken stimulation that Deirdre couldn't. (Dev Alahan – with whom Deirdre had had a fling at Christmas 2001 – similarly had offered Deirdre some rare excitement.) There was a disapproving busybody interfering in this relationship, namely Audrey Roberts, although – in yet another example of the increasingly prevalent *Street* attitude of Continuity Be Damned – no explanation was offered as to what moral high ground the wrecker of Bill and Maureen Websters' marriage imagined she occupied. John Stevenson, now watching The Street as an unconnected viewer, had his own objections. 'I think we'd done enough infidelities with them,' he says. 'There are other ways to make marriages interesting, which we always used to find. The more they do it, the less impact each infidelity has.'

Ken planned to leave Deirdre to sail the canalways with Martha and packed his suitcase. At the last second, he changed his mind and hopped back onto shore – thus proving Peter Barlow, who'd found out about the plan, right: he'd told his father he was 'ridiculous' and that he would be sitting at the table for dinner in No.1 both that night and for the rest of his miserable life. Not that Peter was much less pathetic: his battle with alcoholism was mercilessly and convincingly traced, with a particularly harrowing scene involving him tempted by a half-empty bottle of wine not long after son Simon had nearly lost his life in a fire caused by one of Peter's alcoholic stupors. Peter turned the motion of raising the bottle to his lips into one of smashing it against a wall.

Maggie Jones died in December and The Street hummed and hawed about the necessary act of killing off her character. Not until the following May did Blanche Hunt pass away in the programme, her lack of visibility explained by a foreign sojourn.

There were other celebrity guest appearances. Andrew Sachs played Ramsay Clegg, Norris Cole's long-lost (and despised) half-brother. The former Manuel of *Fawlty Towers* seemed to have only been recruited because of his recent headline status after being the victim of a grubby phone call prank by two DJs. He was alright, but the storyline never caught fire. Screen smoothie Nigel Havers also turned up in The Street, as a male escort to whom Audrey took a shine.

Steve McDonald – long split from Karen – got married this year to Becky Granger, whom Roy and Hayley had taken under their wing. The couple's belief in redemption had been vindicated by the ex-jailbird as she sought with reasonable success to become a law-abiding and considerate individual. The wedding took place on 14 August – five months after the first one was abandoned because Becky turned up pretty in pink but paralytic.

Steve and Becky had a row on their honeymoon and Becky stormed off to join Roy and Hayley, who were holidaying at the home of Frankie Baldwin in Transylvania. An apparently unlikely location for a cockney gal, but somewhere extraordinary was needed as a backdrop for the events of the second *Coronation Street* exclusive material DVD in as many years. Released in October, *Romanian Holiday* featured Frankie in flashback, but not played by Debra Stephenson.

Tony Gordon's dark secret finally emerged this year when, mistakenly believing he was suffering a fatal heart attack, he made a murder confession to Roy Cropper. This was somewhat unfortunate for Maria, Liam Connor's widow. She had initially guessed the truth about Tony, then discounted it and fallen in love with him. If it was any consolation to Maria – which it wasn't – Tony had been humanised by his love for her: he had initially been planning to permanently silence Roy Cropper but instead turned himself in to the police, unable to live anymore with his guilt or face adding to the body count.

Nick Tilsley returned to The Street, confusingly now played not by Adam Rickitt but by Ben Price, a familiar face from *Footballers' Wives* and *Casualty*. (Rickitt in fact was now acting in a soap in his adopted homeland of New Zealand called *Shortland Street*.) Audrey had called Nick back in order to get him to talk his mum out of marrying a loser like

Joe McIntyre (Tina's dad), although even she had no idea of the trouble Joe was in. Joe was living in terror of a take-no-prisoners loan shark named Rick Neelan. Though people who bought loans and added stratospheric interest rates plus menaces to the original debt were increasingly a part of life in Britain – especially in the midst of the latest recession – the storyline was thoroughly annoying. Why Joe didn't just go to the police was mystifying.

Rita found herself falling for Colin, the father of Eileen Grimshaw. Their marriage plans were torn asunder, though, when it emerged that her intended's ne'er-do-well nature wasn't that of the common or garden cheeky chappie: unbeknown even to him, he had got Eileen's 14-year-old schoolfriend Paula Carp in the family way more than 30 years before and had a daughter, Julie Carp, an Underworld machinist and already a regular character. Colin died of a heart attack before the courts could deal with him.

Later in the year, Rita sold The Kabin to her business partner Norris Cole and went off on a cruise. Cue telephone exchanges about what exactly a poop deck is. More comedy was provided by an Indian uncle of Dev Alahan called Umed. A reptilian individual with an accent as thick as mustard, he was an unctuous and grasping presence behind the Corner Shop counter for several months in which the establishment inexplicably failed to go bankrupt.

There was more transmission upheaval for the programme in 2009. When the Sunday episode of The Street had relocated to Friday in January 2008, there was at least a symmetry about the Monday-Wednesday-Friday schedule despite the awkward division of episodes on Mondays and Fridays. That was all blown away by the decision exactly 18 months later to permanently move The Street from the Wednesday slot it had possessed for 49 years to Thursday, with a simultaneous change in the transmission time to 8.30pm. The culprit was football, which had displaced the Wednesday *Street* repeatedly over the years: many were the times, for instance, when the air had turned blue in British living rooms as people had settled down to watch The Street only to find the closing credits rolling because it had been brought forward to 7.00pm to allow a soccer transmission to start at 7.30pm. This new move seemed the final insult. Football might be, to quote a common superlative, a 'game of billions', but – latter-stage World Cup England matches excepted – its TV pulling power in Britain is not in the same league as that of *Coronation Street*.

Part Seven
Coronation Street Now

As *Coronation Street* entered 2010, there was understandable chatter on the internet about how wonderful it would be if Tony Warren were commissioned to write December's 50th anniversary episode. For sentimental reasons, it would indeed be wonderful. For practical reasons – Warren hasn't written a *Coronation Street* episode since March 1976 – it would be close to impossible. (Perhaps a more realistic proposition would be to have this former thespian appear in a speaking role.) However, it does seem reasonable to assume another piece of poetry will be engineered: that the character who has remained with the show from episode one onwards will be central to the anniversary edition.

Utterly unlikely as it would have been to almost all viewers of the first episode of *Coronation Street* that the show would still be around in 50 years, just as unlikely would have been the idea that should it survive that long Ken Barlow would be the sole remaining original character. The unlikelihood of him of all people being still present was down to the fact that he was (although they didn't have the phrase back then) upwardly mobile. This university student who found his father's habit of swilling his meals down with cups of tea excruciatingly non-U (to use a phrase that *was* in circulation at the time) was the sort of person who clearly aspired to leave behind the grimy, humble street in which he'd grown up as soon as he had the necessary degree. Instead, Ken Barlow outlasted every other resident, watching all the people who were on the street in 1960 one by one move away or die. William Roache acknowledges the contradiction of this. 'The problem with Ken always was he's a university graduate from within The Street – why did he stay?' he says. 'So there had to be that element of loser or weakness about him, mainly with his women. He's had his 23 girlfriends and three wives and that's mainly 'cos he can't hang onto them. That was always a problem.'

Ken has had almost as many jobs as partners. Of all the professions in which he's been employed down the years, Roache nominates two as being most appropriate for his character: 'I think his soul is connected to teaching. He's always got this thing about wanting to help people and be the voice of Weatherfield. I think doing the local paper was probably quite near to what he would like to do.' Ken remains an unashamed, old-school socialist. His sometimes pompous collectivist declarations can grate but one can also admire him for sticking to his principles in a world that increasingly dismisses them as antediluvian. Roache himself is a Conservative. He says, 'Bill Roache doesn't necessarily like what Ken says, but I'm an actor and if I play Ken I've just got to believe that he would say it.'

Though he has opinions on the character, Roache admits he has virtually no input. 'The writers write and we act, but if something comes along that you feel you cannot truthfully play, you go and see them and it gets sorted out,' he says. 'It's only happened very rarely over the fifty years for me. Very rarely indeed, 'cos the writers pick up on us and write for us.'

Contrary to common assumption, Roache has neither played just one role all his life nor just one role since joining The Street. As well as his pre-*Street* repertory and TV work, he formed a production company with his second wife after he'd taken on the role of Ken Barlow. 'We produced some plays in Preston,' he says. 'That was really good. It's good to do theatre again and feel the contact with the audience. But it was such hard work and as the schedule stepped up to three and four [episodes] a week, it was just too much. You need time out.' However, it would be fair to say Roache is generally known to the vast mass of the public for his *Coronation Street* role. Just two people in the world can rival Roache for portraying the same character continuously on television, both from the American CBS soap opera *As The World Turns*. Don Hastings has played Bob Hughes therein from October 1960 – i.e., two months before Roache became Barlow. However, his status as holder of the record for continuous portrayal of a character is in doubt, as his appearances since 2006 have been very sporadic. The late Helen Wagner was Nancy Hughes in *As The World Turns* from April 1956 to April 2010, but had a break from the show from 1981 to 1985. The claim of Roache to this appearance crown – he has been in *Coronation Street* every single year of its existence and Ken has always been a regular, not sporadically seen, character – seems therefore the strongest. In light of this, the MBE Roache was awarded in 2001 seems a little paltry, especially when considering Violet Carson's 1965 OBE.

As far back as 40 years ago, Ken Irwin revealed that Roache often debated with himself getting out of *Coronation Street*, a process encouraged by his then agent. 'I go through an agonising, heart-searching thing,' Roache said then of the occasions that his contract came up for renewal. 'It is a marvellous show for me and I love it. But as an actor one sometimes feels one is missing out. I often feel I should get out. Finally, it is economics that count.' By 1970 Roache had financial commitments that included three houses in England and a farm on the island of Elba. Leaving The Street would have certainly affected the economics associated with that set-up. Though he hasn't necessarily publicly cited these as reasons, divorce, a new family and a bankruptcy have subsequently created additional cause to hesitate about leaving the programme. 'We had annual contracts that rolled on,' says Roache now. 'You're lucky if you stay in. Every character is reviewed every year. New producers come in. We don't know. We've no idea what goes on. You get on with the job, you're an actor, you're glad to be employed. I'm really grateful I've got the job. You're never completely secure with just an annual contract.' Nonetheless, he does acknowledge the exquisite dilemma that The Street constitutes for an actor. Thespians by definition want to play different roles; they also by definition want to be seen widely, regularly and in quality product, a desire that *Coronation Street* is seemingly tailor-made to fulfil. 'It worked both ways,' Roache says. 'There was a time when you think about should I move on and so on, but The Street is such a good thing, it's so well written. Every year you'll have two or three really good storylines that are as good as you'll get anywhere. Yes, it is an exquisite thing, but also you'll get new stories and the character gets turned on its head sometimes and gets stretched and the stories are really quite brilliant, the writers are so good, so it's not like playing the same part in a play for fifty years. You're growing, I'm falling to bits in front of everybody's eyes and the character's developing all the time. Even now, this year, at my old age, Stephanie Beacham – another girlfriend. Brilliant.'

Says Roache's former *Street* colleague Geoff Hinsliff, 'I never dared say any of this to Bill, but I used to think that Bill was being kept in reserve. That if ever *Coronation Street* was getting boring and old-fashioned and if those complaints were being made about it, they could always say, "We have got rid of Bill Roache. We are different now." Bill was the pawn that they could discard. It was just a question of why go on and on and on with Bill, bless him. There aren't that many storylines for him, for God's sake, are there? What hasn't he done now in his life?' Hinsliff says, 'I don't think it's a wasted career.' However, he also says, 'Playing the same role for fifty years, [you] can't really say you're an actor – it's something different. When you die: what did you do? "I did this for fifty years and I stayed there and people liked me and they were pleased to see me." That's quite an accomplishment, but as a career as an actor, it doesn't really stack up. But as an achievement, there's nothing like it in the world. Nobody's ever done it.'

The example of his screen brother provides an interesting contrast to Roache's 50-year tenancy of *Coronation Street*. Alan Rothwell's flitting in and out of The Street led ultimately to his permanent writing out of the programme, and therefore by necessity his moving on. The onetime David Barlow says, 'I really wanted to do the different things that you can do, play the different characters. I… discovered more about myself by the things that I've played and it's been that that has fascinated me about working as an actor. If you're stuck playing the same person all the time and then that person's not behaving – because of exigencies in the script – the way you think he would behave, or not even behaving in a way that you think any normal person would behave, then you lose a bit of heart in things.' Through the aegis of The Street, Rothwell was literally one of the most famous faces in the country in the Sixties. Today, many *Coronation Street* fans are completely unaware that Ken Barlow once had a brother. Asked if this causes him a little pang sometimes, Rothwell says, 'Yes it does. But it is only a small pang.' Though he does still get recognised by the public, it is more for his later appearances in children's shows *Picture Box*, *Hickory House* and *Daisy Daisy*. Rothwell: 'During the time of *Coronation Street*, it was enormous really. You were just recognised everywhere you went.' When he informs younger *Coronation Street* fans that he was a founding part of the show, he says, 'They're always surprised and somewhat in awe. That bit's alright, so I can release the news if I want to and get a good reaction.'

Bill Roache needs to explain to nobody his place in The Street's history. But from Rothwell's point of view as a man who wanted to both play different parts and to discover things about himself through his thespian activities, has his screen brother and good friend wasted his career? Rothwell: 'No. Life's much more complicated than that really. Bill's done an awful lot of other things. He's had a good, full life. I've had a good, full life too, but it's been in totally different ways.' He occasionally feels regret about not opting for the security that partly motivated Roache's decision to continue as Ken Barlow. 'Sometimes I wake up in the middle of the night and think to myself, "If I'd have stayed, I'd have been rich now",' says Rothwell. 'I could have provided for my kids a bit better and provided for my wife a bit better.'

Back in 1960, Roache was cast seven years younger than his age. Happily for credibility, he has retained his physical defiance of nature. It's shocking to realise that this full- (if grey-) haired and patently healthy and sturdy man is now pushing 80, and is a decade-and-a-half older than Jack Howarth was when he began playing Albert Tatlock. Howarth had far more of an aura of age to him even in 1960 than Roache does now. Less credible is what Roache's character has been through. Roache has described Ken Barlow as a one-man Greek tragedy. Ken lost to the Grim Reaper not just both parents but two wives and a brother by the age of 36, has outlived his daughter and has lost access to one of his sons. In real life, the actors playing those roles were no longer wanted by the show or vice versa and Roache wanted to stay: at the relevant times it seemed that death was the most plausible or logical way of engineering their exit. Viewed collectively, though, plausibility seems to have gone out the window. Looking at the long list of misfortunes that have afflicted Ken can provoke guffaws not even quelled by the fact of them taking place across the span of 50 years. Isn't this supposed to be a show about recognisably real lives? David Liddiment was the first producer known to have made the character of Ken off-limits to trigger-happy writers, so he clearly doesn't have an issue with how unlikely it is that one person could be so unlucky. 'You've got to live with the characters as they are at that point and you can't start worrying too much about where they've come from,' he says. 'There's a suspension of disbelief. I don't think people watch the show thinking about their past. They think about their immediate past, but it's amazing how much gets forgotten....' However, Liddiment also says, 'Stories do exhaust characters and sometimes you have to rest them a bit before you can come again. There's always some tension between who the characters are, what the stories are and how sustainable characters are over the long term, and Ken Barlow would not have survived had he not had pauses in between all of those things.'

Despite those tragedies, the character of Ken has often been perceived as staid and dull. 'Boring Ken Barlow' is a phrase that became embedded in the nation's psyche as a result of a libel case that Roache brought against the *Sun*, its editor and one of its freelance contributors in 1992; it was a result of an article on Roache in a multi-part series on The Street in that paper in which said sobriquet appeared prominently. The author of the piece was none other than Ken Irwin, that journalist whose career has been so intertwined with the show. As with his infamous first *Street* crit, Irwin decided to tell it like he saw it, casting aspersions on Roache's acting talents. That and a perhaps over-zealous sub-editor did the rest and m'learned friends were consulted. Irwin: 'The headline on the piece that upset Mr Roache was a bit startling and I looked in the copy. I don't write the headlines. I did not make anything up. There was nothing he could deny in the article. Most of it had appeared before and it was factual. He objected to me calling him boring.' Roache actually won the case, but ended up bankrupt for a while because the amount of money paid into court by the *Sun* before the case was the same as that which he had been awarded by the jury, a situation in which the claimant is required to pay costs.

'I don't think he's a particularly good actor,' says Irwin, 'but I don't think he's the worst actor there ever was. He's played the same character for the best part of fifty years. An actor... is supposed to play different parts.' 'Bill's a good actor,' says John Stevenson. 'He's got a good range. He doesn't get much chance to show it but he does light comedy awfully well, as well as straight stuff.' Stevenson, who knows Roache 'Very well', says, 'I don't think Bill regrets staying with the show at all. I'm sure he doesn't. He loves it and he relishes the part still and he still gives it all he's got, which is admirable. He never coasts through it and [he's] always on top.'

Though his character might sometimes be boring, the same cannot be said of Roache, who has very esoteric and unusual interests. He is a staunch believer in spiritualism, a druid who has been known to take part in robed solstice ceremonies around Stonehenge and a man who prompts raised eyebrows even from fellow Conservatives when he posits the somewhat minority theory that John Major was the greatest Prime Minister of the 20th century. However, though to some an odd fellow, he is patently very civilised. As someone in *Coronation Street*'s office remarked to this author, 'He's a lovely chap.'

Sadly, Roache's wife Sara died of a heart attack in 2009 aged just 58, compounding the tragedy of Roache losing an 18-month-old daughter in 1984. Sara was an actress and played the judge who sent Tracy down in 2007, something that completed a remarkable grand slam of *Street* appearances by Roaches: as well as son Linus playing Peter Barlow, Roache's first wife Anna Cropper appeared in the show in 1962 as Joan Akers, who kidnapped Christopher Hewitt. Even Linus Roache's partner Rosalind Bennett has popped up: she played a girlfriend of Curly Watts named Tina Wagstaffe in 1986.

Roache can cite only one point where – whatever outside acting ambitions he might have harboured – he wasn't enjoying being in *Coronation Street*. 'In the middle it sagged a bit,' he says. 'About the twentieth year, somewhere around there, I began to wonder. Probably going through my own sort of crisis. But I didn't seriously think about leaving.... I'm glad I stayed.' He says he never gets bored with the job: 'You don't have a chance. It's very hard work.'

Like Liddiment before her, Carolyn Reynolds also indicated to the show's writers that Ken Barlow was immune from Weatherfield's savage mortality rate. She says, 'I can remember Julian Roach saying that if Bill Roache is brave enough to run with this show to the bitter end, let's hope he has a wonderful exit, fantastic scene in the Rovers, and that we happen to be filming at the time. 'Cos it was so unique to have someone in for that length of time.' Geoff Hinsliff says of Roache, 'Fifty years, that would be a good time for him to say, "Thank you very much".' However, the symmetrical bow-out from the programme that Hinsliff suggests is not something Roache is contemplating. 'Retiring isn't an option,' says Roache. 'I love The Street, I'm very proud of it, and while I can do it and while they want me, I'll be there.'

In his 1970 book *The Real Coronation Street* Ken Irwin said that the programme whose introduction he had lambasted would probably last another three years but expressed doubts that it would survive another decade.

It's easy to scoff at his reasoning on one count – that the original cast was getting old – but it was not so logical to assume then that the programme would or could survive the natural wastage that went with its longevity: it must have seemed to some like suggesting that four new people could replace the constituent parts of The Beatles. Additionally, Irwin made a valid point: that the Independent Television Authority had a remit that involved quality not success, something demonstrated not just in its 1967 decree that *Crossroads* should reduce its output but also its ordering of the actual cancellation of successful shows like *Double Your Money* and *Take Your Pick* because they were getting stale. Though Denis Forman claims that the ITA was delighted with The Street because the show was clean, wholesome and Christian, the body's cancelling of The Street even though it was hitting number one was not by any means out of the question at that point in history. Ultimately *Coronation Street* outlived the ITA in both name and power: the Independent Television Commission, the modern-day equivalent of the ITA, is not an authority with the capacity to take programmes off the air.

The Street was once synonymous with the various Granada 'idents' that immediately preceded it, the most famous of which is probably the yellow-on-blue-background affair with the words 'Granada Colour Production' (later just 'Granada') accompanying a 'G' sprouting an arrow pointing symbolically Northwards. Since 2006, we are informed that the show is a product of 'ITV Studios', the last vestiges of the franchises having disappeared into history in 2003 when Carlton and Granada merged – with the latter taking the majority share – into ITV plc. Carlton and Granada themselves were at that point the final remnants of regional broadcasting on ITV following changes in the law that allowed such companies to gobble each other up. The remit to produce programming resonant for a region that may have helped bring *Coronation Street* into the world no longer exists.

Following a first two decades in which on only three occasions were *Coronation Street* episodes repeated, fans of the programme now never need miss an episode even if they don't possess a VCR or DVD player. *Street* repeats can be seen more than once every day of the week, either on terrestrial television or digital. This is not to mention the episodes' availability as free internet downloads. An omnibus is broadcast on both Saturdays and Sundays.

The programme was heading for some spectacular storylines to mark the half-century, including a plot that dredged up a 50-year-old *Street* secret about a son Ken didn't know he had that was set to feature Roache's actor sons Linus and James. However, the early months of 2010 did not auger well for The Street. Janice Battersby's lodger Trevor Dean (Steve Jackson) was instantly recognisable as a nothing character, the type of failure in casting leading to inevitable quick departure which *Street* viewers by now have a sixth sense about. That he was what we now call a refuse collector reminded older viewers of another *Street* binman (as they were then tagged), Eddie Yeats. The latter's actor Geoffrey Hughes had recognisably had that X-factor that was nothing to do with good looks – or even necessarily anything one could articulate – but which made one want to see him on screen again. Meanwhile, a story in March that saw six-year-old Simon Barlow make his way alone the 50 miles from Blackpool to where Weatherfield notionally stands was simply idiotic – regardless of the scriptwriter's attempt to explain it away with an airy 'I can read a train timetable' from Simon. While the story thread that saw Gail McIntyre (formerly Platt) remanded in custody on suspicion of murdering her husband after Joe made a hash of faking his own death rose reasonably well above its origins in the irritating storyline involving a loan shark, the scenes in a women's prison depicting Gail as an innocent abroad had more than a smack of *déjà vu*: it seemed only five minutes ago that we had been through all this with the Deirdre/Jon Lindsay story. The production team also seemed strangely desperate to make Dev and Sunita Alahan 'real' *Coronation Street* characters by turning them into residents. They had a large house with a garden in leafy Cheshire but Sunita nagged Dev into buying No.7. The extended arguments between the two over it was patently a load of bluster on the part of scriptwriters and storyliners conscious of the illogicality of the desire to live on the same road as their business. The sloppiness and *EastEnders*-like cartoonishness was not a good way to go out for Kim Crowther. Her two-year production reign ended in July when she was replaced by ex-*Doctor Who* producer Phil Collinson.

The year at least proved there were still milestones for a 50-year-old programme. Two different verdicts in Gail's trial were filmed, one of which (guilty) was shown on the internet only. When Sophie Webster puckered up to Sian Powers (Sacha Parkinson) after her friend told her she meant more to her than any lad, The Street's first lesbian story was underway. Meanwhile, Izzy Armstrong (Cherylee Houston) – met by Kirk Sutherland via an internet chat room – was the first disabled regular character whose infirmity was (unlike that of Maud Grimes) not simply a symptom of old age. A new title sequence came at the end of May. The new titles were made necessary by a switch to filming in high definition.

The re-recording of the theme that went with them seemed gratuitous. A dynamic as opposed to sleepy cat summed up the rather flashy nature of the new titles, which opened with shots of a drizzly, busy Manchester that gave way to vistas of The Street that melted into each other. Nonetheless, they ended on a classy shot of Coronation Street chimney pots against a sunset, a very cinematic affair compared to the ground level view of The Street the viewers had long been used to at the climax of the title sequence.

The new recording of the theme tune was less successful. David Browning's intimate knowledge of Granada makes him *au fait* with attempts at the company to update the theme down the years, starting – he estimates – in the mid-1980s. 'Granada have tried several versions,' he claims. 'Believe it or not they even tried a reggae version of it.... Rock 'n' roll, all sorts of versions they tried to update the show.... I wasn't involved in any of those.' None of the alternative recordings ever made the airwaves. Browning: 'Every one has been chucked out by the top floor and they've always decided to retain that Salford brass band feel to it.' Unlike the 1970 rearrangement, the 2010 version was instantly recognisable as different to its predecessor, although having said that it was not a monstrous tampering with perfection like the BBC's updated version of the *Doctor Who* theme tune and did indeed once more retain the Salford brass band flavour. It somehow lacked the mournful dignity of the long familiar arrangement, though, its more prominent clarinet giving it a jauntier tone.

The Street's fake garden fences and chimney pots had to be upgraded to the real thing to withstand the merciless eye of high definition – which must have induced wry chuckles in the stagehands who'd had to make scruffier The Street's sets in 1969 because colour made them look too glamorous.

Being a *Coronation Street* viewer in 2010 to some extent means having to conduct one's life in the way that the protagonists did in the famous episode of *Whatever Happened To The Likely Lads?* in which they desperately attempted to avoid any parts of the media that might tell them the result of the England football fixture whose highlights were due to be screened that evening. Tabloid newspapers and the now almost-as-prolific TV listings magazines consistently run plot spoilers, in the case of the latter often on the front cover and sometimes weeks in advance. Such spoilers are a tradition of course, and the advent of the internet means that anybody – professionally employed in the media or not – can now break a storyline. Additionally, such is the sieve-like nature of TV studios these days – especially with the two-month gap between script delivery and recording now standard on The Street – that spoilt plots would happen anyway to an extent. However, many are surprised and dismayed that these days The Street actively cooperates with such revelations. In 1984, when it was discovered that Esther Rose – storyliner for a quarter-century – had been a mole leaking plots and even actors' home addresses to the press, Bill Podmore was disappointed that her imminent retirement – literally that week – denied him the satisfaction of sacking her. Now it is completely different. Stevenson: 'The producers and ITV seem to think that it's worth blowing the stories in advance just to get on a magazine cover.' The days when a jaw-dropper of a plot development like Martha Longhurst's death could hit the screens without any prior intimation are gone forever.

As are the days when The Street aspired to very lofty heights. Commodification has not yet triumphed over art on The Street, but it would be laughable to suggest that *Coronation Street* in 2010 lives up to the comment of then-*Street* producer Derek Granger in a feature on the programme in a 1962 edition of the television magazine *Contrast*: 'The battle for higher standards will be fought in the area of mass entertainment.'

Fond as he is of the legacy of the show that he helped bring to the airwaves, Sir Denis Forman insists that *Coronation Street* was never realism. 'It conned people into thinking it was documentary but it wasn't, it was unreal,' he says. 'A world was conjured up which was its own world and it had a working class culture which made people think – 'cos it was the only working class show on the air – that it was documentary and realistic. It wasn't. It was highly dramatic. It was a vision of a kind of working class world that never really existed.' Whether or not The Street is realistic is a matter of opinion – other people are convinced that the show, especially in its early days, was as realistic as it's possible to be within the parameters of the artifice of acted drama. However, few today would make great claims for the show being true to life, however enjoyable it remains. Its verisimilitude is gradually being eroded by commercial concerns linked to the massively reduced advertising revenue that ITV is able to generate.

'Recently there was a thing that I read which said people are actually watching as much television as they were, which surprised me,' says Carolyn Reynolds. 'It was a counter-argument against the internet: it's not quite the end of television as we know it.' Perhaps not, but the absolute number of TV viewers being unchanged is scant consolation for ITV as it watches its own ratings tumble – its flagship programme included – in the face of competition unimaginable in 1960 and well beyond. Even over two decades after The Street first hit the screens, ITV was still only having to contend with three other channels.

Viewing statistics have been confused by television technology that means increasing numbers of people delay their consumption of The Street beyond the point where it would be registered by the ratings agency the Broadcasters' Audience Research Board (BARB). Additionally, digital TV means that sometimes ITV is competing with itself. The 'overnight' viewing figures for each *Coronation Street* episode take in first transmissions on ITV1. The ITV1 first broadcast is included in the weekly 'consolidated' viewing figures. Also included in the consolidated figures are Sky Plus and similar timeshifted viewings and DVD/VCR recordings – as long as they are viewed within seven days of the original transmission. The omnibus broadcasts are no longer used to produce an aggregated figure for an episode. ITV2 and ITV2+1 broadcasts of the programme (either single episodes or omnibus editions) are included in those channels' respective viewing figures, not ITV1's. At the time of writing, BARB does not measure the increasingly important internet viewings. For all these reasons, and though much of the country now has access to 200 channels, one wonders whether the official 10-11 million viewers (consolidated) with which *Coronation Street* scales the weekly TV charts is actually an underestimate. Nonetheless, the massive commercial channel competition and the lower official figures have led to a diminution of the amount advertisers are prepared to shell out. The days of ITV being the 'licence to print money' referred to by David Browning are well and truly a thing of the past. This has had inevitable consequences for one of the only shows that can still guarantee the network cash. Reynolds: 'There is enormous pressure on a terrestrial channel that's seen a reduction in share and desperate to try and hold on to what it can and still sees *Coronation Street* as its biggest asset.' John Stevenson says, 'Since the old order changed and Granada was bought out by [Gerry] Robinson and [Charles] Allen and those people, and as ITV went downhill – you know what the debts are now and how little money they make – word keeps coming down the line to the producer saying in effect, "This year we want three murders and a good fire" and all that.' ITV Studios cannot stand up to the ITV network in the way that an independent television company like Granada could. Stevenson: 'The producer can't say, "I don't think it's a good idea." He's actually got to get on with it or move over.'

It seems clear that ITV's obsession with the sensational that it is considered guarantees high ratings explains the recent rise in *Coronation Street* of the dismissal of dramatically inconvenient previously established facts. There are additional commerce-related pressures. Daran Little: 'There's a great push in recent years to have David and Tina and Becky and people like that ending an episode rather than older cast members. If you end an episode, it tends to be the lead story in an episode and is a cliffhanger. You just are aware that there's a drive to make the show more appealing to younger viewers. That comes from conferences when the guys come and give you market research on which characters are popular and stuff like that.' Little says such research is taken 'very seriously, and they're represented at long-term meetings where the network is there and they back these things up.' Another insider, who wishes to be anonymous, says, 'Once [Granada] bought out Carlton and Charles Allen was the undisputed king, producers would come back from a summons to ITV in London – especially after things like the Richard Hillman saga: "Oh, lots more of that." That's why there is so much more crime now. It's always demanded.... The ITV network call every shot. Producers try and dodge the worst demands but it's very difficult. The way things are in television, what do you do now if you fall out with Granada? There's the Sky networks and there aren't many jobs there, and there is the BBC, and the BBC don't want people who've come from ITV anyway. There's enormous pressure to keep your nose clean and smile and do what you're told.'

Little predicts that what he calls the 'suits' will increasingly dictate plot strands. 'If advertisers are less willing to pay money, then less things are going to be made,' he says. 'No one's going to take a risk on a new programme, so more pressure is put onto the established programmes, whether they be light entertainment or soap opera, and ITV network people will interfere more with those programmes because they'll have less programmes to look after.'

For Tom Elliott, things are bad enough now. He says of *Coronation Street*'s big rival, 'Though The Street won many battles, I believe it lost the war because *EastEnders* has imposed that genre of acrimony and hostility on *all* the serial dramas.'

Australia, where The Street was once so massive that the actors were accompanied by outriders and had to be protected from the over-enthusiasm of a public who found them of greater interest than the visiting Queen Mother, is now far more immune to its charms. The Street's popularity Down Under was partly down to great writing and believable characterisation, but it was also partly due to homesickness by expats and a sense of cultural inferiority, both of which are now largely things of history. Antipodean fans can now only see the show on cable and digital channels.

It remains fixed in British viewers' hearts though, while many imitators have fallen by the wayside. *Family Affairs* – despite the Brian Park revamp – bit the dust in 2005. *Brookside*, that programme that once out-proled The Street and did so with more modern techniques, fell victim to declining interest in 2003. Creator Phil Redmond had by the time of its death devised *Hollyoaks*, a younger, zippier soap which has even done well enough to produce spin-off shows. However, its viewing figures come nowhere near the ratings of The Street, which itself these days has pulled away from a flagging *EastEnders*, the only comparable show other than *Crossroads* ever to seriously tussle with it for the public's affections.

Though *Coronation Street* now has to compete with fifth-time repeats of *Top Gear* on Dave and other such delights of the digital age, the viewing figure it attracts for the highest rated of its episodes is second only to the *X Factor* and its variants in the weekly ratings. The latter shows, furthermore, are a here-today, gone-tomorrow proposition: when caustic star judge Simon Cowell leaves, their appeal will be much (possibly ultimately fatally) diminished. From the get-go, *Coronation Street*'s creators decided that 'The Street's the star.' Consequently, no character or actor's departure has ever seriously damaged the show, nor ever will.

An example of how steeped the nation now is in The Street is provided by the fact that the tendency of would-be *Street* writers from down South to come up against an insurmountable obstacle in their non-Northernness has evaporated. Daran Little says, 'The majority of the writing team at the moment aren't Northern. There was a time when I was the only

Coronation Street writer who actually lived in Manchester.' This is clearly testament to the fact that generations all across Britain have been brought up on several doses per week of Northern idiom.

Few of The Street's old guard from whatever vintage seem to feel that it is as good as it was – though their definition of its peak years would seem to vary according to when they worked on it. Denis Forman still watches it occasionally but feels it has made the mistake of dispensing with 'human comedy' as opposed to 'comedy-comedy'. John Finch says, 'I haven't watched The Street now for about fifteen years. It began to upset me. I couldn't adjust to The Street I remembered and The Street that was there. I remember reading an interview Tony Warren gave. They were talking about the difference in The Street then and now and he said, "It's not that The Street's changed. It's life that's changed." And of course that's perfectly true. The last time I saw it I thought the writing was very good.... One of the elements that stopped me watching was the colour. I didn't associate The Street with colour. I always thought of it in terms of black and white.... The acting – it's not acting, they just shout at each other.'

John Stevenson left The Street's writing team permanently in 2005. He both found he disliked the approach of Steve Frost and realised he didn't have the energy any longer to combine writing for it with attending to other projects he wanted to pursue. He still watches at least one episode per week and says regarding his previously stated misgivings about its schedule and approach, 'It's amazing the show's as good as it is.' Brian Park: 'I don't watch *Coronation Street* now. I think there's a time where you've got so big a cast that you can't manage it properly. I think five's [episodes] its maximum in terms of viewer appetite and in terms of the production of an entity like that.' Liddiment says he would not have gone to four weekly episodes, let alone five, but adds, 'That's me being a bit old-fashioned and I'm probably wrong. At the end of the day, I have been delightfully surprised that this volume hasn't damaged the show. One of the tricks of it has been there are two Monday episodes and two Friday episodes, so it doesn't quite feel as many as it would if it was on every day, so it still can feel special.... If The Street loses its touch with reality and its wryness and wit and the richness of its characters then it wouldn't deserve its success and it wouldn't deserve to continue, but there's no sign of that happening.'

Adele Rose: 'One of the Granada researchers rang me recently and said – coming up to the fiftieth – "Would you by any chance have kept any of the original scripts as a memento?" and I said, "Good God, no" – because we had no idea we were building something historic that in fifty years' time was going to be iconic. Of course it has changed, hugely, inevitably. It's like a child. A baby's born, turns into a child, turns into a teenager, turns into a grown-up. It's inevitable that it will change. But the main thing is, it's still there, it's very popular and it's making money for ITV, which badly needs it.'

Alan Rothwell watches The Street 'hardly ever'. Of his infrequent sightings, he says, 'It's admirable in a totally different way. I'm so delighted that it still tries to be funny and upbeat rather than just being doomy and gloomy like *EastEnders*, where everybody seems to be absolutely bloody awful. I still feel proud of it and how well it's done and how well it just seems to manage to continue to do.' However, he sees no thread linking it to the first episode: 'It relates to now. Which it always did. The thread has gone.'

The point made by Finch about actors shouting is also made, unprompted, by both Rothwell and theme tune player David Browning. Rothwell says of this, 'My own experience was, as a child growing up in a working class village in Lancashire, that people were on the whole happy. [Were] they happier than people are today? I suspect they were. Do you know, I think some of it's because of soap operas. I can see kids watching that sort of thing and thinking that's the way to behave. Telly has had a huge influence on all our lives and we should be very careful about it because it's a bit pernicious. It's showing something which is dramatically heightened and showing that as if it is reflecting the life that there is. It's become a circular thing now. It's not reflecting it so much as actually handing back to reality a means of behaving that causes people to fall out with each other much more and not to be so happy.'

The Street's Golden Jubilee year saw an officially sanctioned *Coronation Street* stage play – *50 Years Of Coronation Street Abridged Live* – in which the show's half-century of stories were compressed into two hours by *Street* scriptwriter Jonathan Harvey. Appropriately, the show was launched in Salford before embarking on a nationwide tour. ITV, however, turned down an excellent idea for a much better way to celebrate The Street's half-centenary. Stevenson: 'Daran Little put up the idea for a single play called *Florizel Street* based on the launch and making of *Coronation Street*.' The script was commissioned by BBC Four, although produced by ITV Studios under the supervision of Kieran Roberts, The Street's executive producer since 2006. Stevenson: 'So it may well be that the only real celebrating of *Coronation Street* goes out, instead of its own channel, on the BBC.'

Coronation Street today is a far more corporate proposition than it was 50 years ago. While Ken Irwin continued to have access to *Street* cast members for interviews even after the above-mentioned libel case, he increasingly found that the informality of the days of yore which led him to break the story of Peter Adamson's alcoholism-related suspension – the actor unexpectedly poured out his heart about it during a one-to-one interview – were gone. 'The interviews were set up by the press office,' Irwin recalls. 'Although the actors had always needed to get permission from Granada to speak to the press, you couldn't, like we did in the old days, ring somebody direct and say, "I'll meet you in the pub." What annoyed me is they had press officers sitting in on the interview and [saying], "Don't answer that" or "You don't have to do that".' As late as 1975 (i.e., five years after the issue of Irwin's *The Real Coronation Street* book that had caused Granada some consternation), Granada happily supplied pictures to an outfit called Lang Syne Publishers so that they could illustrate a bizarre pamphlet-cum-book called *Coronation Street Upstairs Downstairs. With Crown Court and the Brothers*, an exploration of four famous UK TV shows with apparently nothing in common. Today, this would be inconceivable – which is why you won't find any Granada/ITV-owned pictures on or in this book. Maximising the revenues from one's intellectual property is no crime, of course, but the loss of the innocence of those days is somehow sad.

Though The Street and ITV Studios are increasingly corporate, philistine interference by the ITV network naturally rankles with them. Another example of this philistine and audience-alienating behaviour was provided in 2010 when the network apparently randomly and with little notice scheduled the odd episode of The Street on Sundays, and in June pushed The Street back to 9pm across an entire week to make room for the semi-finals of *Britain's Got Talent*. (Ironically, the latter plan was wrecked by a real-life mass murder in Cumbria. The week's storyline involving a newly escaped and un-contrite Tony Gordon holding Carla and Hayley at gunpoint before dying in the factory he had set ablaze would have been inappropriate to show at that time, so the episodes were rescheduled.) In the old days The Street could do little about this, but one benefit of the end of the franchise system may be greater bargaining power on the part of programme makers. Back in 1990, when the ITV franchises were up for renewal, Granada chairman David Plowright said that if Granada did not have its transmission licence renewed then Granada – the production company that made *Coronation Street* as opposed to the regional franchise – would take The Street away from ITV and sell it to satellite television. (Granada were subsequently – or possibly consequently – awarded a new licence despite putting in a lower bid than a rival.) This story demonstrates that the programme is not necessarily wedded to ITV in permanence. Under the network agreement between the old ITV companies, it would have been legally impossible for a franchise holder to sell its programmes to any domestic outlet other than the other franchises. Now the contract is between ITV Studios and the ITV network and the complex arrangements of the old franchises don't apply to it. Like any contract it can come to an end and be renegotiated with other clients – for instance, the BBC or Sky. Certainly a BBC1 soap hour comprised of *EastEnders* and *Coronation Street* is culturally intriguing beyond description.

Says Reynolds, 'There was always a rebellious streak in what was Granada that they could go and sell it off to Sky, but the reality was that it was seen by ITV as its flagship and there'd be no way it would accept it. It's never a serious threat. It won't be until ITV Studios is sold off by ITV and when they sell it off there'll be a guaranteed number of years for ITV1 to have the show. ITV Studios is still part of ITV.' Others are less sure that it is as legally impossible as Reynolds seems to be suggesting, but nobody questioned thinks it likely. Park: 'Anything's bloody possible. There was talk of *The Bill* going to Sky for a while or going to Five. It won't sell it to the BBC because they've got *EastEnders*. It'd be a real own goal. Can you imagine everybody's saying how critically moribund the BBC is that they've paid "x" amount to bring over another show? Nah. It's not gonna happen. Plus the argument is, "What are we paying our licence money for when you're not showing diversity and blah blah blah blah".' Little: 'Every time the franchise came up there was always like, "Oh they'll sell it to Sky", but that's just idle talk. It's been on ITV for fifty years. If you move it – like moving things in the schedule – you lose viewers. If you were to do the unthinkable and move *Coronation Street* and put it on the BBC, it would be a very, very different show. They have a completely different way of working at the BBC. Each episode of *EastEnders* goes through about seven more edits than an episode of

Coronation Street. The running time would be longer. And they wouldn't want it – they have *EastEnders*. I think ITV is likely to sell ITV to Disney or something before they sell its crown jewel.'

In the type of coincidence that even soap writers would hesitate to include in a script, the year that *Coronation Street* turned 50 was the one in which its only rival as the world's longest-running television drama was cancelled.

As *The World Turns* started broadcasting in April 1956, so, previously, whatever anniversary The Street was basking in, it could never claim longevity supremacy. With the announcement that *As The World Turns* was to breathe its last in September 2010, there was no attainment left for The Street. Other, of course, than to keep going long enough to surpass that US show's 54 years – and to keep entertaining millions as it has for generations.

Without Sir Denis Forman nudging the Granada Television Committee into a grudging acquiescence to give it at least a short run, *Coronation Street* would probably never have come into existence. Though he says he and everyone else had no way of knowing the programme would last 50 years, Sir Denis changed his mind after a while and now says of its longevity, 'I thought it would run forever. And I think it will.'

Acknowledgments

My grateful thanks are extended to the following people for granting me interviews for this book: Stan Barstow, David Browning, Michael Cox, Tom Elliott, John Finch, Sir Denis Forman, Derek Granger, Geoff Hinsliff, Ken Irwin, Bill Kenwright, David Liddiment, Daran Little, Brian Park, Carolyn Reynolds, William Roache, Adele Rose, Alan Rothwell, John Stevenson and Ernst Walder.

I would also like to thank the following for assistance and/or helping with queries: Caroline Furey of Bolton Museum and Archive Service; Gavin Martin, Ian Penman, Amanda-Jane Read and Janice Troup of ITV Programme Publicity; and Sheila Thompson of Brown Lloyd James for BARB information.

Bibliography

Books

Barstow, Stan, *In My Own Good Time* (Dalesman, 2001)

Condon, Paul; Sangster, Jim, *TV Heaven* (Collins, 2005)

Dyer, Richard, etc., *Television Monograph: Coronation Street* (BFI, 1981)

Finch, John; Cox, Michael; Giles, Marjorie, *Granada Television: The First Generation* (Manchester University Press, 2003)

Forman, Denis, *Persona Granada* (Andre Deutsch, 1997)

Hanson, David, *Access All Areas* (Andre Deutsch, 2004)

Irwin, Ken, *The Real Coronation Street* (Corgi, 1970)

Kay, Graeme; Davis, Anthony; Hayward, Anthony, *Coronation Street: Celebrating 30 Years 1960–1990* (Boxtree Ltd/Granada, 1990)

Kelly, Stephen F.; Jones, Judith, *Forty Years Of Coronation Street* (Boxtree, 2000)

Kershaw, H.V., *The Street Where I Live* (Book Club Associates, 1981)

Kershaw, H.V., *The Street Where I Live (Revised)* (Panther, 1985)

Little, Daran, *40 Years Of Coronation Street* (Andre Deutsch, 2000)

Little, Daran, *Coronation Street: Around the Houses* (Boxtree, 1997)

Little, Daran, *The Coronation Street Story* (Boxtree, 1996)

Little, Daran, *Weatherfield Life* (Boxtree/Granada, 1992)

Nown, Graham, *Coronation Street 1960–1985: 25 Years* (Ward Lock, 1985)

Phoenix, Pat, *All My Burning Bridges* (Arlington, 1974)

Podmore, Bill, *Coronation Street: The Inside Story* (MacDonald, 1990)

Roache, William, *Ken And Me* (Simon & Schuster, 1993)

Roache, William, *Soul On The Street* (Hay House, 2007)

Rosenthal, Jack, *By Jack Rosenthal* (Robson, 2006)

Warren, Tony, *I Was Ena Sharples Father* (Duckworth, 1969)

Warren, Tony, *The Lights Of Manchester* (Arrow, 1992)

Coronation Street Upstairs, Downstairs. With Crown Court and the Brothers (Lang Syne, circa 1975)

TV Times Souvenir Extra: Coronation Street – marking a thousand episodes of Granada's ever-popular serial (Independent Television Publications, 1970)

Websites

coronationstreet.wikia.com

coronationstreetupdates.blogspot.com

en.wikipedia.org

http://corrie.emmerdale.org

http://ftvdb.bfi.org.uk

www.britishtheatreguide.info

www.bbc.co.uk

www.corrie.net

www.digitalspy.co.uk

www.imdb.com

www.itv.com/soaps

Magazines

Blitz

Jazz Professional

Newspapers

Manchester Evening News

Wilmslow Express

All current national UK newspapers

Apologies to anybody inadvertently omitted

Index